749.2

D1493022

modern chairs

Charlotte & Peter Fiell

modern chairs

Benedikt Taschen

Page 2/3 . Seite 2/3

Erwine & Estelle Laverne:

Daffodil and *Jonquil*, 1957

Sessel *Daffodil* und *Jonquil*, 1957

Fauteuils *Daffodil* et *Jonquil*, 1957

Courtesy Fiell International Ltd., London

Page 4/5 . Seite 4/5

Hans Coray:

Landi stacking chairs, 1939

Landi-Stapelstühle, 1939

Chaises émpilables *Landi*, 1939

Courtesy Fiell International Ltd., London

©1993 Benedikt Taschen Verlag GmbH
Hohenzollernring 53, D-50672 Köln
©1993 VG Bild-Kunst, Bonn, for the works of Adolf Loos,
Richard Riemerschmid, Gerrit Rietveld, Le Corbusier,
Jean Prouvé, Douglas Kelley, Roberto Matta Echaurren,
Pierre Paulin and Charlotte Perriand
Edited by Angelika Muthesius, Cologne
Text and idea: Charlotte and Peter Fiell, London
Designed by Mark Thomson, London
Text co-edited by Yvonne Havertz, Cologne
German translation: Bettina Blumenberg, Munich (essay),
Jutta Fanurakis, Munich
French translation: Jacques Bosser, Paris
Reproductions: ORD, Gronau
Printed in Germany
ISBN 3-8228-9451-6

Contents

Inhalt

Sommaire

Marcel Breuer:

Wassily club chair, *Model No. B3*, 1925

Wassily-Stuhl, *Modell Nr. B3*, 1925

Chaise *Wassily*, *modèle n° B3*, 1925

Courtesy Sotheby's, New York

The chair as a twentieth century icon

Der Stuhl als Ikone des 20. Jahrhunderts

Le siège, icône du xxème siècle

In 1873, Dr. Christopher Dresser wrote, "A chair is a stool with a back-rest, and a stool is a board elevated from the ground by supports."[1]

This definition of the chair seems absurdly simplistic today, for over the last hundred years the chair has been subject to a succession of revolutionary transformations, uniquely emerging as an eloquent symbol of our highly complex society. The enduring success of a particular chair design can be evaluated by how skilfully its creator has synthesized aesthetics and function while addressing a specific need. The relevance of an individual design may also be gauged by how well it expresses the spirit of the age in which it was created. Chairs sustain a far greater physical and psychological relationship with their users than do tables or case pieces. For this reason, the design of chairs has to be seen as set apart from that of other furniture. Since the beginning of civilization humans have required something to sit on – and as societies evolve, so does the chair. As a symbolic object, therefore, the chair has few equals – in the form of a throne or the electric chair, it potently expresses power and authority. The chair is an object steeped in connotations; it confers status on its user, it can possess varying degrees of intellectual content.

Im Jahre 1873 schrieb Dr. Christopher Dresser: »Ein Stuhl ist ein Hocker mit einer Rückenlehne, und ein Hocker ist ein Brett, das durch Stützen vom Boden abgehoben ist.«[1]

Diese Definition des Stuhls kommt uns heute fast lächerlich einfältig vor, denn der Stuhl hat im Laufe der letzten hundert Jahre eine Reihe von so revolutionären Wandlungen erfahren, daß er zu einem einzigartigen und beredten Sinnbild unserer überaus komplexen Gesellschaft geworden ist. Ob einem bestimmten Stuhl dauerhafter Erfolg beschieden ist, hängt davon ab, wie gut es seinem Schöpfer gelungen ist, Ästhetik und Funktionalität miteinander zu vereinen und dabei den spezifischen Verwendungszweck nicht aus den Augen zu verlieren. Die Bedeutung eines bestimmten Entwurfs läßt sich auch daran messen, wie treffend er den Geist seiner Entstehungszeit widerspiegelt. Stühle stehen in einer wesentlich engeren physischen und psychologischen Beziehung zu ihren Benutzern als Tische oder Schränke. Deshalb nimmt der Entwurf von Stühlen eine Sonderstellung gegenüber dem übrigen Möbeldesign ein. Seit den Anfängen der Zivilisation haben Menschen etwas gebraucht, worauf sie sitzen konnten – und mit den Gesellschaftsformen entwickelt sich auch der Stuhl. Deshalb

En 1873, Christopher Dresser écrivait: «Un siège est un tabouret avec un dossier et un tabouret est une planche surélevée du sol par le moyen de supports.»[1]

Si cette définition peut sembler absurdement simpliste aujourd'hui c'est que le siège a été soumis à une telle succession de transformations révolutionnaires durant ces cent dernières années qu'il est en fait devenu un symbole de notre société dans toute sa complexité. Le succès durable d'un modèle peut s'évaluer au savoir-faire de son créateur, qui sait réaliser la synthèse de l'esthétique et du fonctionnalisme tout en apportant une réponse à un besoin spécifique, et sa pertinence peut se juger à la manière dont il exprime son époque. Les sièges entretiennent en effet avec leurs utilisateurs une relation physique et psychologique beaucoup plus importante que celle d'une table ou d'un meuble de rangement et c'est pour cette raison que leur création doit être considérée à part de celle des autres éléments du mobilier. Depuis les débuts de la civilisation, les hommes ont toujours eu besoin de quelque chose pour s'asseoir et le siège a évolué de la même façon que la société. En tant qu'objet symbolique, sa puissance n'a que peu d'équivalents. Ainsi, par exemple, sous la forme d'un trône ou d'une chaise électrique, il sait exprimer le pou-

More than any other type of furniture, the chair can be seen as a barometer of social change. While its primary function as an object to sit on remains constant, the specific purposes for which some chairs are designed are mutable. The hall chair, for instance, is all but obsolete today, whereas the operator's chair undergoes continual research and development. The chair more accurately mirrors the social and economic contexts within which design has evolved in the twentieth century, because it best expresses the essence of specific decorative styles. It is also particularly susceptible to the evanescent influences of taste and popular consumerism. In times of economic austerity rationally designed chairs and other durable products will by necessity prevail in the marketplace, while in periods of relative prosperity there is a general tendency towards the anti-rationalism of ornamentation and exaggerated forms.

Chairs are "territorialized" by us in our daily lives; at home, members of a family each have their own particular chair in which they prefer to sit . At work, chairs are used to represent status; manufacturers commonly supply seating systems that incorporate a single standard model which can be variously upgraded – the less costly receptionist's chair is efficiently adapted into an executive's chair with the addition of luxury options. So prevalent and subtle is this symbolism of power that frequently its existence is only registered subconsciously. Chairs also reflect the aspirations and socio-political viewpoints of their owners, laying bare their personalities and social class. More than any other furniture type, the chair offers an insight into the souls of men.

Arne Jacobsen:

Plywood chair, 1955

Sperrholzstuhl, 1955

Chaise contreplaqué, 1955

Courtesy Whitechapel Art Gallery, London

hat der Stuhl als symbolhafter Gegenstand kaum seinesgleichen – in Gestalt eines Throns oder des elektrischen Stuhls ist er ein unmißverständlicher Ausdruck von Macht und Autorität. Der Stuhl ist ein bedeutungsreiches Objekt: Er kann seinem Benutzer Rang verleihen, er kann in unterschiedlichem Maße geistige Inhalte verkörpern.

Mehr als jedes andere Möbelstück kann der Stuhl als Indikator des sozialen Wandels gelten. Zwar bleibt seine Grundfunktion als Sitzmöbel bestehen, doch ist die spezifische Verwendung, für die Stühle entworfen werden, veränderbar. Der Dielenstuhl beispielsweise ist heute völlig veraltet, während der Schreibtischstuhl auf wissenschaftlicher Basis ständig weiterentwickelt wird. Der Stuhl ist ein verläßlicher Spiegel des sozialen und ökonomischen Kontexts, in dem das Design des 20. Jahrhunderts sich entfaltet hat, denn in ihm kommt das Charakteristische bestimmter Einrichtungsstile am deutlichsten zum Ausdruck. Er erweist sich überdies als besonders sensibel für die flüchtigen Einflüsse von Geschmack und Massenkonsum. In Zeiten angespannnter Wirtschaftslage werden stets Stühle mit eindeutig rationalem Design und andere dauerhafte Produkte den Markt beherrschen, während Zeiten relativen Wohlstands durch eine allgemeine Tendenz zum Antirationalismus des Ornamentalen und der übersteigerten Formen gekennzeichnet sind.

In unserem Alltagsleben haben Sitzmöbel für uns etwas von einem »Revier«; zu Hause hat jedes Familienmitglied seinen Lieblingsplatz. Am Arbeitsplatz sind Stühle Rangabzeichen; Hersteller bieten in der Regel Programme an, bei denen sich ein einziges Standardmodell beliebig aufrüsten läßt – aus dem weniger kostspieligen Stuhl für die Empfangsdame wird in der Luxusausführung im Handumdrehen ein Chefsessel. Diese Machtsymbolik ist so weit verbreitet und so subtil, daß man sie oft nur unterschwellig wahrnimmt. Stühle können auch etwas über die Zielvorstellungen und soziopolitischen Standpunkte ihrer Besitzer aussagen, deren Charakter und soziale Herkunft sie offenbaren. Mehr als jedes andere Möbelstück verschafft uns der Stuhl einen Einblick in die menschliche Seele.

voir, l'autorité et la justice. C'est un objet extraordinairement connoté qui peut conférer un statut social ou hiérarchique à son utilisateur, offrir différents niveaux de signification.

Plus que n'importe quel autre type de meuble, le siège peut être considéré comme un baromètre des changements sociaux. Alors que sa première fonction – un objet fait pour s'asseoir – est restée immuable, les buts dans lesquels certains sièges sont conçus évoluent: la cathèdre, par exemple, est aujourd'hui totalement obsolète alors que la chaise de la standardiste fait l'objet de recherches et de développements continus. Le siège reflète avec une grande précision les contextes économiques et sociaux de l'évolution du design au XXème siècle et nul mieux que lui n'exprime l'essence même de chaque style décoratif tout en restant particulièrement sensible aux influences éphémères du goût et de la grande consommation. En période d'austérité économique, les sièges conçus selon des critères rationnels seront appréciés par le marché, tandis qu'en phase de relative prospérité se déploiera une certaine tendance à l'anti-rationalisme, à l'ornementation et aux formes exagérées.

Nous intégrons avec facilité les sièges à notre «territoire». A la maison, chaque membre de la famille dispose de son propre siège sur lequel il préfère s'asseoir. Au travail, les sièges sont des symboles de statut hiérarchique. Très couramment, les fabricants en proposent des lignes qui évoluent à partir d'un modèle de base, la chaise moins coûteuse de la réceptionniste se transformant habilement en fauteuil de dirigeant grâce à quelques options de luxe. Si fort et si subtil est ce symbolisme du pouvoir qu'il n'est souvent perçu qu'inconsciemment. Les sièges révèlent également les aspirations, l'appartenance à une classe sociale et les opinions sociopolitiques de leurs propriétaires. Plus que n'importe quel autre meuble, le siège offre une regard sur l'âme humaine.

Architects and chair design

Architekten und Stuhldesign

Les architectes et la conception du siège

In the quest for a greater unity of design, architects have historically created furniture for specific interiors within their buildings. Although once regarded as subordinate to architecture, the design of furniture and especially that of chairs became a separate discipline when its manufacture was transferred from the domain of the craftsman to that of the industrial process. This shift in the method of production demanded a professional approach to design. Architects, with their background knowledge of engineering, were especially well placed to develop new furniture products that were both functional and aesthetically pleasing within the constraints of modern manufacturing technology. Additionally, furniture design appealed to architects, for through it, more easily than with architecture, they could express their design philosophies in three dimensions. Peter Smithson writes, "It could be said that when we design a chair, we make a society and a city in miniature. Certainly this has never been more true than in this century. One has a perfectly clear notion of the sort of city, and the sort of society envisaged by Mies van der Rohe, even though he has never said much about it. It is not an exaggeration to say that the Miesian city is implicit in the Mies chair".[2]

As a potentially mass-produced and

In ihrem Bemühen um die Schaffung eines einheitlichen Gesamtentwurfs haben Architekten seit jeher entsprechende Möbel für ihre Gebäude entworfen. Obwohl die Gestaltung des Mobiliars einst als der Architektur untergeordnet betrachtet wurde, hat sich der Entwurf von Möbeln, und vor allem von Stühlen, zu einer eigenen Disziplin ausgebildet, als die Herstellung aus dem Bereich des Handwerks in die industrielle Fertigung verlagert wurde. Diese grundlegende Veränderung in der Produktionsweise erforderte eine professionelle Umstellung im Design. Architekten waren aufgrund ihres technischen Wissens und ihrer Konstruktionserfahrung besonders befähigt, neue Möbel zu entwerfen, die sowohl ästhetisch als auch funktional ansprechend waren und gleichzeitig den Erfordernissen der modernen industriellen Fertigung entsprachen. Außerdem kam der Möbelentwurf den Architekten besonders entgegen, weil sie hierin leichter als in der Architektur ihre Entwerferphilosophie in drei Dimensionen zum Ausdruck bringen konnten. Peter Smithson schreibt: »Man könnte sagen, wenn wir einen Stuhl entwerfen, schaffen wir eine Gesellschaft und eine Stadt in miniature. Sicherlich ist dies noch nie so deutlich gewesen wie in diesem Jahrhundert. Man bekommt eine ganz klare Vorstellung von der Art Stadt und der

Historiquement, dans le cadre de leurs recherches d'une plus grande unité de conception, les architectes ont créé des meubles pour l'intérieur des bâtiments qu'ils construisaient. Bien que considéré à une époque comme subordonné à l'architecture, le dessin de meuble et spécialement celui du siège devint une discipline à part lorsque sa fabrication passa du domaine de l'artisan et de son atelier à celui de la production industrielle. Cette modification des méthodes de production réclamait une approche professionnelle du design. Grâce à leurs connaissances techniques, les architectes étaient particulièrement bien placés pour mettre au point de nouveaux meubles à la fois fonctionnels et esthétiques dans le cadre des contraintes technologiques d'une fabrication industrialisée. De plus, la création de meubles exerçait sur eux une forte attraction car ils y voyaient la possibilité d'exprimer leur philosophie d'une conception en trois dimensions plus aisément qu'avec l'architecture. Peter Smithson écrit: «On peut dire que lorsque nous dessinons un siège, nous édifions une société et une ville en miniature. Et ceci n'a sans doute jamais été aussi évident qu'au cours de ce siècle. On possède une notion parfaitement claire du type de société et de cité envisagé par Mies van der Rohe, même s'il ne s'est

Ludwig Mies van der Rohe:

Chaise longue, *Model No. 241*, 1931

Chaiselongue, *Modell Nr. 241*, 1931

Chaise longue, *modèle n° 241*, 1931

Courtesy Knoll Group, New York

thereby more accessible microcosm of the ideological aspirations of the architect, the chair has not surprisingly led many architects to become better known for their furniture designs than for their buildings. Since the 1940s, designers' names have become synonymous with the chairs they have created: for example, the *Mies chair*, the *Eames chair* and the *Le Corbusier chaise longue*.

Art Gesellschaft, die Mies van der Rohe im Auge hatte, wenn er selbst sich dazu auch nicht weiter geäußert hat. Es ist keine Übertreibung zu sagen, daß die Mies-Stadt im kleinen im Mies-Stuhl enthalten ist.«[2]

Darum ist es nicht überraschend, daß der Stuhl als potentielles Massenprodukt und als ein leichter zugänglicher Mikrokosmos der ideologischen Anliegen des Architekten dazu beigetragen hat, daß viele Architekten durch ihre Möbelentwürfe bekannter geworden sind als durch ihre Gebäude. Seit den 40er Jahren des 20. Jahrhunderts sind Designernamen zu Synonymen geworden für die Stühle, die sie entworfen haben: so der *Mies-Stuhl*, der *Eames-Stuhl* und die *Le-Corbusier-Chaiselongue*.

jamais beaucoup exprimé sur ce sujet. Ce n'est pas exagérer que de dire que la ville miesienne est implicite dans les sièges de Mies.«[2]

Image en réduction des aspirations idéologiques de l'architecte, susceptible d'une production en masse et d'accès relativement aisé, il n'est pas surprenant que la création de sièges ait finalement abouti à ce que de nombreux architectes soient plus connus pour leurs meubles que pour leurs bâtiments. Depuis les années 40, certains noms de créateurs sont devenus synonymes de sièges, par exemple la *Chaise de Mies*, la *Chaise des Eames* ou la *Chaise longue de Le Corbusier*.

Modernism and chair design

Modernismus im Stuhldesign

Modernisme et création de siège

The examples we have selected for this survey of the history of the modern chair have been almost exclusively designed by the avant-garde. Those chairs that have no direct bearing on the evolution of Modernism may be considered essentially anti-rational within the context of the classical definition of design. In production or sales terms, modern (with a small "m") designs such as these have only made up a small percentage of the market. Nevertheless, some anti-rational chair designs can be regarded as extremely influential, through either their innovative use of materials and technology, or the aesthetic, political and intellectual agendas they set, while expressing the spirit of the age in which they were created. An analogy could be made with the effect of haute couture on high-street fashion. It should be noted, however, that the concept of rationalism is fluid – what appears to be a rational solution in one era may be considered anti-rational in another. As the needs and concerns of society change, so do designers' and manufacturers' responses to them. To a varying degree, therefore, all design is ephemeral.

The Modern chair is quintessentially an industrial product which has an ancestry that can be traced back to the second quarter of the nineteenth century. Mod-

Die Beispiele, die wir für diesen Überblick über die Geschichte des modernen Stuhls ausgewählt haben, zählen fast ausschließlich zur Avantgarde des Möbeldesigns. Diejenigen Stühle, die nicht unmittelbar zur Entwicklung des Modernismus beigetragen haben, bezeichnen wir als antirational, wohl verstanden vor dem Hintergrund der klassischen Definition von Design. Bezüglich der Produktions- oder Verkaufszahlen machen solche neuzeitlich-modischen Entwürfe nur einen kleinen Prozentsatz des Gesamtmarktes aus. Dennoch haben sich manche antirationalen Stuhlentwürfe als höchst einflußreich erwiesen, sei es durch ihre innovative Verwendung des Materials und der Technologie, sei es durch die ästhetische, politische und intellektuelle Aktualität, die sie umsetzen, indem sie den Zeitgeist zum Ausdruck bringen, in dem sie geschaffen wurden.

Der moderne Stuhl ist ein klassisches Beispiel für ein Industrieprodukt, dessen Vorläufer bis in das zweite Viertel des 19. Jahrhunderts zurückverfolgt werden können. Modernismus ist kein Stil, sondern eine weltanschauliche Bewegung, die eine klassische und menschenwürdige Ideologie propagiert, die auch auf das Möbeldesign angewandt werden kann. Die rationalen Dogmen des Modernismus lauten:

Les exemples illustrant cette histoire du siège moderne sont presque tous l'œuvre de créateurs d'avant-garde. Ces sièges qui n'ont pas de lien direct avec l'évolution du Modernisme peuvent être qualifiés d'anti-rationnels par rapport à la définition classique du design. En termes de production ou de vente, les créations de ce type ne représentent qu'une faible part du marché. Néanmoins, certains de ces modèles ont pu exercer une très grande influence, que ce soit pour leur utilisation de matériaux nouveaux ou de technologies avancées, leur esthétique ou les enjeux politiques ou intellectuels qu'ils soulèvent en exprimant l'esprit de leur époque. Une analogie pourrait être tracée avec la haute-couture et son effet sur la mode de la rue. Il faut noter qu'en tant que concept, le rationalisme peut varier et que ce qui apparaît comme rationnel à un certain moment peut sembler anti-rationnel quelques temps plus tard. Dans une certaine mesure tout design est éphémère.

Le siège moderne est par essence un produit industriel dont l'origine remonte au second quart du XIXème siècle. Le Modernisme n'est pas un style, mais un mouvement philosophique, une idéologie d'essence classique et humaniste applicable à la création de mobilier. Les principes rationalistes du Modernisme sont: l'unification ernism is not a style but a philosophical movement which promotes a classical and humanizing ideology that can be applied to furniture design. The rational tenets of Modernism are: the unification of the physical and the spiritual, the harmonizing of functionalism and aesthetics, internationalism derived through abstraction for greater universality of appeal, innovation, social morality, truth to materials, revealed construction and the responsible use of technology. Design, or as it was referred to in the post-war years, "Good Design", is necessarily a Modernist approach that has little to do with style and everything to do with correctly perceiving social needs.

Within Modernism, there are two distinct approaches to design; geometric abstraction and organic abstraction. The former was widely promoted by the pioneers of the Modern Movement, such as Marcel Breuer, Ludwig Mies van der Rohe and Le Corbusier. The latter approach was founded in the work of pre-World War II Scandinavian designers, initially derived from the teachings of Kaare Klint while he was professor of furniture design at the Academy of Fine Arts, Copenhagen, in the 1920s. Unlike his Bauhaus contemporaries, who urged their students to dissociate themselves from previous styles, Klint believed that his students benefited from studying the decorative arts of the past. The designs that result from this method "do not reveal a craving for newness, but are a restatement of classical solutions combining comfort and dignified simplicity".[3] As such, the work of Alvar Aalto and more significantly the later chair designs of Eero Saarinen and Charles Eames have to be seen as evolutionary in the forms they adopted, while revolutionary in the new production techniques they employed. Although both forms of Modernism are holistic in their intent, organic rationalism is informed by the natural world while the symmetry of rectilinear rationalism is drawn from the classical canons of proportion and formal geometry. Though originally derived from the study of human anatomy, geometric formalism is aesthetically idealizing, extremely rigid and if too strictly adhered to can be perceived as inhuman and thereby alienating.

die Vereinigung des Physischen und des Geistigen, die Harmonisierung des Funktionalen und des Ästhetischen; Internationalismus, der auf Abstraktion beruht, die eine universellere geschmackliche und formale Akzeptanz bewirken soll; wesentlich sind außerdem Innovation, gesellschaftliche Moralität, materialgerechte Verarbeitung, Sichtbarmachung der Konstruktion und verantwortungsbewußter Umgang mit der Technologie. Design, oder wie man es in den Nachkriegsjahren gar nannte, »gutes Design«, verfolgt notwendigerweise ein neuzeitlich-zeitgemäßes Anliegen, das wenig mit Stil zu tun hat, sondern ganz und gar darauf ausgerichtet ist, die gesellschaftlichen Bedürfnisse richtig zu erkennen.

Im Modernismus gibt es zwei unterschiedliche Auffassungen und Richtungen des Designs: die geometrische und die organische Abstraktion. Die erste wurde weitgehend von den Pionieren der modernistischen Bewegung wie Marcel Breuer, Ludwig Mies van der Rohe und Le Corbusier vertreten. Letztere wurde von skandinavischen Designern in der Zeit vor dem Zweiten Weltkrieg begründet, die sie wiederum aus den Lehren von Kaare Klint weiterentwickelt hatten, der in den 20er Jahren Professor für Möbeldesign an der Kunstakademie in Kopenhagen war. Anders als seine Zeitgenossen vom Bauhaus glaubte Klint, daß seine Studenten davon profitieren würden, wenn sie sich mit den dekorativen Künsten aus der Vergangenheit eingehend auseinandersetzten. Die Entwürfe, die aus diesen Lehren hervorgegangen sind, »enthüllen nicht eine krampfhafte Suche nach Neuerungen, sondern sind eine Neuformulierung klassischer Lösungen, die in sich Komfort und würdevolle Einfachheit verbinden«.[3] In diesem Sinne müssen die Arbeiten Aaltos und noch signifikanter die späten Stuhlentwürfe von Eero Saarinen und Charles Eames als evolutionär in ihren übernommenen Formen angesehen werden, hingegen sind sie revolutionär in ihren neuen Produktionstechniken. Wenn auch beide Formen des Modernismus in ihrer Zielsetzung ganzheitlich sind, ist doch der organische Rationalismus von der natürlichen Welt geprägt, während die Symmetrie des geradlinigen Rationalismus ihre Wurzeln aus dem klassischen Kanon von Proportion und formaler Geometrie bezieht. Obwohl sich der geometrische Formalismus ursprünglich aus dem Studium der menschlichen Anatomie entwickelt hat, impliziert er ästhetische Idealisierung, und darin wirkt er einseitig; zu strikt an die Gesetze der Geometrie gebunden, wird er sogar als inhuman und entfremdend angesehen.

du physique et du spirituel, l'harmonisation du fonctionnalisme et de l'esthétique, l'internationalisme dû à une abstraction permettant une plus grande universalité de séduction, l'innovation, la morale sociale, l'authenticité de l'utilisation des matériaux, la mise en évidence de la construction et l'utilisation responsable de la technique. Le design, ou comme on disait dans les années d'après-guerre, le «Good Design» se réfère nécessairement à une approche moderniste qui n'a que peu de rapports avec le style et se trouve étroitement liée à la juste perception des besoins sociaux.

Au sein du Modernisme, coexistent deux approches distinctes du design: l'abstraction géométrique et l'abstraction organique. Les pionniers du mouvement moderniste, comme Marcel Breuer, Ludwig Mies van der Rohe et Le Corbusier, furent les avocats de la première. La seconde approche est née des travaux de designers scandinaves de la période précédant la Seconde Guerre mondiale, euxmêmes influencés par l'enseignement de Kaare Klint, professeur à l'Académie des Beaux-Arts de Copenhague, dans les années vingt. A la différence de ses contemporains du Bauhaus qui pressaient leurs étudiants de rompre avec les styles antérieurs, Klint pensait qu'il fallait savoir tirer parti de l'étude des arts décoratifs du passé. Les créations issues de cette méthode «ne révèlent pas un goût pour la nouveauté mais une relecture des solutions classiques, combinant la recherche du confort et une digne simplicité».[3] Dans cet esprit, l'importance des travaux d'Alvar Aalto et, de façon encore plus significative, les sièges plus tardifs d'Eero Saarinen et de Charles Eames relèvent non seulement d'une évolution formelle mais aussi d'une révolution dans les techniques de production. Bien que les deux écoles du Modernisme soient holistiques dans leur propos, le rationalisme organique s'inspire de l'univers naturel tandis que le rationalisme symétrique et rectiligne s'inspire plutôt des canons classiques de proportions et de géométrie. Bien qu'issu au départ de l'étude de l'anatomie de l'homme, le formalisme géométrique tend vers un idéal esthétique extrêmement rigide qui, poursuivi avec trop de rigueur, peut être perçu comme déshumanisant et aliénant.

12

The use of new technology and materials, frequently developed in other areas of industry and applied to furniture production, has fundamentally shaped the changes that have occurred in chair design this century. How industrial innovation can influence furniture design was identified by George Nelson when defining two diametrically opposed chair types – "the shocking and the soothing".[4] The "shocking" demands attention through the use of contrasts, often, but not exclusively, by manipulating unusual forms or materials, while the "soothing" represents an understated and harmonious unity of design.

Nelson also defined three main influences in modern chair design: "the handicrafted look"," the machine look" and "the biomorphic look".[5] The chair that adopts the handicraft look does not necessarily rely upon craftsmanship in its production and can be made exclusively by machine. Such chairs, which are often only finished by hand, rely on vernacular forms, for example Hans Wegner's *Peacock chair* of 1947. The analysis and subsequent "updating" of existing furniture types originated in the Arts and Crafts movement, whose chief protagonist, William Morris, concluded that evolutionary designs were based on function rather than superfluous ornament.

Die Verwendung neuer Technologien und Materialien, die häufig in anderen Bereichen der Industrie entwickelt und erst dann auf die Möbelproduktion angewandt worden sind, hat grundlegend die Veränderungen bestimmt, die sich im Stuhldesign des 20. Jahrhunderts abgezeichnet haben. In welchem Maße industrielle Innovation das Möbeldesign beeinflussen kann, hat George Nelson in seiner Definition zweier diametral entgegengesetzter Stuhltypen auf den Begriff gebracht: »der Schockierende und der Schmeichelnde«.[4] Der »Schockierende« erfordert Aufmerksamkeit, denn er basiert auf Kontrasten, die häufig, aber nicht ausschließlich, daraus resultieren, daß ungewöhnliche Formen oder Materialien zusammengebracht werden, während der »Schmeichelnde« eine maßvolle und harmonische Einheit des Entwurfs zeigt.

Nelson hat darüber hinaus die drei wesentlichen Einflüsse im modernen Stuhldesign definiert: den »Handwerks-Look«, den »Maschinen-Look« und den »biomorphen Look«.[5] Der Stuhl, der ein handgefertigtes Aussehen hat, muß nicht unbedingt handwerklich hergestellt worden sein, in manchen Fällen kann er sogar ausschließlich maschinell gefertigt sein. Diese Stuhltypen, die meist nur ihren letzten Schliff von Hand erhalten haben, sind

L'utilisation de nouvelles technologies et de nouveaux matériaux dans la production de mobilier, fréquemment mis au point d'ailleurs pour d'autres secteurs industriels, a exercé un rôle fondamental dans les changements qu'a connus la conception des sièges au cours de ce siècle. Le niveau d'influence de l'innovation industrielle a été précisé par George Nelson dans sa tentative de définition de deux types de sièges diamétralement opposés: «le choquant et l'apaisant».[4] Le «choquant» attire l'attention en recourant à des contrastes obtenus souvent, mais pas exclusivement, par la manipulation de formes ou de matériaux inhabituels, tandis que «l'apaisant» repose sur une unité de dessin discrète et harmonieuse.

Nelson définit également les trois principales directions stylistiques du design du siège moderne: le style «artisanal», le style «mécaniste» et le style «biomorphique».[5] Les sièges qui adoptent le style artisanal n'ont pas été forcément réalisés par un artisan et dans certains cas peuvent même avoir été exclusivement fabriqués à la machine. Ils sont d'ailleurs souvent finis à la main et s'inspirent de formes vernaculaires, tels le fauteuil *Peacock* de Hans Wegner (1947). L'étude et la «modernisation» de types de meubles existants trouvent leur origine dans le mouvement

13

The "machine" look is effected either through truly mechanized means of production or by handcrafting representations of the industrial process which express the machine aesthetic. Ludwig Mies van der Rohe's *Barcelona chair* of 1929 is a good example of this type, for although it appears machine-made, it was originally produced almost entirely by hand. Conversely, a chair like the *Polyprop*, designed by Robin Day in 1963, not only looks machine-made but also its design was wholly determined by the most efficient means of standardized industrial production.

Nelson's final category, the "biomorphic look", can be produced by machine or hand using abstracted "biological or organic form – neither homely like the handicraft object nor rigid like the machine form – but amorphous and flowing like living tissue".[6] This type of design was initially influenced by contemporary abstract sculpture in the late 1940s. Ironically, the materials best able to express the abstract essence of nature are synthetic media such as plastic and foam rubber.

Throughout most of this century, the trend in the production of general domestic furniture has been away from the workshop/studio and into the factory. With markets continuing to diversify, however, a

häufig aus regionalen und volkstümlichen Formen entwickelt worden wie etwa Hans Wegners *Pfauenstuhl* von 1947. Studium, Auswertung und zeitgemäße Umsetzung bestehender Möbeltypen, die ihren Ursprung im »Arts and Crafts Movement« haben, einer handwerklich-kunsthandwerklichen Bewegung, deren Kopf William Morris war, haben zu dem Schluß geführt, daß evolutionäres Design auf Funktionalität beruht und nicht auf überflüssigem Ornament.

Der »Maschinen-Look« wird entweder durch rein mechanische Produktionsmittel erzielt oder durch handwerkliche Nachahmung des industriellen Fertigungsprozesses, der die Maschinenästhetik zum Ausdruck bringt. Mies van der Rohes *Barcelona-Stuhl* von 1929 ist ein gutes Beispiel für diesen Typus, denn obwohl er aussieht, als sei er maschinell hergestellt, wurde er ursprünglich fast völlig von Hand gefertigt. Im Gegensatz dazu sieht ein Stuhl wie der *Polyprop*, den Robin Day 1963 entworfen hat, nicht mehr maschinengefertigt aus, sondern auch sein Design ist vollständig bestimmt durch die effizientesten Mittel standardisierter Industrieproduktion. Nelsons dritte Kategorie, der »biomorphe Look«, kann von Maschine oder von Hand hergestellt werden, wobei abstrahierte

Arts and Crafts, dont le principal protagoniste, William Morris, estimait que les projets évolutionnistes devaient plutôt s'appuyer sur la fonction que sur l'ornement inutile.

Le style «mécaniste» résulte, quant à lui, de moyens de production mécanisés ou de versions artisanales du processus industriel traduisant une esthétique mécaniste. La *chauffeuse Barcelona* de Ludwig Mies van der Rohe (1929) en est un bon exemple. Bien qu'elle donne l'impression d'avoir été produite en usine, elle était réalisée à l'origine presque entièrement à la main. Inversement, une chaise comme la *Polyprop* de Robin Day (1963), semble non seulement avoir été fabriquée à la machine mais sa conception a été entièrement déterminée par la recherche des moyens les plus efficaces d'aboutir à une standardisation industrielle de sa production.

La dernière catégorie de Nelson, le style «biomorphique», peut s'obtenir à la machine ou à la main «... à travers des formes biologiques ou organiques pas aussi sensibles que les produits de l'artisanat ni aussi rigides que ceux de la machine, mais lisses comme un tissu vivant.»[6] Cette sorte de conception fut influencée par la sculpture abstraite con-

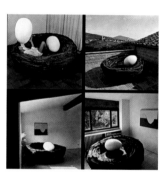

Paolo Ruffi:

La Cova, 1973

La Cova, 1973

La Cova, 1973

Courtesy Poltronova, Milan

Knoll International advertisement for Eero Saarinen's *Tulip* chair

Werbefoto der Firma Knoll International für Eero Saarinens *Tulip*-Stuhl

Knoll International publicité pour la chaise *Tulip* d'Eero Saarinen

Courtesy Knoll Group, New York

Charles & Ray Eames:
670 chair and footstool
670 Sessel und Hocker
670 fauteuil et tabouret
Courtesy Eames office,
Venice, California

reversal of this trend is becoming increasingly apparent. To cope with the popular demand for greater individuality, major manufacturers are currently producing limited editions and short batch runs of anti-rational chair designs, often utilizing low-tech methods of production for the domestic market, while concentrating their research and development budgets on the large and highly lucrative office-furnishings sector. The introduction of Herman Miller's revolutionary *Action Office II* system in 1968 represents one of the most significant benchmarks from which the great divergence of the contract and domestic markets can be measured. Prior to this, a higher percentage of chairs and other furnishings were conceived as multi-functional, efficiently bridging in many successful cases the contract and domestic markets.

»biologische oder organische Formen« verwendet werden, »die weder schlicht und hausbacken wie ein Handwerksobjekt wirken noch strikt und starr wie eine Maschinenform, sondern amorph und fließend wie aus lebendem Stoff«.[6] Diese Art von Design wurde von der zeitgenössischen abstrakten Skulptur Ende der 40er Jahre beeinflußt. Ironischerweise sind synthetische Materialien wie Kunststoff und Schaumgummi am besten geeignet, das abstrakte Wesen der Natur zum Ausdruck zu bringen.

Im Laufe des 20. Jahrhunderts hat sich die Herstellung des häuslichen Mobiliars immer mehr von den Werkstätten und Kunsthandwerkerateliers in die Fabriken verlagert. Je mehr sich jedoch heute unsere Märkte erweitern, desto deutlicher ist eine Umkehrung dieses Trends spürbar. Um der immer stärker um sich greifenden Forderung nach Individualität gerecht zu werden, produzieren große Hersteller immer häufiger limitierte Auflagen und nur kurzfristig produzierte Modelle von antirationalen Stuhlentwürfen, für die häufig Low-Tech-Methoden bei der Produktion angewandt werden, vor allem für das heimische Mobiliar, während sie Forschung und Entwicklung wesentlich auf den höchst lukrativen Büromöbelsektor konzentrieren. Die Einführung von Herman Millers revolutionärem *Action-Office-II-*System im Jahr 1968 markiert einen der bedeutsamsten Schnittpunkte, von dem aus das starke Auseinanderdriften des Firmen- und des Privatkundenmarktes bemessen werden kann. Vor dieser Wende wurde ein größerer Prozentsatz von Stühlen und anderen Möbeln als multi-funktional angesehen, so daß man in vielen erfolgreichen Fällen von einer Brücke zwischen diesen beiden Marktbereichen sprechen könnte.

temporaine à la fin des années 40. D'une façon ironique, les matières synthétiques comme le plastique et le caoutchouc mousse sont les mieux adaptées pour exprimer le caractère abstrait de la nature.

Pratiquement tout au long de ce siècle, la production de meubles pour la maison s'est peu à peu éloignée de l'atelier pour se rapprocher de l'usine, même si, à la suite de la diversification continue des marchés, un renversement de cette tendance s'opère actuellement. Pour s'adapter à la forte demande de plus d'individualisme, les grands fabricants produisent maintenant pour le marché de la maison certains modèles non classiques en éditions limitées ou en petites séries, souvent selon des méthodes très traditionnelles, mais concentrent leurs investissements de recherche et de développement sur le secteur plus vaste et plus rentable de l'équipement de bureau. L'introduction du système révolutionnaire d'Herman Miller, *Action Office II,* (1968), représente l'une des dates décisives à partir de laquelle se constate la divergence des marchés de la maison et du bureau. Auparavant, une grande proportion de sièges et autres meubles s'adaptait avec bonheur aux besoins de la clientèle privée comme à ceux des entreprises.

15

Michael Thonet:

Steam-bent chairs, c. 1836 – 40

Bugholzstühle, um 1836 – 40

Chaises cintrée, vers 1836 – 40

Courtesy Gebrüder Thonet, Vienna

Page from Gebrüder Thonet
catalogue, Vienna, 1904

Seite aus dem Katalog der
Gebrüder Thonet, Wien, 1904

Page du catalogue des Gebrüder
Thonet, Vienne, 1904

During the second half of the nineteenth century, the chair became an industrialized product, mainly as a result of the pioneering research into the steam-bending of wood laminates and later solid wood by Michael Thonet. With the material and structural continuity of his early steam-bent laminated chairs, Thonet set an important precedent in the evolution of the Modern chair – "the elimination of the extraneous, the unification of the essential, the celebration of the natural, the quest for the comfortable, and the popularization of the beautiful".[7] His company, Gebrüder Thonet, manufactured the first truly mass-produced chairs using the newly patented techniques for steam-bending solid wood. These products, however, were not structurally or materially unified, being made in component form for later assembly. Primarily intended for cafés and bars, these innovative chairs were highly successful, owing mainly to the plethora of recently opened coffee houses in Vienna. Thonet's chairs, such as the *Model No. 14*, did not particularly differ in style from the mainly handcrafted contemporary domestic seat furniture and can, therefore, only be seen as Modern in terms of their method of manufacture. Between 1859 and 1914, an astounding 40 million *Model No. 14* chairs were produced, with Thonet employing

In der zweiten Hälfte des 19. Jahrhunderts wurde der Stuhl ein Industrieprodukt, was vor allem der Pionierleistung von Michael Thonet zu verdanken ist, dem es gelungen war, Schichtholz und später auch massives Holz mit Dampf zu biegen. Durch die kontinuierliche Weiterentwicklung von Material und Konstruktion seiner frühen dampfgebogenen Schichtholzstühle hat Thonet einen wichtigen Ausgangspunkt für die Entwicklung des modernen Stuhls markiert – durch die »Eliminierung des Unwesentlichen, die Vereinigung des Wesentlichen, die Zelebrierung des Natürlichen, die Suche nach der Bequemlichkeit und die Verbreitung des Schönen«.[7] In seiner Firma, Gebrüder Thonet, wurden die ersten wirklich massenproduzierten Stühle hergestellt, unter Verwendung der neu patentierten Technik zur Dampfformung von massivem Holz. Diese Produkte wurden aus Einzelteilen zum späteren Zusammensetzen gefertigt. Diese neuen, höchst erfolgreichen Stühle waren vor allem für Cafés und Bars bestimmt und bald aus den zahlreichen Kaffeehäusern nicht mehr wegzudenken. Thonets Stühle, wie etwa das *Modell Nr. 14*, unterschieden sich nicht wesentlich im Stil von den weitgehend handwerklich hergestellten zeitgenössischen Wohnsitzmöbeln; sie können nur bezüglich ihrer Herstellung als modern

Pendant la seconde moitié du XIXème siècle, le siège est devenu un produit industriel, grâce principalement aux avancées décisives dues à Michael Thonet dans le domaine du cintrage à la vapeur de lamellés de bois et, plus tard, de bois massif. En réussissant à se rapprocher avec succès d'une réelle unité de structure et de matériaux, Thonet introduisit un important précédent dans l'évolution du siège: «L'élimination de l'inutile, l'unification de l'essentiel, la célébration du naturel, la recherche du confort et la diffusion de la beauté.»[7] Sa société, Thonet Frères, fut la première a vraiment fabriquer des sièges en série grâce à ses nouvelles techniques qu'il avait fait breveter. Ils étaient cependant encore réalisés en plusieurs éléments séparés puis assemblés. Conçus pour des cafés, ces sièges novateurs connurent un vif succès. Au plan du style, les sièges de Thonet, comme le *modèle n° 14*, ne sont pas fondamentalement différents des sièges de l'époque réalisés selon des méthodes artisanales et ne peuvent donc être considérés comme modernes qu'au regard de leur méthode de fabrication. De 1859 à 1914, le chiffre étonnant de 40 millions de *modèle n° 14*, furent produits, tandis que Thonet employait plus de 25 000 personnes dans soixante usines implantées dans toute l'Europe. Cette

25,000 people in sixty factories scattered across Europe. This incredible capacity was achieved through the implementation of a factory line system of production which separated the stages of the manufacturing process. Systemized production meant that a worker had little part in the creative process or contact with the product through to its completion.

During the nineteenth century, furniture manufacturers generally used technical innovations in industry to mimic handcrafted items. These products were thus neither true to the materials nor the technology they employed in their manufacture. By mid-century, however, it was being acknowledged in certain quarters that beauty could lie in function and honestly expressed materials rather than extraneous ornament. At a meeting of the Freemasons of the Church in 1849, Mr. William Smith Williams delivered a lecture entitled "Importance of the Study of Design" suggesting that, "The adaptation of the thing to its purpose, so far from producing ugliness, tends to beauty, and it also induces new forms. The problem to be solved is simply this: given the use and material of the article, to find a beautiful shape. In the commonest, rudest, and oldest implements of husbandry – the plough, the scythe, the sickle – we have examples of simple yet beautiful curves. The most elementary and simple of forms, if well-proportioned and of graceful contour, are the most pleasing".[8]

Growing sentiments such as these, combined with some acknowledgement of the deceptive use of the industrial process, culminated in a rejection of the machine and the formation of the Arts and Crafts Movement, whose advocates initially proposed handcrafted methods of production which could be operated through a guild system. Although virtuous in its aspirations, this approach failed in its objective of providing the masses with well-designed and affordable furniture. William Morris was forever frustrated by the fact that most of his business was conducted through a private clientele composed of the privileged classes. When asked why he was in such an agitated mood while working on the interior scheme of a house owned by Sir Louther Bell, Morris fiercely replied, "It is only that I spend my life ministering to the swinish luxury of the rich."[9] Although Morris must have recognized that his ideology was flawed in practice, he did make a significant contribution towards the foundations of Modernism in that his designs were based on a reductivist aesthetic. The promotion of vernacular forms and handcrafted techniques made honesty and

angesehen werden. Zwischen 1859 und 1914 wurden nicht weniger als vierzig Millionen Stück vom *Modell Nr. 14* hergestellt, und Thonet beschäftigte inzwischen 25 000 Mitarbeiter in sechzig Fabriken, die über Europa verstreut lagen. Diese unglaubliche Produktionskapazität konnte dadurch möglich werden, daß ein Fabrikationssystem eingeführt wurde, in dem die einzelnen Stadien der Herstellung in verschiedenen Fabriken vorgenommen wurden. Diese systematisierte Reihenproduktion bedeutete für den Arbeiter, daß er nur geringen Anteil am kreativen Prozeß und nur wenig Kontakt mit dem Produkt auf dem Weg bis zu seiner Fertigstellung hatte.

Im späten 19. Jahrhundert verwandten Möbelfabrikanten technische Neuerungen in der Industrie dazu, handwerklich hergestellte Gegenstände nachzuahmen. Diese Produkte waren also weder materialgetreu, noch entsprachen sie der Technologie, die in den Fabrikationsstätten verwandt wurde. In der Mitte des Jahrhunderts wurde jedoch von mancher Seite anerkannt, daß Schönheit auch in der Funktion liegen dürfe und auch im solide verarbeiteten, klar zur Geltung gebrachten Material, nicht aber im überflüssigen Ornament. Bei einem Treffen der Freimaurer im Jahre 1849 hielt William Smith Williams eine Rede mit dem Titel »Die Bedeutung des Studiums des Designs«, in der er folgendes sagte: »Die Anpassung des Stils an seinen Zweck, weit entfernt von der Herstellung von Häßlichkeit, strebt nach Schönheit, und sie führt zur Gestaltung neuer Formen. Das Problem, das es zu lösen gilt, ist ganz einfach dies: Verwendungszweck und Material des Gegenstands vorausgesetzt, muß eine schöne Form gefunden werden. Bei den gebräuchlichsten, gröbsten und ältesten Geräten der Landwirtschaft – dem Pflug, der Sense, der Sichel – haben wir Beispiele für einfache und doch schöne geschwungene Formen. Die elementarsten und einfachsten Formen sind, sofern sie gut proportioniert und elegant in ihren Umrissen sind, die gefälligsten.«[8]

Zunehmend wurden solche Ansichten populär, und außerdem wurde der industrielle Fortschritt immer mehr als Enttäuschung empfunden. Dies gipfelte schließlich in einer Ablehnung der Maschinen, und aus dieser abweisenden Haltung formierte sich das »Arts and Crafts Movement«, eine Bewegung zur Erhaltung und Förderung des Handwerks und Kunsthandwerks, deren Verfechter für Herstellungsmethoden eintraten, die durch organisierte Gilden am Leben erhalten werden sollten. So ehrgeizig dieses Vorhaben auch war, es scheiterte an seiner Zielset-

incroyable capacité de production fut permise par la mise au point d'un système de chaîne de production qui séparait les diverses étapes de la production. Mais la rationalisation de la production signifiait aussi qu'un ouvrier n'avait plus guère de rôle créatif ou même de contact avec le produit.

A la fin du XIXème siècle, les fabricants de meubles, se contentaient généralement de tirer parti des progrès de l'industrie pour reproduire les articles jusquelà faits à la main. Ces produits n'étaient donc pas «authentiques» que ce soit dans leurs matériaux ou leur technologie. Vers le milieu du siècle cependant, on commença à prendre conscience dans certains cercles que la beauté pouvait naître d'une réponse adéquate à une fonction et de l'utilisation honnête des matériaux plutôt que d'une ornementation superfétatoire. En 1849, lors d'une réunion de francsmaçons, William Smith Williams put ainsi tenir une conférence intitulée «L'importance de l'étude du dessin» qui suggérait que: «L'adaptation d'une chose à son objet, loin de produire de la laideur, tend vers la beauté et induit également de nouvelles formes. Le problème à résoudre est tout simplement celui-ci: étant donné l'usage et les matériaux dont est fait l'objet, il s'agit de lui trouver une forme superbe. Dans les accessoires les plus communs, les plus grossiers et les plus anciens de l'agriculture, comme une charrue, une faux, ou une faucille, nous trouvons des exemples de courbes simples et cependant magnifiques. Les formes les plus simples et les plus élémentaires, si elles sont bien proportionnées et de contour gracieux, sont les plus plaisantes.»[8]

La diffusion de ce type de raisonnement et quelques déceptions rencontrées par l'industrialisation culminèrent pour certains dans un rejet de la machine et expliquent la naissance du mouvement Arts and Crafts, qui se fit au départ le défenseur de méthodes artisanales de production dans le cadre d'un système corporatiste. Bien que vertueuse dans ses aspirations, cette approche échoua dans son objectif d'offrir aux masses des meubles bien dessinés et de prix abordable. William Morris fut à jamais frustré de ce que l'essentiel de son travail soit surtout apprécié par les classes privilégiées. A quelqu'un qui lui demandait les raisons de sa nervosité alors qu'il travaillait sur l'aménagement intérieur d'une maison appartenant à Sir Louther Bell, il répliqua avec fureur: «C'est parce que je passe ma vie à travailler pour le sale luxe des riches.»[9] Bien que Morris ait reconnu l'échec pratique de ses idées, il a néanmoins apporté simplicity in design desirable to society's affluent elite.

Charles Voysey, a later proponent of the Arts and Crafts Movement, argued that it was the manufacturers' inappropriate use of the machine and not the machine itself that was to blame for the production of poor quality, excessively embellished objects in the High Victorian style. He believed that if the machine was used responsibly it could provide high-quality furniture at a reasonable cost. Although Voysey did produce furniture such as this, the machine was never wholeheartedly accepted in Britain. Nevertheless, for all its inbuilt contradictions, the Arts and Crafts Movement expanded the debate on design reform and, by doing so, influenced the Glasgow School, the Wiener Werkstätte, the American Arts and Crafts Movement and the architect Frank Lloyd Wright, all of which had an impact on the origins of the Modern Movement.

The Glasgow School can be seen as an offshoot of the Arts and Crafts Movement in Britain for, although it shared many of the same principles, such as truth to materials and revealed construction, it employed different forms. The abstracted, geometric and elongated chairs designed by Charles Rennie Mackintosh in the latter part of his career were highly influential on the Continent, where they were exhibited to great acclaim. Predominantly three-dimensional spatial exercises, the uncanny appearance of these chairs led Mackintosh and his followers to be dubbed "the spook school".[10]

Josef Hoffmann and other Wiener Werkstätte designers also used pared down geometric forms which were customarily pierced with square or rectangular motifs. This abstraction of form into linear planes, as so manifest in Josef Hoffmann's *Sitzmaschine* of c. 1908, was to have some bearing on later designers, especially Gerrit Rietveld. The Deutsche Werkbund, of which Hoffmann was a member, was founded in 1907 in opposition to the perceived backwardness of the prevalent Art Nouveau style with its excessive ornamentation. The members of this group urged "the improvement of industrial products through the combined efforts of artists, industrialists and craftsmen" in an effort to promote a more meaningful mode of design. In 1908, a member of the group, Adolf Loos, wrote a seminal paper entitled, "Ornament und Verbrechen" ("Ornament and Crime") which asserted the notion that the inordinate use of applied decoration could lead to the debasing of society and ultimately to crime. Later, in 1924, the Werkbund published

zung, die Massen mit gut gestalteten und erschwinglichen Möbeln zu versorgen. William Morris war sehr bald zutiefst über die Tatsache enttäuscht, daß der größte Teil seiner Unternehmung durch eine private Klientel aufrechterhalten wurde, die zur privilegierten Klasse gehörte. Als er gefragt wurde, warum er sich in einer so aufgewühlten Verfassung befände, während er mit der Innenausstattung eines Hauses beschäftigt war, das sich im Besitz von Sir Louther Bell befand, antwortete Morris grimmig: »Das kommt daher, weil ich mein Leben damit verbringe, zum saumäßigen Luxus der Reichen beizutragen.«[9] Obwohl Morris erkennen mußte, daß seine Ideologie in der Praxis scheitern mußte, leistete er sehr wohl einen bedeutenden Beitrag zur Grundlegung des Modernismus, vor allem hinsichtlich seiner Gestaltungsprinzipien, die auf einer reduktionistischen Ästhetik basierten. Seine Förderung volkstümlicher, regionaler Formen und handwerklicher Techniken bewirkte, daß Strenge und Einfachheit der Gestaltung auch für die wohlhabende Gesellschaftsschicht zu einem wünschenswerten Prinzip wurden.

Charles Voysey, ein späterer Förderer des »Arts and Crafts Movement«, gab zu bedenken, daß es an dem unangemessenen Umgang der Hersteller mit den Maschinen läge und nicht an der Maschine selbst, die also nicht für die schlechte Qualität und exzessiv verzierten Objekte im hochviktorianischen Stil verantwortlich gemacht werden könnte. Er war überzeugt, daß die Maschine, wenn sie verantwortungsvoll eingesetzt würde, qualitativ hochwertige Möbel zu angemessenen Preisen produzieren könnte. Obwohl Voysey seine Möbel unter dieser Voraussetzung herstellte, wurde die Maschinenproduktion in England niemals mehr voll akzeptiert. Trotz all seiner Widersprüchlichkeit gelang es dem »Arts and Crafts Movement«, die Debatte über die Design-Reform über ihre Grenzen hinaus auszudehnen; sie beeinflußte die Glasgow School, die Wiener Werkstätte, das amerikanische »Arts and Crafts Movement« und den Architekten Frank Lloyd Wright, die alle einen wichtigen Beitrag zur Entstehung des »Modern Movement« geleistet haben.

Die Glasgow School kann als ein Ableger des »Arts and Crafts Movement« in Großbritannien angesehen werden; sie machte sich viele Gestaltungsprinzipien zu eigen, etwa die materialgerechte Verarbeitung und die Offenlegung der Konstruktion, sie bediente sich dabei aber unterschiedlicher Formen. Die abstrakten, geometrischen und langgestreckten Stühle, die Charles Rennie Mackintosh in der

une contribution significative au Modernisme à travers sa recherche d'une esthétique épurée. Par ailleurs, la promotion des formes vernaculaires et des techniques artisanales sensibilisèrent l'élite aisée à l'authenticité et la simplicité du design.

Charles Voysey, défenseur plus tardif du mouvement Arts and Crafts soutint quant à lui que c'était l'utilisation inappropriée de la machine pour produire – mal – des objets excessivement décorés dans le goût victorien et non la machine elle-même qui était à blâmer. Il pensait qu'utilisée de façon responsable, elle pouvait produire des meubles de haute qualité à faible coût. Bien que Voysey ait réussi à produire des meubles dans cet esprit, la machine ne fut jamais vraiment bien acceptée en Grande-Bretagne. En dépit de ses contradictions internes, le mouvement réussit cependant à diffuser le débat sur la réforme du design et, ce faisant, influença l'Ecole de Glasgow, les Wiener Werkstätte, le mouvement américain Arts and Crafts et l'architecte Frank Lloyd Wright, qui tous jouèrent un rôle important dans les origines du mouvement moderniste.

L'Ecole de Glasgow peut être considérée comme une branche des Arts and Crafts britanniques même si, bien que ces deux mouvements aient partagé de nombreux principes en commun dont la vérité des matériaux et la mise en évidence de la construction, elle suivit des chemins différents. Les chaises «abstraites», géométriques et élongées que Charles Rennie Mackintosh dessina dans la dernière partie de sa carrière eurent beaucoup d'influence sur le continent où elles furent exposées. Exercices de style en trois dimensions, leur apparence étrange fit que l'on qualifia vite Mackintosh et ses suiveurs d'«école des fantômes».[10]

Josef Hoffmann et d'autres designers des Wiener Werkstätte utilisèrent également des formes géométriques épurées, ajourées de motifs rectangulaires ou carrés. Ce traitement de la forme selon des plans rectilignes, si manifeste dans la *Sitzmaschine* d'Hoffmann (vers 1908) devait avoir une certaine influence sur des designers ultérieurs, en particulier Gerrit Rietveld. Le Deutsche Werkbund, dont Hoffmann était membre, fut fondé en 1907 par opposition au caractère considéré comme rétrograde d'un Art nouveau surdécoré alors au sommet de sa gloire. Les membre de ce groupe appelaient de leurs vœux «l'amélioration des produits industriels grâce aux efforts combinés d'artistes, d'industriels et d'artisans» pour tenter de promouvoir un mode de design plus signifiant. En 1908, Adolf Loos, membre du groupe, écrivit un article remarqué:

Frank Lloyd Wright:

Chair designed for Midway
Gardens, 1914

Stuhl, entworfen für Midway
Gardens, 1914

Chaise dessinée pour Midway
Gardens, 1914

Courtesy Cassina, Milan

Gerrit Rietveld:

Beugelstoel, 1927

Courtesy Fischer Fine Art Ltd., London

Spätphase seines Schaffens entworfen
hat, haben einen starken Einfluß auf den
Kontinent ausgeübt, wo sie unter großem
Beifall ausgestellt wurden. Diese Stühle
sind vor allem dreidimensionale Raum-
experimente, das heißt Umsetzungen von
Mackintoshs räumlichen Vorstellungen,
und ihr geradezu unheimliches Aussehen
hat dazu geführt, daß er und seine Anhän-
ger den Spitznamen »Die Spukschule«
erhielten.[10]

Josef Hoffmann und andere Designer
der Wiener Werkstätte benutzten ebenfalls beschnittene geometrische Formen,
die meist mit quadratischen oder recht-
eckigen Motiven durchsetzt waren. Diese
Abstrahierung der Form in linear geglie-
derte Flächen, wie sie bei Josef Hoffmanns
Sitzmaschine von ca. 1908 zu sehen ist,
sollte einige Auswirkung auf spätere Designer haben, vor allem auf Gerrit Rietveld.
Im Jahre 1907 wurde der Deutsche Werkbund gegründet, in dem Hoffmann Mitglied war. Die Gründung erfolgte in er-
klärter Opposition zu den als rückwärts
gewandt und veraltet empfundenen, aber
dennoch vorherrschenden Stilrichtungen
der Art Nouveau und des Jugendstils, die
sich exzessiver Ornamentierung bedienten.
Die Mitglieder dieses Bundes drangen auf
»die Verbesserung von Industrieprodukten
durch die vereinten Anstrengungen von
Künstlern, Industriellen und Handwerkern«
und setzten sich zum Ziel, dem Design
eine ernsthaftere Bedeutung beizumessen
und sich mehr auf die wesentlichen Elemente zu konzentrieren. 1908 verfaßte
Adolf Loos, Mitglied der Gruppe, ein
Grundsatzpapier mit dem Titel »Ornament
und Verbrechen«, in dem er die Behaup-
tung aufstellte, daß der wuchernde Gebrauch von dekorativen Elementen zum
Verderben der Gesellschaft und schließlich sogar zum Verbrechen führen könnte.
1924 veröffentlichte der Werkbund die
Schrift »Form ohne Ornament«, in der die
Illustrationen die Vorzüge eines Industriedesigns vorführten, das ausschließlich auf
Funktionalität basierte.

Die Architektur und das von Frank
Lloyd Wright entworfene Mobiliar basierten ebenfalls auf einfachen, geradlinigen
geometrischen Formen. Seine Vorliebe für
vollständig vereinheitlichtes Design sollte
auch in den späteren Arbeiten von Charles
Eames und Eero Saarinen von vorrangiger
Bedeutung werden. Wahrscheinlich von
noch größerer Bedeutung ist Wrights Pio-
nierarbeit für ein einheitliches Design im
Hinblick auf George Nelson, auf den er
einen entscheidenden Einfluß bei der Entwicklung integrierter Möbelsysteme für
den Wohnraum und den Arbeitsplatz
ausübte.

«Ornament und Verbrechen» (Ornementation et crime) dans lequel il affirmait que le
recours désordonné à une décoration arti-
ficielle pouvait mener à la désagrégation
de la société et, en dernier recours, au
crime. Plus tard, en 1924, le Werkbund
publia «Form ohne Ornament» (Forme
sans ornementation) dans lequel les illustrations démontraient les vertus d'un design industriel essentiellement fondé sur
la fonction.

L'architecture et le mobilier de Frank
Lloyd Wright reposaient également sur
une géométrie simple et rectiligne. Sa
préférence pour une conception globale-
ment unificatrice devait être de première
importance pour les travaux ultérieurs de
Charles Eames et d'Eero Saarinen. Mais
peut-être plus remarquable encore est
l'exploration par Wright de cette approche
globalisante du design qui se retrouvera
dans le concept de George Nelson de
systèmes de mobilier intégré pour la maison et les lieux de travail.

Le *fauteuil rouge-bleu* de Gerrit
Rietveld (1917/18) est généralement considéré comme le premier siège vraiment
moderne. Bien que Rietveld n'ait pas fait
appel à de nouveaux matériaux ou de nouvelles techniques dans sa conception, il
ouvrit la porte à une nouvelle réflexion sur
la façon dont un siège pouvait être conçu.
Avec ses plans géométriques nettement
marqués, le *fauteuil rouge-bleu* remettait
en question le besoin traditionnel de ressorts et de rembourrage. Ce remarquable
dessin, qui brisait tant de règles établies,
contestait avant tout le recours à une di-
versité de matériaux. L'utilisation volontaire
de panneaux de bois de taille standardisée
et la simplicité de l'assemblage étaient
révolutionnaires dans le climat de l'époque
où les fabricants se faisaient une gloire de
leurs techniques artisanales. Il est important de noter que sa facilité de construction le rendait susceptible d'une production à grande échelle. Cependant, son
esthétique était trop avant-gardiste pour
plaire à un vaste public. Son dessin suggérait qu'un fauteuil ne devait pas forcément posséder le «poids» matériel et visuel
associé au luxe et au coût élevé des
meubles traditionnels. Après avoir réalisé
un premier modèle en frêne naturel, Rietveld décida de peindre le suivant pour la
maison Schröder-Schrader (1924). Le
siège et le dossier furent rouge et bleu, la
coupe des extrémités en jaune et la structure en noir. Il plaça ensuite le siège sur un
sol noir et contre un mur noir pour donner
l'impression que les parties siège et dossier flottaient dans l'espace. Cette recherche d'une plus grande transparence
structurelle allait devenir l'un des signes

"Form ohne Ornament" ("Form without Ornament"), in which illustrations demonstrated the virtues of industrial designs based solely on function.

The architecture and furniture of Frank Lloyd Wright was also based on simple, rectilinear geometry. His preference for unified design was to be of primary significance to the later work of Charles Eames and Eero Saarinen. Perhaps even more importantly, however, Wright's pioneering approach to design influenced George Nelson's concept of integrated furniture systems for the home and the workplace.

The *Red-and-blue-chair* designed by Gerrit Rietveld in 1917/18 is generally regarded as the first truly Modern chair. Although Rietveld did not incorporate new materials or construction techniques in the chair's design, he gave rise to a new insight into how a chair could be conceived – with its simple geometric planes the *Red-and-blue-chair* questioned the need for traditional springing and upholstery. This remarkable design, which broke all pre-existing rules, essentially contested the use of anything but a minimum of materials. The intentional use of roughly cut wood of standard sizes and the simplistic joining of elements were revolutionary in a climate in which mainstream manufacturers prided themselves on their conventional craft-based techniques. Importantly, the ease of its construction made it viable for full-scale mass-production. However, its aesthetics were too avant-garde for popular appeal. The design suggested that a chair did not have to possess the visual and material weight that associated traditional furniture with luxury and high cost. Initially, the chair was constructed of natural beech, and later, in 1924, for the interior of the Schröder-Schrader house, Rietveld painted the seat and back blue and red, and the cut ends yellow, while staining the supporting structure black. He then placed the chair on a black floor and against a black wall to create the impression that the seat and back sections were floating in air. This quest for a greater structural transparency was to become one of the central endeavours of Modernism. The date of the *Red-and-blue-chair* is highly significant, for it was "a natural turning point in modern history. It was a moment at which – after cubism, abstraction, Dada – art could never be the same again; at which – after the massive displacements of the First World War – society could never be the same again; at which – after the terrible destruction of economic means – the techniques of architecture and the objectives of industrial design could never be the same again."[11]

Der von Gerrit Rietveld 1917/18 entworfene *Rot-Blau-Stuhl* wird allgemein als der erste wirklich moderne Stuhl angesehen. Obwohl Rietveld bei seinem Entwurf keine neuen Materialien oder Konstruktionstechniken angewandt hat, eröffnete er mit diesem Modell neue Einsichten für die Gestaltung von Stühlen – mit seinen einfachen geometrischen Flächen stellte der *Rot-Blau-Stuhl* die Notwendigkeit traditioneller Federung und Polsterung grundsätzlich in Frage. Dieser bemerkenswerte Entwurf, der mit allen bestehenden Regeln brach, sollte vor allem beweisen, daß man mit einem Minimum an Material auskommen konnte. Die Verwendung von grob zugeschnittenem Holz in standardisierter Größe und die höchst einfache Verbindung der Elemente galten als revolutionär, denn bis dahin herrschte ein Klima, in dem die weithin anerkannten Hersteller ihre konventionellen, vom Handwerk entlehnten Techniken priesen. Es ist von besonderer Bedeutung, daß die einfache Konstruktion dieses Stuhls ihn bestens geeignet machte für eine voll technisierte Massenproduktion. Doch seine Ästhetik war zu avantgardistisch für den allgemeinen Geschmack. Das Design brachte zum Ausdruck, daß ein Stuhl nicht das optische und materielle Gewicht in Anspruch zu nehmen habe, das vor allem solche traditionellen Möbelstücke für sich beanspruchen – oder das man ihnen beimißt – die gemeinhin mit Luxus und hohen Preisen in Verbindung gebracht werden. Ursprünglich war der Stuhl aus naturbelassenem Buchenholz gebaut, doch später, im Jahre 1924, malte Rietveld für die Innenausstattung des Schröder-Schrader-Hauses Sitz und Lehne blau und rot an, die abgeschnittenen Enden gelb und die tragende Struktur schwarz. Er stellte den Stuhl auf einen schwarzen Fußboden und vor eine schwarze Wand, um den Eindruck zu erwecken, daß Sitz und Lehne in der Luft schwebten. Dieses Bemühen um eine größere Transparenz der Konstruktion sollte zu einem zentralen Anliegen des Modernismus werden. Der Zeitpunkt, zu dem der *Rot-Blau-Stuhl* entstand, ist höchst bezeichnend, denn es war »ein natürlicher Wendepunkt in der modernen Zeitgeschichte. Es war ein Zeitpunkt, zu dem die Kunst – nach Kubismus, reiner Abstraktion und Dada – nicht mehr das sein konnte, was sie gewesen war; ein Moment, in dem auch die Gesellschaft – nach den massiven Umwälzungen durch den Ersten Weltkrieg – nicht mehr dieselbe bleiben konnte; ein Zeitpunkt, zu dem – nach der entsetzlichen Zerstörung der wirtschaftlichen Mittel – die Technik und die Architektur und die Zielsetzungen des

Mart Stam:

Side chair and table, 1926/27

Stuhl und Tisch, 1926/27

Chaise et table, 1926/27

from Werner Gräff, "Innenräume",
Verlag Dr. Fr. Wedekind, Stuttgart, 1928

Le Corbusier:

Basculant chair,
Model No. B301, c. 1929

Basculant-Stuhl,
Modell Nr. B301, um 1929

Chaise *Basculant*,
modéle n°. B301, vers 1929

Courtesy Sotheby's, New York

This culture of turmoil demanded new solutions to existing problems but did not offer significant industrial innovation, unlike the period following the Second World War. Instead, progress had to be made ideologically rather than technically. The *Red-and-blue-chair* was shown at a general exhibition at the Bauhaus in 1923, and as "a three-dimensional realization of the philosophy of the De Stijl movement"[12] it was the first chair to express a radical Modern ideology. The design disseminated the movement's vision of utopia, the basis of which was founded in Dutch puritanism. The members of De Stijl advocated the purification of art and design through abstracted cubism, or as Piet Mondrian described it, Neo-Plasticism, which in its search for honesty and beauty would bring harmony and enlightenment to humanity.

Although the potential mass-production of modern furniture through the application of new technology was first explored at the Bauhaus, the founding fathers of the Modern Movement, such as Ludwig Mies van der Rohe and Marcel Breuer, still primarily viewed furniture as integral to unified architectural schemes. Their designs, such as the *Barcelona chair* of 1929 and the *Wassily chair* of 1925, were initially created within the context of specific interior plans – the German Pavilion at the Barcelona International Exhibition of 1929 and the painter Wassily Kandinsky's staff accommodation at the Dessau Bauhaus. Ironically, chair designs such as these, which very much appear to be machine-made, were labour-intensive to produce and, therefore, costly to manufacture – an aspect that ran counter to Bauhaus philosophy. It was realized that the true mass-production of democratic Modern furniture would only be possible if a form of mechanized standardization was adopted. However, it was not until the post-World War II years that it was economically or technically feasible to achieve this on a wide scale.

Modern architecture and design that addressed the pressing requirement for public housing and low-cost furnishings was the central theme explored at the Deutsche Werkbund exhibition, "Die Wohnung" ("The Dwelling") held at the Weissenhofsiedlung in 1927. A year earlier, all the architects who were to take part in the exhibition met in Stuttgart. At this gathering of kindred spirits, the Dutch architect Mart Stam presented drawings of a prototype chair that incorporated the architectural cantilever principle. Visually simpler while structurally and materially more unified than those with four legs, Stam's chair

Industriedesigns nicht mehr dieselben sein konnten«.[11] In dieser Zeit der Umwälzungen verlangten Kunst und Kultur nach neuen Lösungen für die bestehenden Probleme, doch sie bewirkten keine nennenswerten industriellen Neuerungen, wie es in der Zeit nach dem Zweiten Weltkrieg der Fall war. Jetzt mußte der Fortschritt eher auf ideologischer als auf technischer Ebene stattfinden. Der *Rot-Blau-Stuhl* wurde 1923 auf einer Ausstellung im Bauhaus gezeigt; als »eine dreidimensionale Realisierung der Philosophie der De-Stijl-Bewegung«[12] war er der erste Stuhl, der auf radikale Weise die Ideologie der Modernität zum Ausdruck brachte. Der Stuhlentwurf propagierte die utopische Vision der Bewegung, die ihre Wurzeln im niederländischen Puritanismus hatte. Die Mitglieder von De Stijl setzten sich für die Reinheit von Kunst und Design ein und entwickelten aufgrund dieser Haltung einen abstrakten Kubismus, oder, wie Piet Mondrian es nannte, einen Neoplastizismus, der in seinem Streben nach Strenge und Schönheit der Menschheit Harmonie und Klarheit bringen sollte.

Es war am Bauhaus, wo die Möglichkeit der Massenproduktion moderner Möbel durch die Anwendung neuer Technologien zuerst erforscht wurde; doch es waren die Gründungsväter der Moderne wie Ludwig Mies van der Rohe und Marcel Breuer, die als erste das Mobiliar als einen integralen Bestandteil einer einheitlichen architektonischen Planung ansahen. Ihre Stuhlentwürfe, etwa der *Barcelona-Stuhl* von 1929 und der *Wassily-Stuhl* von 1925, waren ursprünglich als Elemente bestimmter innenarchitektonischer Konzeptionen geplant – der eine für den deutschen Pavillon auf der Weltausstellung von 1929 in Barcelona, der andere für die Mitarbeiterrunde des Malers Wassily Kandinsky am Dessauer Bauhaus. Ironischerweise sind Stuhlentwürfe wie diese, die so aussehen, als seien sie maschinell gefertigt, sehr arbeitsintensiv in der Herstellung und verursachen daher hohe Kosten – ein Gesichtspunkt, der der Bauhausphilosophie zuwiderlief. Man war sich darüber im klaren, daß eine sinnvolle Massenproduktion moderner Möbel nur dann möglich wäre, wenn eine Form von mechanisierter Standardproduktion erreicht werden könnte. Es dauerte jedoch noch bis in die Jahre nach dem Zweiten Weltkrieg, bis es ökonomisch und technisch möglich war, dies in größerem Umfang zu verwirklichen.

Moderne Architektur und Design, die speziell auf die drängenden Bedürfnisse des sozialen Wohnungsbaus und kostengünstiger Möbel ausgerichtet waren,

distinctifs du Modernisme. La date de création du *fauteuil rouge-bleu* est très significative car elle marque «une inflexion naturelle de l'histoire moderne. Ce fut le moment – avec le cubisme, l'abstraction pure, Dada – après lequel l'art ne pouvait plus jamais être le même; après lequel, si l'on pense aux grands mouvements de population de la Première Guerre mondiale, la société n'allait plus jamais être la même, et, après les terribles destructions du conflit, les techniques de l'architecture et les objectifs du design industriel n'allaient plus jamais être les mêmes».[11] Cette culture de crise réclamait de nouvelles solutions mais ne proposait pas d'innovations industrielles significatives, à la différence de l'après-Seconde Guerre mondiale. Le progrès allait emprunter des voies idéologiques plutôt que techniques. Le *fauteuil rouge-bleu* fut présenté lors d'une grande exposition du Bauhaus en 1923. Matérialisation en trois dimensions de la philosophie du mouvement De Stijl[12], il fut le premier à exprimer une idéologie radicalement moderne. Le design fit connaître la vision utopique de ce mouvement qui prenait ses racines dans le puritanisme néerlandais. Les membres de De Stijl réclamaient la purification de l'art et du design grâce au cubisme abstrait ou, comme le déclara Piet Mondrian, le néo-plasticisme qui allait apporter l'harmonie et illuminer l'humanité à travers sa recherche de la vérité et de la beauté.

Bien que la problématique de la production de meubles en série grâce aux progrès de la technique ait été initialement explorée par le Bauhaus, les pères fondateurs du mouvement moderniste, comme Ludwig Mies van der Rohe et Marcel Breuer, considéraient encore essentiellement le mobilier comme part intégrante de leurs projets architecturaux pris dans leur globalité. La chauffeuse *Barcelona* de 1929 et le fauteuil *Wassily* de 1925 furent d'abord créés pour des aménagements intérieurs spécifiques, en l'occurrence le pavillon allemand de la Foire Internationale de Barcelone de 1929 et les bureaux de Wassily Kandinsky au Bauhaus de Dessau. Ironiquement, ces projets semblent devoir beaucoup à la machine, alors qu'ils demandaient de nombreuses heures de travail augmentant considérablement leur prix et les éloignant de ce fait de la philosophie du Bauhaus. On comprit alors qu'une véritable production en série de mobilier moderne démocratique ne pouvait être possible que si l'on adoptait une forme de standardisation autorisant la mécanisation. Mais pourtant ce ne fut pas avant la fin de la Seconde Guerre mondiale qu'il fut économiquement ou techniquement was the first of its kind. Such was the magnitude of this breakthrough in design that its significance is comparable in sculpture to Michelangelo's realization of the first full unsupported contraposto since Antiquity in his "David".

At the Weissenhof exhibition, Stam first displayed his cantilevered side chair which was being produced by the L.&C. Arnold company in rigid cast tubular steel, reinforced with metal rods. Controversially, Ludwig Mies van der Rohe also exhibited a cantilevered chair, the *Model No. MR10*, a refined version of Stam's precedent which later became known as the Weissenhof chair. The more elegant *MR10* was constructed of resilient bent tubular steel which allowed a greater degree of flexibility, affording the sitter comfort without the need of springing or upholstery. A year later, Marcel Breuer produced two further cantilevered chairs, the *Model No. B32*, known as the *Cesca* (named after his daughter, Francesca) and the *Model No. B33*, which was highly derivative of Stam's earlier design. Reputedly inspired by the handlebars of his newly purchased Adler bicycle, it was Breuer who had first incorporated resilient tubular steel in the design of chairs with his *Model No. B3 Wassily chair* of 1925. With this landmark design, Breuer paid homage to the linearity and reductivist aesthetics of Gerrit Rietveld's earlier *Red-and-blue-chair*.

Even if cost-efficient industrial mechanisms had been in place to facilitate the high-volume manufacture of Modernist furniture, it is highly debatable whether the masses for whom these designs were intended would have embraced them with widespread enthusiasm. Tubular metal, for instance, was still generally associated with industry and did not, therefore, mesh with the working classes' bourgeois aspirations. The Modern designs of the Bauhaus were not only too avant-garde for industrial production, but also too forward-looking and aesthetically challenging for widespread public acceptance. The philosophical morality promoted by the Bauhaus, however, formed the bedrock on which Modernism would grow into an international movement. In the 1930s, several important members of the Bauhaus emigrated from Germany to the United States of America via Britain, disseminating Modernist ideology and widely influencing the next generation of architects and designers.

A less stringent form of geometric rationalism was adopted by the pioneers of the so-called "International Style" in France – Le Corbusier, Pierre Jeanneret and Charlotte Perriand. These designers

bildeten das zentrale Thema auf der Ausstellung »Die Wohnung«, die der Deutsche Werkbund 1927 in der Weißenhof-Siedlung ausrichtete. Ein Jahr zuvor hatten sich alle Architekten, die an dieser Ausstellung teilnehmen sollten, in Stuttgart getroffen. Bei dieser Zusammenkunft von Gleichgesinnten präsentierte der niederländische Architekt Mart Stam Zeichnungen von einem Stuhlprototypen, der auf dem architektonischen Prinzip der freitragenden Fläche beruhte. Stams Stuhl wirkte optisch einfacher als herkömmliche Stühle mit vier Beinen, und gleichzeitig wirkte er einheitlicher in Konstruktion und Material; es war der erste Stuhl in dieser Art. Dieser Entwurf bedeutete für das Design einen derart entscheidenden Durchbruch, daß er in seiner Bedeutung zu vergleichen ist mit Michelangelos Verwirklichung der ersten vollkommen ungestützten Kontrapost-Skulptur seit der Antike, mit seinem »David«.

Auf der Weißenhof-Ausstellung führte Stam seinen Stuhl mit freitragender Sitzfläche zum erstenmal vor; er wurde von der Firma L. & C. Arnold aus unelastischem Stahlrohr, das mit Metallstäben verstärkt war, hergestellt. Als Gegenentwurf stellte auch Ludwig Mies van der Rohe einen freitragenden Stuhl aus, das *Modell Nr. MR10*, eine veredelte Version von Stams Vorläufer, die später als der *Weißenhof-Stuhl* bekannt wurde. Der eleganter wirkende *MR 10* war aus federndem, gebogenem Stahlrohr gebaut, das eine stärkere Biegsamkeit gestattete und den Sitzkomfort erhöhte, ohne daß eine Federung oder Polsterung notwendig war. Ein Jahr später produzierte Marcel Breuer zwei weitere freitragende Stühle, das *Modell Nr. B32*, das als *Cesca* (benannt nach seiner Tochter Francesca) bekannt ist, und das *Modell Nr. B33*, das deutlich aus Stams früherem Entwurf abgeleitet war. Breuer war angeblich durch die Lenkstange seines neuerworbenen Adler-Fahrrades dazu angeregt worden, als erster federndes Stahlrohr für seine Stuhlentwürfe zu verwenden, und so entwickelte er 1925 sein *Modell Nr. B3 Wassily*. Dieser Stuhl bedeutete einen Markstein im Design. Breuer erwies damit seine Reverenz an die Linearität und reduktionistische Ästhetik von Gerrit Rietvelds früherem *Rot-Blau-Stuhl*.

Selbst wenn kostengünstige industrielle Fertigungsverfahren zur Verfügung gestanden hätten, um die aufwendige Herstellung moderner Möbel zu erleichtern, so ist es doch höchst fraglich, ob die Massen, für die diese Entwürfe gedacht waren, sie mit der entsprechenden Begeisterung aufgenommen hätten. Stahlrohr wurde

possible d'y arriver, du moins à grande échelle.

L'architecture et le design modernes, qui répondaient aux besoins pressants du public en logements et en mobilier économiques, furent le thème central de l'exposition du Deutsche Werkbund «Die Wohnung», (l'habitation) qui se tint à la cité de Weissenhof en 1927. Un an plus tôt, tous les architectes qui devaient y prendre part se rencontrèrent à Stuttgart. A cette réunion, le Néerlandais Mart Stam montra le dessin d'un prototype de siège en porte-à-faux. D'aspect et de structure plus simples que les modèles classiques à quatre pieds et faisant appel à un nombre de matériaux réduit, cette chaise était la première de ce type. Telle fut l'importance de cette percée du design que l'on peut comparer sa signification à la sculpture du David de Michel-Ange, premier «contraposto» sans aucun soutien.

A l'exposition de Weissenhof, Stam présenta donc sa chaise en porte-à-faux, produite par la L.& C. Arnold Company en tubes de fonte d'acier rigide renforcés de tiges de métal. Ludwig Mies van der Rohe exposa également son *modèle n° MR10*, une version raffinée de celui de Stam et qui prit plus tard le nom de Weissenhof. Plus élégant, le *MR10*, était construit en tube d'acier cintré flexible, qui permettait davantage de souplesse et offrait à la personne assise un réel confort malgré l'absence totale de ressorts ou de rembourrage. Un an plus tard, Marcel Breuer sortit deux autres sièges en porte-à-faux, le *modèle n° B32*, connu sous le nom de Cesca (d'après le prénom de sa fille, Francesca) et le *modèle n° B33*, très directement dérivés du modèle initial de Stam. Inspiré, d'après ce que l'on disait, par le guidon de son nouveau vélo Adler, Breuer avait été le premier à se servir de tube d'acier flexible pour la fabrication d'un siège, dès son *modèle n° B3 Wassily* en 1925. A travers cette création d'importance historique, Breuer rendait hommage à la linéarité et au minimalisme du *fauteuil rouge-bleu* de Rietveld.

Même si la structure industrielle capable de fabriquer les meubles modernistes en grande série avait été en place, on peut se demander si les masses auxquelles ces créations étaient destinées les auraient adoptées avec enthousiasme. Le tube de métal, par exemple, rappelait le plus souvent l'industrie et s'associait mal, pour cette raison, aux aspirations bourgeoises des classes travailleuses. Les projets modernistes du Bauhaus n'étaient pas seulement trop avant-gardistes pour la production industrielle de l'époque mais également trop avancés et esthétiquement trop collaborated on many projects, including several chair designs such as the *Grand Confort* and the *Model No. 2072 chaise longue*. Like their German counterparts, they used a combination of tubular metal and leather in their designs. However, their use of these materials was less utilitarian in nature. Influenced by the contemporary Art Deco style, these designs bear the unmistakable hallmark of Parisian chic. Nevertheless, the interior schemes and chair designs of Le Corbusier, Jeanneret and Perriand must be considered Modern, for they encapsulate many of the same principles as their Bauhaus counterparts yet in a less doctrinaire way. By associating luxury and style with industrial materials, the Modern chair became more desirable to the affluent and increasingly sophisticated furniture-buying public.

Unlike those at the Bauhaus, Scandinavian designers such as Alvar Aalto and, slightly later, Bruno Mathsson relied on the use of natural woods and other organic materials in their approach to Modernism. Aalto made a significant contribution to the history of the Modern chair with his bent laminated wood *Paimio chair* of 1931/32. Where the design required greater pliancy, such as in the scrolls of the seat and back, Aalto removed several layers of veneer, thereby increasing the material's malleability. The Scandinavian's gentler and more tactile form of rationalism was well received in America and Britain during the 1930s and 1940s.

Importantly, the prominent Finnish architect, Eliel Saarinen emigrated to the United States in 1923 and a year later took up a visiting professorship at the University of Michigan – one of the main furniture-producing regions in America. In 1927, the Cranbrook Foundation was established by the philanthropist and newspaper proprietor, George G. Booth, and in 1932, Eliel Saarinen became the director of the Cranbrook Academy of Arts. As the democratic counterpart to the Bauhaus, Cranbrook was founded with the intention of bringing unity to the arts. Both institutions operated studios and workshops dedicated to the teaching of the various disciplines within the fine and applied arts and an exchange of ideas between these fields of study was strongly promoted. The Cranbrook Academy of Arts was the pre-eminent design institute in America during the inter-war years, with many of its alumni and staff becoming leaders in their fields of design and architecture. The significance of Eliel Saarinen's directorship of Cranbrook cannot be overstated, for he inculcated the principles of Modernism to a small but extremely

immer noch weitgehend als Material zur industriellen Verarbeitung angesehen und ließ sich daher kaum mit den bürgerlichen Sehnsüchten der arbeitenden Klasse in Einklang bringen. Das moderne Design des Bauhauses war nicht nur zu avantgardistisch für die industrielle Produktion, sondern auch zu sehr in die Zukunft gerichtet; außerdem bedeutete es ästhetisch eine zu große Herausforderung für die breite Akzeptanz des Publikums. Doch die moralischen Grundlagen einer Weltanschauung, die vom Bauhaus propagiert wurde, bildeten das Fundament, auf dem der Modernismus sich zu einer internationalen Bewegung auswachsen sollte. In den 30er Jahren emigrierten viele bedeutende Mitglieder des Bauhauses über England in die Vereinigten Staaten und verbreiteten ihre Ideologie der Moderne. Sie übten einen weitreichenden Einfluß auf die folgende Generation von Architekten und Designern aus.

Eine weniger stringente Form des geometrischen Rationalismus wurde von den Pionieren des sogenannten »internationalen Stils« in Frankreich entwickelt; zu ihnen gehörten Le Corbusier, Pierre Jeanneret und Charlotte Perriand. Diese Architekten und Designer arbeiteten bei vielen Projekten zusammen und entwarfen mehrere Stühle, etwa den *Grand Confort* und das *Modell Nr. 2072 Chaise Longue*. Wie ihre deutschen Kollegen verwendeten sie in ihren Entwürfen eine Kombination aus Metallrohr und Leder. Jedoch war die Verwendung dieser Materialien bei ihnen weniger zweckgebunden. Sie unterlagen noch immer den Einflüssen des zeitgenössischen Art-Déco-Stils, und daher weisen diese Entwürfe unverkennbar die Merkmale des pariserischen Chics auf. Dennoch kann man die Innenausstattungen und Stuhlentwürfe von Le Corbusier, Jeanneret und Perriand als modern bezeichnen, denn sie beruhen in vieler Hinsicht auf denselben Prinzipien, denen auch ihre Bauhaus-Kollegen folgten, wenn auch in der französischen Variante auf weniger doktrinäre Weise. Indem sie bei ihren Entwürfen Luxus und Stil mit Industriematerial wie etwa Stahlrohr in Verbindung brachten, wurde der moderne Stuhl auch für das wohlhabende und zunehmend anspruchsvollere Publikum zum begehrenswerten Kaufobjekt.

Im Unterschied zu den Mitgliedern des Bauhauses wandten sich skandinavische Designer wie Alvar Aalto und, etwas später, Bruno Mathsson, bei ihrer Auseinandersetzung mit dem Modernismus natürlichen Materialien zu, vor allem der Verwendung von Naturhölzern. Aalto leistete mit seinem *Paimio-Stuhl* von 1931/32 aus

Charles & Ray Eames:

Plywood lounge chair (prototype), 1946

Sperrholzstuhl (Prototyp), 1946

Chaise en contreplaqué (prototype), 1946

Courtesy Eames Office, Venice, California

24

gebogenem Schichtholz einen wichtigen Beitrag zur Geschichte des modernen Stuhls. An den Stellen, wo die Konstruktion größere Biegsamkeit erforderte, etwa in den Vertiefungen von Sitz und Rückenlehne, entfernte Aalto mehrere Schichten des Furniers und erhöhte so die Geschmeidigkeit des Materials. Die weichere und taktilere Spielart des skandinavischen Rationalismus wurde in den 30er und 40er Jahren in Amerika und England sehr gut aufgenommen. Ein folgenreiches Ereignis war die Emigration des prominenten finnischen Architekten Eliel Saarinen im Jahre 1923 in die Vereinigten Staaten; ein Jahr später übernahm er eine Gastprofessur an der Universität von Michigan – in einer der wichtigsten möbelproduzierenden Regionen Amerikas.

1927 gründete der Zeitungsverleger und Mäzen George G. Booth die Cranbrook Foundation; im Jahr 1932 wurde Eliel Saarinen Direktor der Cranbrook Kunstakademie. Cranbrook, das man als demokratisches Gegenstück zum Bauhaus bezeichnen kann, wurde mit dem Ziel gegründet, eine Einheit in die Künste zu bringen. Beide Institutionen unterhielten Ateliers und Werkstätten, die dafür bestimmt waren, in den verschiedenen Disziplinen innerhalb der schönen und angewandten Künste zu unterrichten, und es wurde größter Wert darauf gelegt, daß ein Ideenaustausch zwischen diesen beiden Bereichen stattfand. Die Cranbrook Academy of Arts war die beste und einflußreichste Schule für Design in Amerika in den Jahren zwischen den Kriegen, und viele ihrer Studenten und Lehrer wurden die führenden Köpfe in ihren Bereichen von Design und Architektur. Man kann Eliel Saarinens Leistung als Direktor der Cranbrook Academy gar nicht hoch genug einschätzen, denn er vermittelte einer kleinen, äußerst talentierten Gruppe von jungen Männern und Frauen die Prinzipien des Modernismus. Es war diese Generation von Designern, die einige der wichtigsten und beispielhaftesten Neuerungen in die Geschichte des Stuhldesigns einführte: Sie trieb die moralischen Überzeugungen des Modernismus weiter voran und brachte sie in drei Dimensionen in massenhafter Verbreitung zum Ausdruck; die Anwendung künstlerisch anspruchsvoller Technologie blieb dabei oberstes Gebot.

Der Zweite Weltkrieg hatte enorme Auswirkungen auf die Möbelindustrie, vor allem in den Vereinigten Staaten. Da in der Kriegszeit Forschung und Entwicklung in erheblichem Maße in kriegswichtige Produktionsbereiche investiert wurden, vor allem in die Luftfahrtindustrie, hatte dies für die Nachkriegszeit zur Folge, daß

osés pour être acceptés par le grand public. La morale philosophique du Bauhaus, cependant, constituait une base solide sur laquelle le Modernisme allait s'épanouir et devenir un mouvement international. Dans les années 30, plusieurs membres importants du Bauhaus émigrèrent d'Allemagne vers les Etats-Unis en passant par l'Angleterre et diffusèrent l'idéologie moderniste qui allait influencer profondément la génération suivante d'architectes et de designers.

Une forme moins rigoureuse de rationalisme géométrique fut adoptée par les pionniers français du «Style international». Le Corbusier, Pierre Jeanneret et Charlotte Perriand collaborèrent sur de nombreux projets dont plusieurs sièges, le *Grand Confort* et la chaise longue *modèle n° 2072*. Comme leurs homologues allemands, ils utilisaient une association de tubes de métal et de cuir mais dans un esprit moins utilitaire. Influencées par le style Art déco de l'époque, ces créations portent la marque indélébile de l'élégance parisienne. Néanmoins, les projets d'aménagement intérieurs et de sièges de Le Corbusier, Jeanneret et Perriand doivent être considérés comme modernistes, car ils font la synthèse de nombreux principes du Bauhaus quoique d'une façon moins doctrinaire. En mariant le luxe et le style à des assemblages de matériaux industriels comme le tube d'acier, le siège moderne put alors séduire une clientèle aisée qui commença à acheter des meubles de plus en plus sophistiqués.

A la différence de ceux du Bauhaus, les designers scandinaves comme Alvar Aalto et, légèrement plus tard, Bruno Mathsson suscitèrent une approche moderniste différente qui faisait appel au bois et à d'autres matériaux naturels. Aalto apporta une contribution significative à l'histoire du siège moderne avec sa chaise de bois lamellé cintré, la *Paimio* (1931/32). Aux endroits où son dessin réclamait un cintrage techniquement audacieux, comme dans les enroulements du siège et du dossier, Aalto fit enlever plusieurs couches de placage pour augmenter la souplesse du matériau. Cette forme de rationalisme scandinave plus douce et plus tactile fut bien reçue en Amérique et en Grande-Bretagne tout au long des années 30 et 40. Il est important de noter que le grand architecte finlandais Eliel Saarinen émigra vers les Etats-Unis en 1923 et devint, un an plus tard, professeur invité à l'Université du Michigan, l'une des premières régions américaines pour la production de meubles.

En 1927, le propriétaire de journaux et philanthrope George G. Booth créa la

Gaetano Pesce:

Up 1 chair, 1969

Stuhl *Up 1*, 1969

Chaise *Up 1*, 1969

Courtesy Whitechapel Art Gallery, London

talented group of young men and women. It was this generation of designers who would set some of the most important precedents in the history of chair design by carrying forward the moral certainties of Modernism and expressing them in three dimensions on a mass scale through the application of state-of-the-art technology.

The Second World War had an enormous impact on the furniture industry, particularly in the United States. The dramatic increase in wartime research and development in other manufacturing fields, especially the aircraft industry, meant that after the war furniture designers and manufacturers had the opportunity of applying the latest and most efficient technology to the peacetime production of durable products. During this period, the interdisciplinary science of ergonomics, founded by Kaare Klint in 1917, was still in its infancy, with wartime research having been conducted by the military into what was then known as "human engineering".[13] After 1945, designers for the first time were able to quantify data which provided a new insight into the relationship between man and machine. Chairs could adopt forms that were more suited to accommodating the human body. The seat and back of the plywood series of chairs designed by Charles and Ray Eames, for example, were moulded in a way that closely followed the line of the seated body, thus affording a high degree of comfort without the use of padding. During the war, the Eameses' research into the production of low-cost wood laminates and mouldings led to a commission by the US Navy to design and produce leg splints, arm splints and stretchers in moulded plywood. Using their specially developed "Kazam" machines, so named because of the noise they made when operated, the Eameses were the first designers to mould plywood into three-dimensional compound curves – a technical breakthrough that would have enormous implications for chair design.

In postwar America and slightly later in Europe, there was a huge demand for domestic furniture at the same time as much of the Western World was enjoying an unprecedented economic boom. This era was a hopeful and forward-looking period in history, with many designers firmly believing that science and technology could bring about a brave new world. During this period many architect-designers concentrated their talents on the development of innovative furniture rather than on architectural projects. As a consequence, enlightened manufacturing companies, such as Herman Miller and

Möbeldesigner und -hersteller nun die Möglichkeit hatten, die neuesten und wirkungsvollsten Technologien auf die Herstellung bestimmter dauerhafter Produkte für friedliche Zwecke anzuwenden. Zu dieser Zeit steckte die interdisziplinäre Wissenschaft der Ergonomie, die 1917 von Kaare Klint begründet worden war, noch in ihren Kinderschuhen; zumal die Forschungen der Kriegszeit, die von Militärs betrieben wurden, zu dem geführt hatten, was man dann »human engineering« (Menschenmanipulation) nannte.[13] Nach 1945 sahen sich Designer zum erstenmal in der Lage, Daten auszuwerten, die neue Einsichten in die Beziehung zwischen Mensch und Maschine brachten. Das machte es ihnen möglich, Stühle so zu formen, daß sie besser geeignet waren, eine Paßform für den menschlichen Körper zu bilden. Zum Beispiel bei der Serie von Sperrholzstühlen nach Entwürfen von Charles und Ray Eames waren Sitz und Rückenlehne so geformt, daß sie genau den Umrissen des sitzenden Körpers angepaßt waren, so daß sie dem Sitzenden ein hohes Maß an Bequemlichkeit verschafften, ohne daß eine Polsterung erforderlich war. Während des Krieges führte die Forschung der Eames-Brüder im Bereich der kostengünstigen Schichthölzer und Formbretter dazu, daß sie von der US-Marine den Auftrag erhielten, Bein- und Armschienen und Tragbahren aus geformtem Sperrholz zu entwerfen und zu produzieren. Unter Verwendung ihrer speziell entwickelten »Kazam«-Maschinen – ein lautmalerischer Name – formten sie als erste Designer komplexe dreidimensionale Ausbuchtungen in Sperrholz; dies bedeutete einen technischen Durchbruch, der unabsehbare Folgen für das Stuhldesign haben sollte.

Im Amerika der Nachkriegszeit und wenig später auch in Europa bestand eine gewaltige Nachfrage nach Haushalts- und Wohnraummöbeln, denn zugleich erlebte der größte Teil der westlichen Welt einen nie dagewesenen wirtschaftlichen Aufschwung. Diese Ära war eine hoffnungsvolle und vorwärtsgewandte Periode in der Geschichte, und viele Designer glaubten fest daran, daß Wissenschaft und Technik eine schöne neue Welt hervorbringen würden. In dieser Zeit konzentrierten viele Architekten-Designer ihr Talent ganz auf die Entwicklung innovativer Möbel und weniger auf architektonische Entwürfe. Das hatte zur Folge, daß aufgeklärte und weitsichtige Möbelhersteller wie etwa Herman Miller und Knoll International in der Lage waren, einem großen Publikum revolutionäre, kostengünstige und qualitativ hochwertige moderne Möbel anzubieten.

Cranbrook Foundation et, en 1932, Eliel Saarinen devint le directeur de la Cranbrook Academy of Arts. Equivalent démocratique du Bauhaus, Cranbrook fut fondé dans l'intention de militer pour une vision unificatrice dans les arts. Les deux institutions disposaient de même de studios et d'ateliers consacrés à l'enseignement de diverses disciplines et multipliaient les échanges entre les beaux-arts et les arts appliqués. La Cranbrook Academy of Arts fut l'institut de design prééminent de l'Amérique de l'entre-deux-guerres et beaucoup de ses anciens étudiants et de ses animateurs occupèrent une place de premier plan dans leur domaine d'activité. L'importance de la direction d'Eliel Saarinen ne doit pas être négligée, car il inculqua les principes du Modernisme à un groupe d'étudiants et d'étudiantes peu nombreux mais extrêmement talentueux. Ce fut de cette génération de designers qu'allaient sortir certains des modèles qui, en traduisant la philosophie du Modernisme et en particulier la volonté de production à grande échelle et celle de recourir à des technologies d'avant-garde, allaient exercer un rôle fondamental dans l'histoire du siège.

La Seconde Guerre mondiale exerça un impact énorme sur l'industrie du meuble et avant tout aux Etats-Unis. L'important accroissement de la recherche et du développement dans certains domaines d'activités, en particulier l'industrie aéronautique, signifiait qu'après la guerre, les designers et les fabricants de mobilier allaient avoir la possibilité d'appliquer les technologies le plus récentes et les plus efficaces à la production de biens de consommation durables. Par ailleurs, pendant cette période, la science interdisciplinaire de l'ergonomie, fondée par Kaare Klint en 1917, fit des débuts prometteurs à l'occasion de certaines recherches militaires sur ce que l'on appelait alors l'«human engineering».[13] Après 1945, les designers purent pour la première fois disposer de données quantifiables qui leur donnaient une nouvelle vision des relations entre l'homme et la machine. Ceci déboucha sur des formes de sièges mieux adaptées au corps humain. Le siège et le dossier de la série «Contreplaqué» de Charles et Ray Eames, par exemple, furent moulés selon une technique qui suivait au plus près la ligne d'un corps assis, assurant un meilleur degré de confort sans avoir recours au rembourrage. Pendant la guerre, les recherches des Eames dans le domaine de la production économique de lamellés et de moulages de bois furent encouragées par une commande de l'US Navy pour la conception et la fabrication de gouttières

Knoll International, were able to offer the general public revolutionary, low-cost, yet high-quality, Modern furniture.

In the 1950s, through the emergence of a new Scandinavian-influenced approach to Modernism, ergonomics and advanced technology, particularly in the plastics industry, the chair uniquely became more unified in design. Unlike the geometric formalism adhered to by the early Modern Movement, which at best only offered the possibility of structural and material unity, a truly functional unification of the chair with its user could be realized through an organic approach to design. More concerned with the way people actually sat than with how they were compelled to sit according to convention, Eero Saarinen and Charles Eames, after intensive research in the late 1940s and early 1950s, developed several seminal chair designs in fibreglass-reinforced plastic that achieved a hitherto unrealized organic unity of design. Concurrently in Italy, designers such as Marco Zanuso began exploring the potential of foam rubber as a suitable material for upholstery, and its successful application led to a new confidence of expression in chair design. By the mid 1950s, the chair became more sculptural in form to better accommodate the human body while counteracting the geometric regularity of the novel and increasingly prevalent built-in storage units. In doing so, the chair became one of the central points of the modern interior.

The mass-production of low-cost durable products for the huge domestic and contract requirement after the Second World War was viewed as an essential and, therefore, worthy social objective. Throughout the 1950s manufacturers in both Europe and the United States emphasized in their marketing strategies the quality, cost efficiency and universality of their products. With domestic interiors becoming generally smaller in scale, individual chair designs were by necessity multi-functional, being used for such purposes as writing, dining and lounging. This concern for flexibility enabled companies in America, such as Knoll International and Herman Miller, to secure dominant market shares as their seat furniture in particular could be used successfully within both domestic and contract environments.

With the rise and celebration of popular culture in the 1960s, the status of the chair was profoundly altered by the avantgarde: it became a disposable product. In this age of booming consumerism, when it was believed that built-in obsolescence would increase productivity and thereby economic prosperity, the modern chair

Durch einen neuen, von Skandinavien beeinflußten Zugang zur Moderne, durch den Einsatz von Ergonomie und fortschrittlicher Technologie, vor allem in der Kunststoffindustrie, wurde der Stuhl in den 50er Jahren einheitlicher im Design. Im Gegensatz zum geometrischen Formalismus, dem die Verfechter des frühen Modernismus anhingen, der aber bestenfalls nur die Möglichkeit einer Vereinheitlichung von Konstruktion und Material bot, konnte nun durch die Auseinandersetzung mit den organischen Bedingungen des Designs eine wirklich funktionale Verbindung des Stuhls mit seinem Benutzer erreicht werden. Entwerfer wie Eero Saarinen und Charles Eames beschäftigten sich nun mehr mit der Frage, wie die Leute tatsächlich saßen, als mit der Frage, wie sie der Konvention entsprechend zu sitzen hatten. Nach ausgedehnten Studien in den späten 40er und frühen 50er Jahren entwickelten sie mehrere zukunftsweisende Stuhlentwürfe in fiberglasverstärktem Kunststoff, durch den sie eine unübertroffene organische Einheit erreichten. Zur gleichen Zeit begannen in Italien Designer wie Marco Zanuso, die Möglichkeiten von Schaumgummi als geeignetem Polstermaterial näher zu beleuchten; die erfolgreiche Verwendung dieses Materials führte zu einer ganz neuen Perspektive in der Formensprache des Stuhldesigns. In der Mitte der fünfziger Jahre wurde der Stuhl skulpturaler in seiner Gestaltung und setzte zugleich einen Gegenakzent gegen die geometrische Regelmäßigkeit der neu aufgekommenen und immer beliebter werdenden Einbaumöbel. In seiner Funktion als Raumakzent wurde der Stuhl zum Blickpunkt des modernen Innenraums.

Die Massenproduktion von dauerhaften Tiefpreisprodukten für den riesigen häuslichen und professionellen Bedarf nach dem Zweiten Weltkrieg wurde als eine wesentliche und daher notwendige Zielsetzung angesehen. Sowohl europäische als auch amerikanische Hersteller setzten in den 50er Jahren in ihren Vermarktungsstrategien auf Qualität, günstige Preise und weltweiten Vertrieb ihrer Produkte. Da die Wohnungseinrichtungen zu jener Zeit im allgemeinen bescheidenere Ausmaße hatten, erwies es sich als sinnvoll, multifunktionale Stühle zu entwerfen, die sowohl zum Schreiben als auch zum Essen und für den Wohnbereich zu verwenden waren. Dieses Bedürfnis nach Flexibilität ermöglichte es Firmen in Amerika, zum Beispiel Knoll International und Herman Miller, sich beherrschende Marktanteile zu sichern, da vor allem ihre Sitzmöbel sowohl im privaten häuslichen Bereich als auch in Büros und professio-

et de civières en contreplaqué moulé. Utilisant des machines spécialement mises au point à cet effet, les «Kazam», ainsi nommées pour le bruit qu'elles faisaient, les Eames furent les premiers designers à mouler le contreplaqué selon des formes complexes tridimensionnelles, percée technique qui allait avoir d'énormes implications sur le design du siège.

Dans l'Amérique d'après-guerre et légèrement plus tard en Europe, alors que la plupart des pays du monde occidental connaissaient une expansion économique sans précédent, se dessinait une énorme demande pour le mobilier de maison. Cette époque était pleine d'espoir et de croyance en l'avenir et de nombreux designers pensaient fermement que la science et la technologie réunies pouvaient conduire au meilleur des mondes. Pendant cette période, de nombreux architectes-designers s'orientèrent vers la mise au point de meubles innovateurs plutôt que de projets architecturaux. C'est ainsi que des entreprises particulièrement éclairées, comme Herman Miller et Knoll International furent en mesure d'offrir à un vaste public des meubles modernes de haute qualité à un coût relativement raisonnable. Au cours des années cinquante, profitant de la convergence de la nouvelle approche scandinave, de l'ergonomie et des nouvelles techniques, en particulier de l'industrie des plastiques, le siège fit des progrès décisifs vers son unification conceptuelle. A la différence du formalisme géométrique auquel adhéraient les tenants historiques du mouvement moderniste, qui ne pouvait qu'offrir au mieux une plus grande unité de structure et de matériaux, une véritable symbiose du siège et de son utilisateur était enfin à portée de la main grâce à l'approche organique. Plus intéressés par la façon dont les gens s'assoient réellement que par la manière dont les conventions leur enseignent de s'asseoir, Eero Saarinen et Charles Eames, après des recherches intensives à la fin des années 40 et au début des années 50, mirent au point plusieurs sièges en matériaux plastiques renforcés de fibre de verre qui atteignirent à une cohérence de design jusque-là inconnue. Dans le même temps, en Italie, des designers comme Marco Zanuso commencèrent à explorer le potentiel de la mousse de caoutchouc dans le rembourrage et leurs réussites ouvrirent de nouvelles possibilités d'expression à la conception du siège. Vers le milieu des années 50, il prit des formes plus sculpturales pour mieux s'adapter au corps humain tout en jouant un rôle de contrepoint face à la sécheresse géométrique des rangements intégrés, de plus en plus

27

became just another short-lived gimmick as expendable as a paper dress. Peter Murdoch and Peter Raacke, among others, challenged the tradition that associated furniture with high cost and permanence by producing designs constructed of paperboard and cardboard. Aimed at a youth-based and socially liberated market, the chair was no longer seen as a durable product for the home, but as a lifestyle accessory subject to the ephemeral demands of fashion. This approach was exploited in Italy through the introduction of novel seating formats such as the inflatable *Blow chair* designed by Scolari, D'Urbino, Lomazzi and De Pas in 1967, the *Sacco* beanbag designed by Gatti, Paolini & Teodoro in 1968 and the vacuum-packed *Up* series designed by Gaetano Pesce in 1969. These revolutionary innovations combined with the increasing availability of "flat-pack" or "knock-down" furniture greatly simplified the act of purchasing – one could now literally buy a chair off the shelf.

In Britain during the 1960s, fuelled by the emergence of colour supplement magazines, there was a reaction against the rational austerity of "Good Design" which had until then been widely promoted, not least by the Government, as "good" taste. Having been forced to accept an unrelenting State form of Modernism and a steady diet of Scandinavian functionalism for a decade, the British public longed for something more exciting and less responsible. Through a media explosion and the early manifestations of the Global Village, this decade first witnessed the manipulative capabilities of the manufacturer to design the consumer to fit the product. While the design and manufacture of attention-grabbing evanescent and gimmicky products flourished, popular culture and rampant consumerism became widespread throughout America and, slightly later, Europe. In Italy, furniture manufacturers realized that the only way to maintain their already prominent position within the market was to accelerate research and development projects with more funding. "Concept factories" were established by companies such as Cassina, Zanotta, Poltronova and Artemide with the objective of creating new seating formats. The quest for technical novelty for its own sake ensured that considerable advances were made, especially in the area of injection-moulded plastics. With the advent of thermoplastics such as Polypropylene and ABS, first applied to furniture production in 1963 and 1967 respectively, a new world of possibilities was opened to the manufacturer of Modern furniture. During this period of

nellen Bereichen erfolgreich Verwendung fanden.

Mit dem Aufkommen und der Verherrlichung der Popkultur in den 60er Jahren erfuhr der Status des Stuhls durch die Avantgarde eine grundlegende Veränderung: Er wurde zum Wegwerfprodukt. In diesem Jahrzehnt des Konsumbooms war man überzeugt, daß die in dem Produkt mitgelieferte schnelle Veraltung die Produktivität und damit den ökonomischen Wohlstand erhöhen würde; der moderne Stuhl wurde zu einem weiteren kurzlebigen Werbegag, ebenso entbehrlich wie ein Papierkleid. Peter Murdoch, Peter Raacke und andere Designer forderten die Tradition heraus, die Möbel mit hohen Kosten und langer Haltbarkeit in Verbindung gebracht hatte, indem sie Stühle entwarfen, die aus Pappkarton und Pappdeckeln gebaut waren. Zielgruppen waren junge Leute und ein sozial unabhängiger Markt, der den Stuhl nicht länger als ein dauerhaftes Produkt für die Inneneinrichtung betrachtete, sondern als ein Life-Style-Accessoire, das den vergänglichen Bedürfnissen der Mode unterworfen war. Diese Ideen fanden in Italien großen Anklang und wurden sofort in neue Entwürfe umgesetzt, zum Beispiel den aufblasbaren *Blow-Stuhl* nach Entwürfen von Scolari, D'Urbino, Lomazzi und De Pas aus dem Jahr 1967, den *Sacco*-Bohnensack, entworfen von Gatti, Paolini und Teodoro im Jahr 1968, und die vakuumverpackten *Up*-Serien nach Entwürfen von Gaetano Pesce von 1969. Diese revolutionären Neuerungen und das wachsende Angebot an »Flachpack«- oder »Zusammenklapp«-Möbeln vereinfachten das Einkaufen ganz erheblich – jetzt konnte man buchstäblich den Stuhl aus dem Regal nehmen.

In Großbritannien erhob sich in den 60er Jahren eine spürbare Abwehr gegen die rationale Nüchternheit des »Guten Designs«, das bis dahin stark gefördert worden war, zumal von der Regierung, die es als »guten Geschmack« propagierte. Dem britischen Volk war ein Jahrzehnt lang eine phantasielose, staatlich geförderte Form von Modernität und eine ständige Versorgung mit skandinavischem Funktionalismus aufgenötigt worden, und nun sehnte es sich nach aufregenderen und weniger einengenden Produkten. Durch das explosionsartige Anwachsen der Medien und die ersten Anzeichen einer weltweiten Verstädterung wurde man sich in den 60er Jahren der manipulativen Fähigkeiten der Fabrikanten bewußt, die den Verbraucher so »umzuprogrammieren« verstanden, daß er sich ihrem Produkt anpaßte. Während Entwurf und Herstellung von kurzlebigen Blickfang- und Wegwerf-

Piero Gilardi:
Model *Pavé*, 1965
Modell *Pavé*, 1965
Modèle *Pavé*, 1965
Courtesy Gufram, Turin

Gruppo Strum:
Pratone (Big Meadow), 1962
Courtesy Gufram, Turin

Robert Venturi:

Sheraton chair, 1984

Stuhl *Sheraton*, 1984

Chaise *Sheraton*, 1984

Courtesy Knoll Group, New York

George Sowden:

Oberoy chair designed for
Memphis, 1981

Stuhl *Oberoy*, entworfen für
Memphis, 1981

Chaise *Oberoy*, dessinée pour
Memphis, 1981

Courtesy Memphis, Milan

produkten ihre Blüten trieben, verbreiteten sich die Popkultur und eine hemmungslose Konsumlust über ganz Amerika und später auch über Europa. In Italien hatten die Möbelhersteller bald begriffen, daß die einzige Möglichkeit, ihre bereits beherrschende Marktposition zu behaupten, darin bestand, Forschung und Entwicklung ihrer Projekte durch höhere Investitionen zu beschleunigen. Firmen wie Cassina, Zanotta, Poltronova und Artemide richteten sogenannte »Konzeptionsfabriken« ein mit dem Ziel, neue Sitzmöbelformate zu entwickeln. Die Suche nach technischen Neuerungen um jeden Preis bewirkte, daß beachtliche Fortschritte erzielt wurden, vor allem im Bereich gespritzter Kunststofformen. Durch das Aufkommen von Thermokunststoffen wie Polypropylen und ABS, die erstmals 1963 beziehungsweise 1967 bei der Möbelherstellung verwandt wurden, eröffnete sich eine neue Welt der Möglichkeiten für die Hersteller moderner Möbel. In dieser Zeit erneut auflebender Aktivitäten in der italienischen Möbelindustrie spielten Designer wie Vico Magistretti, Marco Zanuso und Joe Colombo eine Vorreiterrolle; ihren ausgefallenen modernen Stuhlentwürfen ist es zu verdanken, daß Kunststoff als luxuriöses und hochwertiges Material einen gehobenen Status erhielt. Der erste Stuhl, der als vorbildliches Einzelstück Furore machen sollte, wurde von Verner Panton entworfen, der bezeichnenderweise aus Skandinavien stammte. Mit seinem freischwingenden *Stapelstuhl* von 1960, der erst 1968 in die Produktion ging, verwirklichte Panton Eero Saarinens bisher nicht umgesetzte Vorstellung einer vollkommenen Einheitlichkeit des Designs.

Das immer stärkere Auseinanderdriften des Möbelmarktes in Wohnbereich und Büroausstattung in den späten 60er und frühen 70er Jahren hatte zur Folge, daß, wenn auch in begrenztem Umfang, immer eigenwilligere avantgardistische Wohnmöbel hergestellt wurden. Ein extremes Beispiel für diese Entwicklung war das Auftauchen höchst surrealistischer Möbel, die von den Popskulpturen des Künstlers Claes Oldenburg inspiriert waren. Sie bestanden aus geformtem Polyurethan-Schaum, überdimensioniert in der Größe und als Einzelstücke gedacht; zu ihnen gehörte *Capitello*, ein Stuhlentwurf von Studio 65 aus dem Jahr 1971, der alle bisherigen Vorstellungen vom Aussehen eines Stuhls über Bord warf. Doch dies war bereits die Dämmerzeit der Popkultur, und als sich in der Mitte der 70er Jahre die Ölkrise abzuzeichnen begann, wandte sich die öffentliche Meinung immer stärker gegen die Exzesse der allgemeinen Konsumlust.

à la mode. Ce faisant, il devint l'un des principaux points d'attraction esthétique de l'habitation moderne.

Après la Seconde Guerre mondiale, la production en série de produits durables et économiques pour répondre aux énormes besoins des marchés domestiques et de l'équipement de bureau fut considérée comme un véritable projet de société. Tout au long des années 50, les fabricants, que ce soit en Europe ou aux Etats-Unis, mirent en valeur dans leurs stratégies de commercialisation le coût et la polyvalence de leurs produits. Avec des logements dont la taille s'était généralement réduite, les sièges devinrent par nécessité multifonctionnels, utilisés aussi bien pour écrire et se détendre que pour manger. Ce souci de la polyvalence permit à des sociétés américaines, comme Knoll International et Herman Miller, de s'assurer des parts importantes du marché, en particulier grâce à des sièges utilisables aussi bien à la maison que dans l'entreprise.

Avec l'explosion de la culture pop dans les années 60, le statut du siège fut profondément modifié par l'avant-garde: il devint un produit que l'on pouvait jeter. En cette période de folie de consommation, où l'on pensait que l'obsolescence programmée allait permettre d'accroître la production et donc la prospérité économique, le siège devint un gadget supplémentaire, d'aussi peu de valeur qu'une robe en papier. Peter Murdoch et Peter Raacke, entre autres, défièrent la tradition du mobilier de prix que l'on conservait pendant des générations en lançant des modèles en carton. Destinés à un public jeune et socialement libéré, ces sièges n'étaient plus considérés comme des produits durables, mais comme des accessoires de style de vie sujets aux foucades éphémères de la mode. Cette approche fut exploitée en Italie qui vit apparaître des types de sièges entièrement nouveaux, comme le fauteuil gonflable *Blow* de Scolari, D'Urbino, Lomazzi et De Pas en 1967, le *Sacco*, fauteuil-sac dessiné par Gatti, Paolini et Teodoro en 1968, et la gamme *Up*, emballée sous vide, dessinée par Gaetano Pesce en 1969. Ces innovations révolutionnaires combinées à l'envahissement des meubles en kit, à monter soi-même, simplifiaient grandement l'acte d'achat et l'on pouvait littéralement choisir son siège comme n'importe quel autre produit de grande consommation.

En Grande-Bretagne, les années 60 virent se dessiner une réaction animée par les suppléments en couleur de la grande presse, contre l'austérité du rationalisme du «Good Design». Celui-ci était alors largement soutenu par l'Etat pour lequel il renewed vigour within the Italian furniture industry, designers such as Vico Magistretti, Marco Zanuso and Joe Colombo were instrumental in establishing the status of plastics as materials of quality and luxury through their sophisticated Modern chair designs. The first chair to achieve a crucial single-piece construction, however, was designed by Verner Panton, ironically a Scandinavian. With his cantilevered *Stacking chair* of 1960, which was not fully manufactured until 1968, Panton accomplished Eero Saarinen's unrealized ambition of total design unity.

One of the results of the ever-growing divergence of the domestic and contract markets in the late 1960s and early 1970s was the production, though limited, of increasingly expressive avant-garde furniture for the home. An extreme example of this was the appearance of highly surreal furniture inspired by the Pop Art sculptures of Claes Oldenburg. Constructed of moulded polyurethane foam, oversized and out-of-context designs, such as *Capitello* created by Studio 65 in 1971, completely altered previously held perceptions of what a chair could look like. These were the twilight years, however, of Pop Culture, and when the reality of the mid-1970s oil crisis dawned there was an enormous backlash of public opinion against the excesses of popular consumerism.

The global recession of the 1970s hailed a more austere and conscientious approach to design within the industrial mainstream – the chair was now more commonly seen as equipment for sitting. Dwindling markets and cost constraints, which compelled designers and manufacturers to return to a rational approach to design, prompted the minority style known as High Tech. As somewhat of a reinterpretation of Modern Movement rationalism, High Tech furniture, such as Rodney Kinsman's *Omkstak chair* of 1971, integrated utilitarian industrial materials while expressing a machine aesthetic. In less talented designers' hands than Kinsman's, however, the High Tech style, which is limited by geometric formalism, is characterless and bland.

The pervasive conservatism within the furniture industry during the 1970s, however, fuelled the emergence of several radical design groups in Italy with decidedly utopian aspirations. Global Tools, Superstudio, Archizoom and Gruppo Strum all questioned the assumptions of Modernism and signalled a mode of design based on spontaneous creativity and philosophical pluralism. Their design "projections" were a means of subversion in a mainstream immobilized by economic constraints and

Mit der weltweiten Rezession in den 70er Jahren besann man sich in der Industrieproduktion wieder auf einen nüchterneren und vernünftigeren Aspekt des Designs. Der Stuhl wurde jetzt vor allem als praktisches Sitzmöbel angesehen. Schrumpfende Märkte und Kostendämpfungen, durch die Designer und Hersteller gezwungen waren, sich wieder auf das Machbare zu besinnen, förderten das Klima für eine neue Stilrichtung, genannt High Tech, die wiederum nur von einer Minderheit angenommen wurde. High-Tech-Möbel wie etwa Rodney Kinsmans Stuhl *Omkstak* aus dem Jahr 1971 waren eine Art Neuinterpretation des rationalen Modernismus; sie bestanden aus zweckdienlichen, industriell gefertigten Materialien und brachten eine Maschinenästhetik zum Ausdruck. Wenn jedoch weniger talentierte Designer als Kinsman ans Werk gingen, geriet der High-Tech-Stil, der sich durch geometrischen Formalismus auszeichnet, ins Beliebige, er wurde langweilig und charakterlos.

Doch in den 70er Jahren machte sich in der Möbelindustrie zunehmend ein Konservatismus breit, der in Italien mehrere radikale Designergruppen auf den Plan rief, die entschieden utopische Ziele vor Augen hatten. Vereinigungen wie Global Tools, Superstudio, Archizoom und Gruppo Strum stellten die Errungenschaften des Modernismus radikal in Frage und propagierten eine Richtung im Design, die auf spontaner Kreativität und weltanschaulichem Pluralismus basierte. Ihre Designprojekte waren als Mittel gedacht, die gängige Hauptrichtung zu unterwandern, die durch wirtschaftliche Beschränkungen und intellektuelle Apathie zum Stillstand gekommen war. Gegengruppen wie diese, die sich zum üblichen Design in Opposition setzten, hielten die Debatte über modernes Design lebendig und ebneten den Weg für die Einrichtung des Studios Alchimia im Jahre 1976. Alessandro Mendini war der führende Kopf dieser höchst einflußreichen Designergruppe, die die Trennung von Kunst und Design von Grund auf in Frage stellte. Seine »Neuentwürfe« von Joe Colombos *4867*-Stuhl, den er mit einem falschen Marmorüberzug versah, und Gio Pontis *Superleggera*, den er respektloserweise mit Bootsflaggen verzierte, machten sich über die Anspruchshaltung des »Guten Designs« lustig. Das Studio Alchimia, das sich bei all seinen Entwürfen um die physikalische Funktion am wenigsten scherte, unterlegte diese Designs mit sozialen und politischen Kommentaren – der Stuhl war nun zu einem symbolischen und provokanten Objekt geworden. Das Studio Alchimia verkündete lautstark seine

était devenu le «bon goût». Soumis à une version officielle de Modernisme et à un régime sévère de fonctionnalisme scandinave pendant dix ans, le public britannique avait envie de quelque chose de plus enthousiasmant et de moins sérieux. Sous la pression des médias et des premières manifestations du «village global», cette décennie fut tout d'abord le champ d'expérience de la capacité des fabricants à manipuler le consommateur pour qu'il s'adapte à leurs produits. Un design tout de séduction et une abondante production industrielle de meubles aussi superficiels qu'éphémères, contribuèrent à la diffusion de la culture pop et du goût pour la consommation aux Etats-Unis puis, légèrement plus tard, en Europe. En Italie, les fabricants de meubles réalisèrent que la seule façon de maintenir leur position déjà prééminente sur le marché était d'accélérer la recherche et le développement. «Des usines-concept» furent construites par des sociétés comme Cassina, Zanotta, Poltronova et Artemide dans le but de créer de nouveaux standards de sièges. La recherche de la nouveauté technique à tout prix déboucha sur des progrès considérables, en particulier dans le domaine de l'injection plastique. Avec l'arrivée des thermoplastiques, tels le polypropylène (1963) et l'ABS (1967), de nouvelles possibilités s'ouvrirent. Pendant cette période de vigueur renouvelée de l'industrie du meuble italienne, des designers comme Vico Magistretti, Marco Zanuso et Joe Colombo et leurs créations sophistiquées jouèrent un rôle fondamental dans la montée en puissance des plastiques enfin reconnus comme matériaux de qualité et même de luxe. Le premier siège à avoir été produit en une seule opération, fut cependant l'œuvre de Verner Panton, un Scandinave. Avec sa chaise en porte-à-faux, la *Stacking Chair* de 1960, qui ne fut réellement produite qu'à partir de 1968, il réalisa l'ambition inaboutie d'Eero Saarinen d'unité totale du design.

L'un des résultats de la divergence grandissante entre les marchés de la maison et du bureau de la fin des années 60 et du début des années 70 fut la production, quoique limitée, d'un mobilier pour la maison de plus en plus avant-gardiste et expressionniste avec, pour exemple extrême, l'apparition de meubles surréalistes inspirés par les sculptures pop de Claes Oldenburg. Souvent en mousse de polyuréthane moulée, sur-dimensionnées et hors contexte, ces créations, comme le *Capitello* du Studio 65 (1971), modifièrent complètement les perceptions que l'on avait pu avoir jusqu'alors d'un siège. Mais la pop culture en était déjà à son crépusintellectual apathy. Counter-design groups such as these kept the Modern design debate lively and paved the way for the establishment of Studio Alchimia in 1976. Alessandro Mendini was the leading propagandist of this highly influential design group, which challenged the distinctions between art and design. His "redesigns" of Joe Colombo's *4867* chair, to which he applied a faux marble finish, and Gio Ponti's *Superleggera*, to which he wryly attached yachting ensigns, mocked the pretensions of Good Design. With physical function the least of its considerations, Studio Alchimia infused these designs with social and political commentary – the chair had been intentionally transformed into a symbolic object. Blatantly anti-commercial and self-consciously intellectual in content, Studio Alchimia exploited decorative embellishment to mark what it believed to be the death of Modernism.

Founded in 1981, the Memphis design studio was central to the promotion of post-modernism within the decorative arts. Like its anti-design paradigm, Studio Alchimia, Memphis created furniture that ran against the accepted tenets of design and culture, using decoration, however, for its own sake and not for the promotion of a coherent ideology. Borrowing ornamental references from previous styles, Memphis successfully popularized anti-design, contributing to its general acceptance within the furniture industry's mainstream.

Against the background of a credit-fuelled economic boom and the perceived failure of Modernism, post-modernism emerged in the 1980s in response to the demand for a new mainstream international style. Divorcing industry from design and relating it more to fine art, post-modern furniture designers viewed styling rather than functionalism as paramount in importance. Often employing visual puns and decorative motifs borrowed from historic styles amalgamated in a single design, post-modern furniture, unlike that of the Pop era, was intended to possess a physical durability through the use of expensive materials and lavish construction. While drawing inspiration from eclecticism rather than consumerism, post-modern designers acknowledged the architect and critic Charles Jenck's rallying cry for double-coding mixed references and hybrid themes. Ultimately, these anti-design sentiments led to the kitsch vulgarity of Las Vegas being lauded for its honesty, while furniture designers created *Mickey meets Sheraton* chairs. A new visual language had indeed been created but at the expense of any real meaning or value to the consumer.

antikommerziellen und bewußt intellektuellen Anliegen und wucherte mit Dekor und Zierwerk, um deutlich ins Auge springen zu lassen, was es für den Tod der Moderne hielt.

Das 1981 gegründete Memphis-Design-Studio hatte eine zentrale Bedeutung für das Aufkommen der Postmoderne in der dekorativen Kunst. Wie der Protagonist des Anti-Design, Studio Alchimia, schuf Memphis Möbel, die den gängigen und allgemein anerkannten Strömungen in Design und Kultur zuwiderliefen; es verwendete den Dekor jedoch um seiner selbst Willen und nicht zur Propagierung einer stimmigen Ideologie. Memphis entlehnte ornamentale Elemente aus früheren dekorativen Stilen und machte Anti-Design populär; es trug sogar dazu bei, daß es in der gängigen industriellen Möbelmode akzeptiert wurde.

Vor dem Hintergrund eines durch Kredite gespeisten Wirtschaftsbooms und dem endgültig konstatierten Scheitern der Moderne kam in den 80er Jahren die Postmoderne auf, die ursprünglich eine Bewegung in der Architektur war; sie war die Antwort auf die Forderung nach einer neuen, international akzeptierten Stilrichtung. Postmoderne Möbeldesigner praktizierten eine klare Trennung zwischen Industrie und Design, das sie wieder mehr der Kunst annähern wollten; sie sahen die stilistische Gestaltung als ihre wichtigste Aufgabe an, nicht den Funktionalismus. Sie verwendeten häufig optische Spielereien und dekorative Motive, die sie von historischen Stilen entlehnt hatten und in einem postmodernen Design zu etwas Neuem verschmolzen; anders als in der Pop-Ära sollten postmoderne Möbel von dauerhafter Haltbarkeit sein, was durch die Verwendung teurer Materialien und aufwendiger Konstruktionen erreicht wurde. Die postmodernen Designer gewannen ihre Inspiration mehr aus dem Eklektizismus als aus dem Konsumbedürfnis der Menschen, denn sie hörten auf die lautstarke Forderung des Architekten und Kritikers Charles Jenck, die nach vielfältig verschlüsselten Verweisen und der Vermischung unterschiedlicher Themen verlangte. Letztlich führten diese Anti-Design-Theorien zu dem vulgären Kitsch von Las Vegas, der für seine Aufrichtigkeit gelobt wurde, während Möbeldesigner Stühle entwarfen wie *Mickey meets Sheraton*. Diese neue optische Sprache blieb aber für den Verbraucher letztlich ohne besonderen Wert.

In den 80er Jahren kam mit dem allgemeinen wirtschaftlichen Wohlstand ein Pluralismus im Design auf, der auch vom Verbraucher akzeptiert wurde und eine

cule. Avec la crise du pétrole du milieu des années 70 se manifesta une réaction massive de l'opinion contre les excès de la société de consommation.

La récession générale des années 70 déboucha sur une approche plus austère et plus responsable du design devenu «industriel», le siège étant tout simplement considéré comme un équipement pour s'asseoir. La mauvaise santé des marchés et l'accroissement des contraintes de coût forcèrent les designers et les fabricants à revenir à une approche rationnelle du design et donnèrent naissance à un nouveau style de modernité, le High Tech. Sorte de réinterprétation du rationalisme moderniste, le mobilier High Tech, comme la chaise *Omkstak* de Rodney Kinsman (1971), intégrait des matériaux industriels et exprimaient une esthétique mécaniste. En des mains moins talentueuses, cependant, ce style limité par son formalisme géométrique se révèlera vite sans caractère.

En Italie, par réaction, le conservatisme affirmé de l'industrie du meuble pendant les années 70 fit éclore plusieurs groupes de design radical aux aspirations résolument utopistes. Global Tools, Superstudio, Archizoom et Gruppo Sturm remirent en question les certitudes du Modernisme et installèrent un mode de design reposant sur la créativité spontanée et le pluralisme philosophique. Leurs «projections» de design étaient autant de moyens de subversion dans un courant principal immobilisé par des contraintes économiques et l'apathie intellectuelle. Des groupes d'anti-design permirent ainsi au débat sur la modernité de continuer et ouvrirent la voie à l'apparition du Studio Alchimia en 1976. Alessandro Mendini fut le premier propagandiste de ce groupe de design très influent qui défiait les distinctions entre art et design. Ses «redesigns» de la *chaise 4867* de Joe Colombo à laquelle il appliqua une finition de faux-marbre et de la *Superleggera* de Gio Ponti, qu'il décora avec humour de symboles de yachting, se moquaient des prétentions du «Good Design». La fonction étant son moindre souci, le Studio Alchimia formulait à travers ses œuvres des commentaires politiques et sociaux au bénéfice desquels le siège était alors transformé en objet-symbole provocant, profondément anticommercial et d'un intellectualisme affiché. Le Studio Alchimia exploita l'ornementation pour marquer ce qu'il pensait être la mort de la modernité.

Fondé en 1981, le Groupe Memphis a joué un rôle central dans la promotion du post-modernisme dans le domaine des arts décoratifs. Comme son équivalent de

By the mid 1980s an accepted pluralism in design emerged, with the general economic prosperity sustaining an ever greater stylistic diversification in the decorative arts. Working outside of the industrial process, independent designers explored unconstrained spontaneous creativity, producing ever more fanciful chair designs while the patrons of avant-garde furniture became increasingly concerned with expressing their own individuality through the acquisition of these pieces. Producing highly poetic "one-off" and batch production furniture, comprising mainly chairs, designers such as Ron Arad, Tom Dixon, Danny Lane and André Dubreuil flourished, becoming internationally renowned. In this period of relative excess, specialized furniture galleries were established to exhibit these experimental and challenging designs. The reticence of mainstream manufacturers to become involved with such anti-rationalism, regarded as of limited appeal even within the high-end domestic furniture market, ebbed in the mid 1980s as the work of many independent designers began to receive considerable recognition by the international design press.

Avant-garde designers working within the industry, such as Philippe Starck, continually produced new chair designs to sate the public's desire for novelty during the 1980s. Like the 1960s, this was a decade when domestic furniture design followed fashion rather than the quest for solutions to real needs. Well-established manufacturers were content to fund the production of anti-rational furniture which grabbed the attention of the press, thus indirectly publicizing the company's static range, which often consisted of contract seating and systems products. This publicity-motivated funding, coupled with an increasing competition for the spotlight, meant that many manufacturers were distracted from concentrating their resources on the worthwhile research and development of more ecologically conscious products.

The beginning of the 1990s, however, has seen a shift of attitude in the approach of some designers and manufacturers towards the production of environmentally sound furniture design. Philippe Starck's *Louis 20 chair* for instance, is an innovative construction of recyclable materials, while the highly rational *Ensemble chair* by Alfred Homann, with an even wider functional application, is primarily constructed of a newly developed plastic that is also recyclable. Admirable as these designs are in addressing the environmental concerns of today, the most effective guiding

immer größere stilistische Vielfalt in der dekorativen Kunst bewirkte. Unabhängige Designer, die außerhalb der industriellen Fertigungsprozesse tätig waren, loteten die Möglichkeiten ihrer freien Kreativität aus und produzierten immer witzigere Möbelentwürfe, während die Initiatoren der Avantgarde-Möbel zunehmend dazu übergingen, ihre Individualität durch den Erwerb solcher Stücke zum Ausdruck zu bringen. Designer wie Ron Arad, Tom Dixon, Danny Lane und André Dubreuil produzierten höchst poetische »Unikate« und Möbelentwürfe in begrenzter Stückzahl, vor allem Stühle, und erwarben sich damit internationales Ansehen. In dieser Zeit exzessiver Kreativität entstanden in ganz Europa spezielle Möbelgalerien, in denen diese experimentellen und provokanten Designs ausgestellt wurden. Die Möbelhersteller der gängigen Marken zeigten große Zurückhaltung, sich mit solch antirationalen Produkten einzulassen, denn sie wurden als wenig erfolgversprechend für den Markt angesehen, selbst in der gehobenen Klasse; diese Zurückhaltung löste sich Mitte der 80er Jahre allmählich auf, als die Arbeit vieler unabhängiger Designer große Anerkennung durch die internationale Designpresse erhielt.

Avantgarde-Designer wie Philippe Starck, die für die Industrie tätig waren, produzierten unablässig neue Stuhlentwürfe, um das Bedürfnis des Publikums nach Neuerungen in den 80er Jahren zu befriedigen. Wie die 60er Jahre war auch dies ein Jahrzehnt, in dem sich Wohnmöbel-Design mehr nach der Mode richtete als nach der Befriedigung tatsächlich bestehender Bedürfnisse. Hersteller mit gefestigten Marktpositionen förderten mit Vorliebe die Produktion antirationaler Möbel, die die Aufmerksamkeit der Medien auf sich zogen und dadurch indirekt Reklame machten für das fest umrissene Firmenprogramm, das häufig aus Bürositzmöbeln und Einbausystemen bestand. Diese publicity-orientierte Förderung, gepaart mit einem wachsenden Wettbewerb um das Rampenlicht, hatte zur Folge, daß viele Hersteller ihre Forschungsmittel nun nicht mehr ausschließlich auf die Entwicklung ökologisch sinnvoller Produkte konzentrierten.

Zu Beginn der 90er Jahre ließ sich jedoch eine Veränderung in der Haltung mancher Designer und Hersteller feststellen: Ihr Interesse galt nun verstärkt der Produktion umweltfreundlicher Möbel. So ist Philippe Starcks Stuhl *Louis 20* eine innovative Konstruktion aus recyclefähigem Material, und ebenso ist der höchst funktionale *Ensemble-Stuhl* von Alfred Homann, der einen breiteren

l'anti-design, Studio Alchimia, Memphis créa des meubles qui allaient à l'encontre des règles ambiantes, utilisant cependant le décor pour lui-même et non pour la promotion d'une idéologie cohérente. Empruntant ses références ornementales à d'anciens styles décoratifs, Memphis popularisa avec succès l'anti-design et contribua à le faire accepter par l'industrie du meuble.

C'est sur un fond d'expansion économique à crédit et d'échec patent du Modernisme que le post-modernisme émergea dans les années 80. Il se fit d'abord remarquer en architecture où il apportait une réponse à l'attente impatiente d'un nouveau grand style international. Poussant au divorce de l'industrie et du design qu'ils tiraient vers les beaux-arts, les designers post-modernes attachaient une importance majeure au style, au détriment du fonctionnalisme. Employant souvent d'un même élan astuces visuelles et motifs décoratifs empruntés, le mobilier postmoderne, à la différence de celui de la période pop, se voulait posséder une certaine durabilité en employant des matériaux chers et des constructions sophistiquées. Tirant leur inspiration de l'éclectisme plutôt que de la société de consommation, les designers post-modernes se reconnurent dans les textes de l'architecte et critique Charles Jenck qui défendait un mélange de références à double codage et de thèmes hybrides. Ces attitudes antidesign firent, par exemple, que l'esthétique de Las Vegas, se vit portée aux nues pour son «honnêteté», tandis que des créateurs dessinaient des chaises portant des noms comme *Mickey au Sheraton*. Un nouveau langage visuel s'était bien créé mais aux dépens de toute réelle signification ou de toute valeur pour le consommateur.

Vers le milieu des années 1980, émergea dans le monde du design un pluralisme nouveau qui allait de pair avec une prospérité économique retrouvée et une diversification stylistique artistique de plus en plus marquée. Loin de l'univers industriel, des designers indépendants se moquant des contraintes, dessinèrent des sièges pleins de fantaisie qui plaisaient à une clientèle d'avant-garde heureuse d'exprimer sa personnalité à travers l'acquisition de ces œuvres. Produisant des pièces très poétiques en exemplaire unique ou en édition très limitée – essentiellement des sièges d'ailleurs – des designers comme Ron Arad, Tom Dixon, Danny Lane et André Dubreuil se firent connaître dans le monde entier. Pendant cette période, marquée de nombreux excès, des galeries spécialisées dans le mobilier s'ouvrirent dans toute l'Europe pour exposer des principle in confronting the longer term ecological requirement would be to simply make less last longer. To quote Marcel Breuer – "A piece of furniture, (and above all the chair), is not an arbitrary composition: it is a necessary component of our environment… the outward expression of our everyday needs; it must be able to serve both those needs that remain constant and those which vary. This variation is possible only if the very simplest and most straightforward pieces are used; otherwise changing will mean buying new pieces. Let our dwelling have no particular 'style', but only the imprint of the owner's character."[14]

Verwendungsspielraum zuläßt, hauptsächlich aus einem neuentwickelten Kunststoff konstruiert, der ebenfalls recyclefähig ist. So bewundernswert diese Entwürfe in ihrem Bemühen um eine umweltfreundliche Verarbeitung auch sind, müßte doch der Grundgedanke bei der Umsetzung heutiger ökologischer Erfordernisse sein, eine Langzeitplanung im Auge zu behalten, nach dem Motto: weniger, aber haltbarer. Um Marcel Breuer zu zitieren: »Ein Möbelstück (und vor allem ein Stuhl) ist keine beliebige Komposition: Es ist ein notwendiger Bestandteil unserer Umwelt… der äußere Ausdruck unserer alltäglichen Bedürfnisse; er müßte in der Lage sein, sowohl jene Bedürfnisse zu befriedigen, die gleich bleiben, als auch solche, die sich verändern. Diese Wechselbeziehung ist nur möglich, wenn die einfachsten und unkompliziertesten Möbelstücke verwendet werden; andernfalls würde Veränderung bedeuten, neue Stücke zu kaufen. Unser Wohnzimmer sollte keinen speziellen › Stil ‹ haben, sondern nur die persönliche Note des Besitzers zum Ausdruck bringen.«[14]

projets audacieux et souvent expérimentaux. La réticence des fabricants à s'impliquer dans ce mouvement qu'ils considéraient comme d'intérêt limité, même pour le marché du meuble domestique de luxe, cessa vers le milieu des années 80 lorsque le travail de nombreux designers indépendants commença à se faire reconnaître par la presse internationale du design.

Des designers d'avant-garde proches de l'industrie, comme Philippe Starck, produisirent de multiples modèles de sièges qui satisfaisaient le besoin de nouveauté du public. Comme pendant les années 60, le mobilier pour la maison suivit la mode plutôt que de chercher à répondre à des besoins réels. Des fabricants connus furent heureux d'utiliser ces meubles remarqués par la presse pour faire indirectement parler de leurs modèles plus classiques, en l'occurrence souvent des meubles ou des systèmes d'équipement pour le bureau. Ce financement à caractère publicitaire, couplé à une course effrénée pour la célébrité, empêcha en réalité de nombreux fabricants d'investir suffisamment dans une recherche valable pour des produits plus respectueux de l'environnement.

Le début des années 90, cependant, a vu un changement d'attitude dans l'approche écologique de certains designers et fabricants. La chaise *Louis 20* de Philippe Starck, par exemple, est réalisée à partir de matériaux recyclables, tandis que le siège *Ensemble* d'Alfred Homann, tout à fait rationnel et encore plus polyvalent, est essentiellement construit dans un nouveau plastique également recyclable. Aussi remarquables puissent être ces créations dans leur prise en compte des enjeux écologiques, on peut penser que la réponse la plus efficace à long terme, serait tout simplement d'arriver à faire durer ces meubles davantage. Pour citer Marcel Breuer: «Un meuble, et par dessus tout un siège, n'est pas une composition arbitraire: c'est une composante nécessaire de notre environnement … l'expression extériorisée de nos besoins de tous les jours; il doit être capable de servir à la fois les besoins qui ne changent pas et ceux qui peuvent varier. Cette variation n'est possible que si les éléments les plus simples et les plus sincères sont utilisés; autrement, le moindre changement voudra dire acheter de nouveaux meubles. Que nos habitations n'aient pas de ‹ style › particulier, mais reflètent simplement l'empreinte de la personnalité de leur propriétaire!»[14]

Alfred Homann:

Ensemble chair, 1992

Ensemble-Stuhl, 1992

Chaise *Ensemble*, 1992

Courtesy Fritz Hansen, Copenhagen

Ross Lovegrove:

FO8 chairs (prototype), 1991

FO8-Stühle (Prototyp), 1991

Chaises *FO8* (prototype), 1991

Courtesy Ross Lovegrove, London

The Chairs . Die Stühle . Les Chaises

1885–1992

Michael Thonet

1796–1871

Austria . Österreich . Autriche

Side chair, Model No. 14
c. 1855

Stuhl, Modell Nr. 14
um 1855

Chaise, modèle n° 14
vers 1855

Bent solid beechwood, moulded laminated wood and solid beechwood, with wooden seat

Rahmen aus Buche; Bügel verformtes Schichtholz und Buche massiv; Sitzfläche aus Holz

Hêtre massif cintré, bois lamellé moulé et hêtre massif, siège en bois

Gebrüder Thonet, Vienna, after 1860

Early *Model No. 14* variations, c. 1855

Varianten des frühen *Modells Nr. 14*, um 1855

Variations du modèle antérieur, *n° 14*, vers 1855

Through its minimal use of materials and suitability for mass-production, *Model No. 14* embodies some of the principles associated with the Modern Movement. The pared-down forms of early Thonet chairs such as *Model No. 14*, however, were simplified for commercial reasons from contemporaneous period styles, Biedermeier in particular[1], and, therefore, can only be viewed as "modern" in terms of their production method.

Mit seinem minimalen Materialaufwand und seiner Eignung für die Massenproduktion verkörpert das *Modell Nr. 14* einige Prinzipien der Moderne. Allerdings sind die frühen Thonet-Stühle mit ihrer klaren Linienführung, zu denen dieses Modell zählt, eher als »Sparversionen« zeitgenössischer Nachahmungen historischer Stilarten zu verstehen.[1] Sie wurden aus kommerziellen Gründen vereinfacht und können daher nur in bezug auf die Herstellungsmethode als »modern« bezeichnet werden.

Parce qu'il utilise un nombre réduit de matériaux et qu'il est adapté aux procédés de production en série, le *modèle n° 14* illustre certains des principes du Mouvement moderniste. Les formes dépouillées des premiers sièges Thonet, tel ce *modèle n° 14*, correspondaient en réalité à des versions simplifiées (pour des raisons commerciales) des styles de l'époque, en particulier le Biedermeier[1], et ne peuvent guère être considérées comme «modernes» qu'en termes de méthodes de fabrication.

In 1852 the Shakers founded a factory in New Lebanon, New York, to produce furniture for sale outside their communities. The Shakers' belief that "regularity is beauty" and "beauty rests on utility" paralleled the ideals of the Arts and Crafts movement.[2]

1852 gründeten die Shaker in New Lebanon, New York, eine Möbelmanufaktur, in der sie Möbel für den Verkauf außerhalb ihrer Siedlungen herstellten. Ihre Überzeugungen – »Regelmäßigkeit ist Ordnung« und »Schönheit beruht auf Nützlichkeit« – standen im Einklang mit den Idealen der Arts-and-Crafts-Bewegung.[2]

En 1852, les Shakers créèrent un atelier à New Lebanon, dans l'Etat de New York, pour produire et vendre des meubles hors de leurs communautés. La croyance des Shakers que «la vérité est beauté» et que «la beauté repose sur l'utilité» rappelle les idéaux du mouvement Arts and Crafts.[2]

Licensed reissue of Shaker chairs

Lizensierter Nachbau der Shaker-Stühle

Rééditions des chaises Shaker

Licensed reissue of Shaker bench

Lizensierter Nachbau einer Shaker-Bank

Réédition de banc Shaker

Reconstruction of a Shaker interior

Rekonstruktion einer Inneneinrichtung der Shaker

Reconstruction d'un intérieur Shaker

Shaker

USA . Etats-Unis

Rocking-chair 1890
Schaukelstuhl 1890
Chaise à bascule 1890

Solid wood construction, rush seat

Holz massiv, Sitzfläche Binsengeflecht

Bois massif, siège en jonc tressé

Shaker Factory, New Lebanon, New York

Henry
van de Velde

1863–1957

Belgium . Belgien . Belgique

Bloemenwerf chair 1895

Stuhl Bloemenwerf 1895

Chaise Bloemenwerf 1895

Solid walnut frame with rush seat

Rahmen Nußbaum massiv; Sitzfläche Bastgeflecht

Cadre de noyer massif, siège en raphia

Société van de Velde, Brussels

Henry van de Velde:

Padouk armchair with batik upholstery, 1898/99

Padouk-Armlehnstuhl, Polsterung mit Batikbezug, 1898/99

Fauteuil *Padouk*, revêtu de batik, 1898/99

This chair was designed for Van de Velde's own house, Bloemenwerf, near Brussels. He designed the house and all its contents as part of an organic and unified whole.

Den *Bloemenwerf*-Stuhl entwarf Van de Velde für sein eigenes Haus in Uccle bei Brüssel. Er hat es, einschließlich der Ausstattung, als organisches, einheitliches Ganzes konzipiert.

Cette chaise fut spécialement dessinée pour la propre maison de Van de Velde, Bloemenwerf, à Uccle, près de Bruxelles. Il conçut cette maison et l'ensemble de son contenu comme un tout organique et unifié.

Charles Rennie Mackintosh

1868–1928
Great Britain . Großbritannien .
Grande-Bretagne

Side chair 1897
Stuhl 1897
Chaise 1897

Solid oak construction with
upholstered seat

Rahmen aus Eiche massiv, Sitzfläche gepolstert

Cadre en chêne massif, siège
rembourré

**Manufacturer unknown
(reissued by Cassina, Italy,
from 1973)**

Charles Rennie Mackintosh:

Dining room. Drawing from the
collections of designs submitted
for the "House of an Art Lover"
competition, 1901

Speisezimmer. Zeichnung aus
den von Alexander Koch veröffent-
lichten Entwurfsunterlagen für die
Ausschreibung zum »Haus eines
Kunstfreundes«, 1901

Salle à manger. Dessin provenant
des esquisses publiées par
Alexander Koch pour le
concours «Intérieur d'un
ami des artistes», 1901

Reconstruction of a Mackintosh
room

Rekonstruktion eines Mackintosh-
Raums

Reconstruction d'une chambre de
Mackintosh

Designed for the Luncheon Room at
Miss Cranston's Argyle Street Tea-
Rooms, Glasgow, these high-backed
chairs functioned as screens when
placed around a table, affording greater privacy. "Given the diminutive stat-
ure of the Scotswomen who patronised this establishment at the turn of
the century, the light passing through
the pierce-work on the elliptical crest
rails would have ideally imparted a
halo-like glow about their heads…
Mackintosh endowed these comman-
ding chairs with a mystical quality
through the manipulation of form."[3]

Die von Mackintosh für den Lunch
Room in Miss Cranston's Tea-Rooms
in der Argyle Street, Glasgow, entwor-
fenen Stühle mit den hohen Rückenlehnen wirkten wie Wandschirme und
schützten die Gäste vor neugierigen
Blicken. »Bei der winzigen Statur
schottischer Damen kann man sich gut
vorstellen, daß der ovale Lichtschein,
der durch die durchbrochenen Bekrö-
nungen der Lehnen fiel, eine Art Hei-
ligenschein um ihre Köpfe zeichnete…
Mackintosh hat diese alles überragen-
den Stühle durch kunstvolle Gestaltung mit mystischer Qualität
ausgestattet.«[3]

Spécialement créées pour la salle à
manger de Miss Cranston's Tea-
Rooms de Argyle Street, à Glasgow,
ces chaises jouaient un rôle d'écran
qui permettait aux clients de mieux
s'isoler. «Etant donné la petite taille
des clientes écossaises, la lumière qui
filtrait à travers la découpe pratiquée
dans l'écusson elliptique devait normalement envelopper leur tête d'une
sorte de halo lumineux. Grâce à cette
manipulation des formes, Mackintosh
conféra à ces chaises une sorte de
qualité mystique.»[3]

Adolf Loos

1870–1933

Austria . Österreich . Autriche

Chair c. 1898

Stuhl um 1898

Chaise vers 1898

Stained, bent beech frame with woven cane seat

Rahmen Bugholz, gebeizt; Sitzfläche aus Rohrgeflecht

Structure de hêtre cintré teinté, siège canné

Jacob & Josef Kohn, Vienna

Although based on earlier precedents set by Thonet[4], this chair, designed for the Café Museum in Vienna, represents the first of a new generation of architect-designed bent wood products. The Café Museum, designed by Loos in 1899, was subsequently nicknamed the "Café Nihilismus" because of its rather stark, undecorated interior scheme.

Obwohl dieser speziell für das Café Museum in Wien entworfene Stuhl von Adolf Loos auf früheren Entwürfen von Thonet[4] basiert, gehört er zu einer neuen Generation von Bugholzmöbeln, die von Architekten für einen bestimmten Platz geschaffen wurden. Das Café Museum, das Loos 1899 entworfen hat, erhielt wegen seiner betont kargen Innenausstattung den Spitznamen »Café Nihilismus«.

Bien qu'inspirée de précédents sièges de Thonet[4], cette chaise créée spécialement pour le Café Museum à Vienne, représente le point de départ de la nouvelle génération de meubles en bois cintré dessinés par des architectes. Le Café Museum, créé par Loos en 1899, fut rebaptisé «Café Nihilisme» du fait d'un décor intérieur particulièrement dépouillé.

Adolf Loos:

Café Museum, 1899

40

Richard Riemerschmid:

Music Room for the "Deutsche Kunstausstellung Dresden", 1899

Musikzimmer für die »Deutsche Kunstausstellung Dresden«, 1899

Le Salon de Musique pour la «Deutsche Kunstausstellung» de Dresde, 1899

Richard Riemerschmid:

Sketch for an armchair, 1899

Entwurfszeichnung für einen Lehnsessel, 1899

Dessin pour un fauteuil, 1899

Richard Riemerschmid:

Beechwood chair, 1900

Bugholzstuhl, 1900

Chaise en bois de hêtre, 1900

Richard Riemerschmid

1868–1957

Germany . Deutschland . Allemagne

Side chair 1899

Stuhl 1899

Chaise 1899

Solid oak frame with upholstered leather seat

Eiche massiv; Sitzfläche gepolstert, mit Leder bezogen

Structure en chêne massif, siège rembourré, recouvert de cuir

Vereinigte Werkstätten für Kunst im Handwerk, Munich (also manufactured by Liberty & Co., London, after 1899)

Designed for the 1899 Dresden Art Exhibition, this elegant chair, which was intended for use by musicians, helped to establish Riemerschmid's reputation. The lack of arms allows the freedom of movement necessary when playing musical instruments. It is generally regarded as the most significant German Jugendstil chair design.

Dieser elegante Musikzimmerstuhl, den Riemerschmid für die Dresdner Kunstausstellung von 1899 entwarf, begründete seinen Ruf als Designer. Das Fehlen von Armlehnen ermöglichte optimale Bewegungsfreiheit beim Musizieren. Aufgrund seines Designs gilt dieser Stuhl im allgemeinen als das wichtigste Sitzmöbel des deutschen Jugendstils.

Dessiné pour l'Exposition artistique de Dresde en 1899, cet élégant siège de musicien contribua à établir la réputation de Riemerschmid. L'absence d'accoudoirs permet la liberté de mouvement nécessaire lorsque l'on joue d'un instrument. Il est généralement considéré comme le modèle de chaise le plus élaboré du Jugendstil allemand.

Koloman Moser

1868–1918

Austria . Österreich . Autriche

Wooden slatted chair 1902

Holzlattenstuhl 1902

Fauteuil en lattes de bois 1902

Painted beech frame with wicker-work seat

Rahmen Buche massiv, lackiert; Sitzfläche Korbgeflecht

Structure de hêtre peint avec siège en vannerie

Prag-Rudniker Korbwaren, Vienna

Similar designs to this were exhibited at the Vienna Secession's 1903 exhibition of Gustav Klimt's work and were also used in the entrance lobby of Josef Hoffmann's sanatorium "Westend" in Purkersdorf. The chair's cubic form and restricted use of colour are signs of the mature Secessionist style and anticipate the geometric abstraction employed by Modern Movement designers in the 1920s and 1930s.

Ähnliche Entwürfe waren in der Klimt-Ausstellung der Wiener Sezession von 1903 und in der Eingangshalle des Sanatoriums Westend von Josef Hoffmann im niederösterreichischen Purkersdorf zu sehen. Die kubische Form und das zurückhaltende Farbkonzept sind typisch für den reifen Stil der Sezession und nehmen das geometrisch-abstrakte Design der Moderne der 20er und 30er Jahre vorweg.

Des modèles similaires avaient été présentés lors de l'Exposition des travaux de Gustav Klimt par la Sécession Viennoise et figuraient également dans l'entrée du sanatorium de Purkersdorf de J. Hoffmann. La forme cubique de ce siège et le recours limité à la couleur illustrent le style sécessionniste de la maturité et anticipent l'abstraction géométrique des créateurs modernistes des années 20 et 30.

Josef Hoffmann:

Sanatorium Purkersdorf, 1904–06

Koloman Moser:

Writing cabinet with integrated chair, Vienna, 1904

Schreibschrank mit integriertem Stuhl, Wien, 1904

Secrétaire avec fauteuil encastrable, Vienne, 1904

Koloman Moser:

Armchair, rear view, 1903

Armlehnsessel, Rückansicht, 1903

Fauteuil, vue de dos, 1903

Oak armchair c. 1903

Armlehnstuhl aus Eiche
um 1903

Fauteuil de chêne vers 1903

Stained, solid oak frames with
fabric-covered, upholstered
horsehair seats

Konstruktion Eiche massiv, gebeizt; Sitzflächen mit Roßhaar-
polsterung, mit Stoff bezogen

Structure de chêne massif teinté
avec sièges rembourrés de crin
de cheval et recouverts de tissu

Maker unknown

Charles Rennie Mackintosh:

Chair, 1903

Stuhl, 1903

Chaise, 1903

"From 1897 to 1916 (Mackintosh) was occupied with designing, decorating and furnishing a chain of Tea-Rooms, established in Glasgow by the Misses Cranston as part of a campaign started in the 1880s with the founding of the Glasgow Temperance Movement, to combat widespread daytime drunkenness. The Tea-Rooms were provided with billiard tables and smoking-rooms for the amusement of the customers but few, if any, of the Glasgow drunks patronised the new establishments with their elegant and original furniture and fittings."[5]

»Von 1897 bis 1916 war er (Mackintosh) mit dem Entwurf, der Ausstattung und der Einrichtung einer Kette von Tea-Rooms beschäftigt, die die Damen Cranston in Glasgow eröffnet hatten – im Rahmen der um 1880 gegründeten Glasgower Temperenzlerbewegung zur Bekämpfung der damals weit verbreiteten Trunksucht. Die Tea-Rooms waren zur Unterhaltung der Gäste mit Billardtischen und Rauchzimmern ausgestattet, aber nur wenige Glasgower Trunkenbolde, wenn überhaupt, besuchten die neuen eleganten Etablissements.«[5]

«De 1897 à 1916, Mackintosh dessine, décore et meuble une chaîne de salons de thé. Elle avait été créée à Glasgow par les demoiselles Cranston dans le cadre d'une campagne qui avait débuté dans les années 80 par la fondation d'une ligue de combat contre l'alcoolisme alors très répandu. Les salons de thé abritaient des billards et des fumoirs pour la distraction des clients, mais peu d'alcooliques de Glasgow – si jamais il y en eut – fréquentèrent ces établissements élégants, décorés et meublés avec originalité.»[5]

Charles Rennie Mackintosh:

Interior of Willow Tea-Rooms
c.1904

Inneneinrichtung der Willow-Tea-
Rooms, um 1904

Vue intérieure des Willow Tea-
Rooms, vers 1904

Frank Lloyd Wright

1869–1959

USA . Etats-Unis

Dining chair
c. 1904

Eßzimmerstuhl
um 1904

Chaise de salle à manger
vers 1904

Solid oak frame with fabric-covered, upholstered seat

Rahmen Eiche massiv; Sitzfläche gepolstert, mit Stoff bezogen

Structure de chêne massif, avec siège rembourré recouvert de tissu

Matthews Bros. Manufacturing Co., Milwaukee, Wisconsin

The sophisticated design of this dining chair, designed for the Darwin D. Martin House in Buffalo, New York, shows Wright's preference for geometric regularity, simplicity and the harmonious synthesis of the American Arts and Crafts style with Japanese art and design.

Die elegant-einfache Gestaltung dieses Speisezimmerstuhls für das Haus von Darwin D. Martin in Buffalo, New York, demonstriert Wrights Vorliebe für geometrische Regelmäßigkeit, Einfachheit und die harmonische Verschmelzung des amerikanischen Arts-and-Crafts-Stils mit japanischer Kunst und japanischem Design.

Le dessin sophistiqué de cette chaise de salle à manger pour la maison Darwin D. Martin à Buffalo, New York, témoigne de la préférence de Wright pour la rigueur géométrique, la simplicité et la synthèse harmonieuse du style Arts and Crafts américain et des tendances du design japonais.

Frank Lloyd Wright:

Interior of the Darwin D. Martin House, Buffalo, New York, 1904/05

Inneneinrichtung des Hauses von Darwin D. Martin, Buffalo, New York, 1904/05

Intérieur de la maison Darwin D. Martin, Buffalo, New York, 1904/05

Frank Lloyd Wright:

High-backed side chair, c.1906

Stuhl mit hoher Rückenlehne, um 1906

Chaise à haut dossier, vers 1906

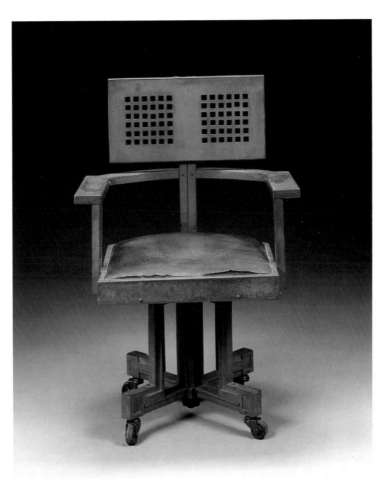

Frank Lloyd Wright

1869–1959

USA . Etats-Unis

Office swivel chair 1904

Bürodrehstuhl 1904

Siège de bureau pivotant 1904

Painted steel frame with leather-covered upholstered seat, supported on a swivelling steel base terminating on castors

Stahlrahmen, farbig lackiert; Sitzfläche gepolstert und leder-bezogen; Untergestell auf einer beweglichen Stahlbasis, auf Rollen

Structure d'acier peint avec siège rembourré recouvert de cuir sur une base pivotante en acier mon-tée sur roulettes

Von Dorn Iron Works Company, Cleveland, Ohio

Frank Lloyd Wright:

Interior of the Larkin Company Administration Building, Buffalo, New York, 1903–05

Das Innere des Verwaltungs-gebäudes der Larkin Company, Buffalo, New York, 1903–05

Intérieur de bureau de la Larkin Company, Buffalo, New York, 1903–05

Without architectural precedent, Frank Lloyd Wright's Larkin Company Administration Building in New York revolutionised the concept of the work-place environment, heralding the birth of the modern, integrated office. The Larkin Co. office chair was designed specifically for this project and its for-mal geometry was echoed throughout the surrounding building. Wright's in-tention with this regularity of form was to create a space that was both vis-ually and functionally unified.

Mit seinem Bürogebäude für die Larkin Company in New York revolutionierte Frank Lloyd Wright die Gestaltung von Arbeitsplätzen und schuf eine moderne Bürolandschaft mit großen, ungeteilten Büroflächen. Den Bürostuhl für die Larkin Company hatte er speziell für dieses Projekt entworfen; seine streng geometrische Konstruktion korrespon-dierte mit den ihn umgebenden Ge-bäuden. Durch diese Regelmäßigkeit der Formen wollte Wright Räume schaffen, die visuell und funktionell eine Einheit bilden.

Sans précédent architectural connu, le Larkin Company Administration Buil-ding de Frank Lloyd Wright à New York révolutionne le concept de l'en-vironnement du travail et annonce la naissance du bureau intégré moderne. Ce siège de bureau fut spécialement conçu pour ce projet et sa géométrie formelle faisait écho à l'architecture environnante. A travers cette rigueur formelle, l'intention de Wright était de créer un espace unifié tant visuelle-ment que fonctionnellement.

Frank Lloyd Wright:

Office armchair designed for the Larkin Company Administration Building, 1904

Bürodrehstuhl für das Verwal-tungsgebäude der Larkin Company, 1904

Fauteuil de bureau pivotant dessiné pour la Larkin Company, 1904

Frank Lloyd Wright:

Interior of the Larkin Company Administration Building, Buffalo, New York, 1903–05

Das Innere des Verwaltungs-gebäudes der Larkin Company, Buffalo, New York, 1903–05

Intérieur de bureau de la Larkin Company, Buffalo, New York, 1903–05

45

Josef Hoffmann

1870–1956

Austria . Österreich . Autriche

Sitzmaschine, Model No. 670
c. 1908

Sitzmaschine, Modell Nr. 670
um 1908

Sitzmaschine, modèle n° 670
vers 1908

Stained, laminated wood, bent solid beechwood, turned wood and brass fittings

Schichtholz gebeizt, Bugholz und gedrechseltes Holz, Messingbeschläge

Bois lamellé teinté, hêtre massif cintré, bois tourné et accessoires en cuivre

Jacob & Josef Kohn, Vienna

Josef Hoffmann:
Sanatorium Purkersdorf, 1904–06

Manufactured by J. & J. Kohn from about 1908 to 1916, the *Sitzmaschine*, with an adjustable back, was sold both with and without large horsehair-filled cushions. The latter was the more popular option, suggesting that the chair may have been more often purchased purely for its aesthetic qualities than for its functionalism. The *Sitzmaschine*'s stringent geometric formalism predicts Gerrit Rietveld's later *Red-and-blue chair* of 1917/18.

Die *Sitzmaschine* mit verstellbarer Rückenlehne wurde von J. & J. Kohn von 1908 bis 1916 hergestellt und mit oder ohne große, roßhaargefüllte Sitzkissen verkauft. Die Käufer zogen im allgemeinen die letzte Version vor, vermutlich weil sie den Stuhl eher wegen seiner ästhetischen Qualitäten als wegen seiner Funktionalität erwarben. Die *Sitzmaschine* mit ihrem streng geometrischen Formalismus nimmt Gerrit Rietvelds *Rot-Blau-Stuhl* von 1917/18 vorweg.

Fabriqué par J. & J. Kohn de 1908 environ à 1916, cette *Sitzmaschine* (machine à s'asseoir) à dossier inclinable, fut commercialisée avec ou sans grands coussins bourrés de crin de cheval. Le modèle sans coussin fut le plus vendu, ce qui laisse à penser que ce siège était plus acheté pour ses qualités esthétiques que son fonctionnalisme. Le strict formalisme géométrique annonce le *fauteuil rouge-et-bleu* de Rietveld de 1917/18.

Josef Hoffmann:
Sitzmaschine, 1905

Josef Hoffmann:
Side chair *Model No. 371*, c. 1906
Stuhl *Modell Nr. 371*, um 1906
Chaise *modèle n° 371*, vers 1906

46

Gerrit Rietveld

1888–1964

Netherlands . Niederlande . Pays-Bas

Red-and-blue chair
1917/18

Rot-Blau-Stuhl
1917/18

Fauteuil rouge-et-bleu
1917/18

Painted solid beechwood and plywood construction

Konstruktion aus Buche massiv und schichtverleimtem Sperrholz, farbig lackiert

Hêtre massif peint et contre-plaqué

G.A. van de Groenekan, De Bilt (reissued by Cassina, Italy, from 1971)

The ancestry of the *Red-and-blue chair*'s essential form can be traced back to the *Morris* chair, via the designs of Josef Hoffmann and Frank Lloyd Wright.[6] The *Red-and-blue chair* is viewed as the first truly modern chair because of the revolutionary philosophical agenda it set. While expressing reductivist aesthetics, the design speculated on standardised mass production through a geometrically abstracted construction of regular and simply joined machined materials.

Die Form des *Rot-Blau-Stuhls* geht im wesentlichen auf den *Morris*-Stuhl und die Entwürfe von Josef Hoffmann und Frank Lloyd Wright zurück.[6] Der *Rot-Blau-Stuhl* gilt als erster wirklich »moderner« Stuhl wegen der radikal neuen Gestaltungsphilosophie, die hinter dem Design steckt. Mit der geometrisch-abstrakten Form strebte Rietveld eine puristische Konstruktion an, die durch ihre einheitlich gestalteten, maschinell bearbeiteten und einfach verzapften Einzelteile eine genormte Massenproduktion erleichtern sollte.

L'hérédité de la forme de base du *fauteuil rouge-et-bleu* peut être retracée jusqu'à la chaise *Morris*, en passant par certains dessins de Hoffmann et de Frank Lloyd Wright.[6] Il est considéré comme le premier siège vraiment moderne du fait des enjeux révolutionnaires qu'il soulève. Tout en exprimant une esthétique de réduction, sa conception laissait entrevoir la possibilité de production en série, grâce à une construction géométrique abstraite en matériaux standard usinés et assemblés avec simplicité.

Gerrit Rietveld, G.A. van der Groenekan, Adriaen van Ostadelaan

Gerrit Rietveld:

Red-and-blue-chair, designed in 1918, executed in 1919

Rot-blau-Stuhl, entworfen 1918, ausgeführt 1919

Fauteuil rouge-et-bleu, dessiné en 1918 et réalisé en 1919

47

Marcel Breuer

1902–81

Germany . Deutschland .
Allemagne

**Wassily Club chair,
Model No. B3** 1925

**Sessel Wassily,
Modell Nr. B3** 1925

**Fauteuil Wassily,
modèle n° B3** 1925

Bent, nickeled tubular steel frame
(later chrome-plated) with fabric,
canvas or leather

Rahmen: Stahlrohr, vernickelt
(später verchromt); Sitzfläche,
Arm- und Rückenlehnen mit
Eisengarnstoff, Kanvas oder
Leder bespannt

Structure en tubes d'acier cintrés
et nickelés (plus tard chromés),
tissu, toile ou cuir

**Standard-Möbel Lengyel & Co.,
Berlin, and Gebrüder Thonet,
Frankenberg, Germany, from
c.1928 (reissued by Gavina,
Italy from 1962 to 1968 and
Knoll International, Inc., New
York, from 1968 to present)**

Designed for the painter Wassily
Kandinsky's staff quarters at the
Dessau Bauhaus, the *Model No. B3*
was revolutionary both in materials and
method of manufacture. Breuer's Adler
bicycle is said to have inspired his use
of tubular steel, while Constructivist
sculpture must surely have influenced
the chair's form. The *Wassily* and many
other Modern Movement designs were
first mass-produced in the 1950s and
1960s, when there was a general
reassessment of pre-war Modernist
furniture.

Das *Modell Nr. B3*, von Breuer ursprünglich für den Maler Wassily Kandinsky, Mitglied des Dessauer Bauhauses, entworfen, hat das Design in
bezug auf Material und Herstellung
radikal verändert. Zur Verwendung von
Stahlrohr soll Breuer sein neues Adler-
Fahrrad inspiriert haben, während die
Form des Sessels an konstruktivi-
stische Skulpturen erinnert. Der *Wassily* und viele andere Entwürfe der
Klassischen Moderne wurden erst in
den 50er und 60er Jahren, als man das
Vorkriegs-Möbeldesign wiederentdeckt
hatte, produziert.

Créé pour les bureaux du peintre
Wassily Kandinsky au Bauhaus de
Dessau, ce *modèle n° B3* était révolutionnaire aussi bien au niveau des
matériaux que de la fabrication. On ra-
conte que le vélo Adler que Breuer
venait d'acheter lui avait fait penser aux
tubes d'acier, mais la sculpture cons-
tructiviste a certainement tout autant
influencé les formes de ce siège. Le
Wassily, comme beaucoup d'autres
projets, ne fut réellement produit en
série que dans les années 50 et 60, à
la faveur d'une remise en perspective
de l'importance du siège moderniste.

Marcel Breuer:

Furnishing for a lady gymnastics
teacher, Berlin, 1930

Einrichtung für eine Gymnastik-
lehrerin, Berlin, 1930

Ameublement pour une
professeuse de gymnastique,
Berlin, 1930

Photograph of a woman seated in
a *Wassily* chair wearing a mask
by Oskar Schlemmer, c. 1927

Foto einer Frau mit »Schlemmer«-
Maske in dem Sessel *Wassily*, um
1927

Photo d'une femme avec masque
de Schlemmer dans le fauteuil
Wassily, vers 1927

Eileen Gray

1878–1976
France . Frankreich

Transat chair 1926
Armlehnstuhl Transat 1926
Fauteuil Transat 1926

Upholstered sling seat supported
on a solid sycamore frame with
chrome-plated metal fittings

Rahmen Sykomorenholz massiv,
verchromte Beschläge; Polster-
auflage, mit Leder bezogen

Siège suspendu rembourré dans
un cadre de sycomore massif,
accessoires en métal chromé

**Jean Désert, Paris (reissued by
Ecart, France from 1978)**

Eileen Gray's elegant *Transat* folding chair was based on the traditional steamer chair. The French architect, Jean Badovici, wrote of Gray in the June 1924 issue of "Wendingen", the Dutch design journal: "She is modern in every possible aspect of her style, vision and expression, in her disdain of the old emotional, aesthetic and traditional plastic forms. She has understood that our own times have brought, along with new patterns of life, the necessity of new ways of thinking; that the machine age must transform our sensibilities."[7]

Grays eleganter Armlehnstuhl *Transat* ist den traditionellen Liegestühlen großer Passagierdampfer nachempfunden. Der französische Architekt Jean Badovici schrieb in der niederländischen Zeitschrift »Wendingen« im Juni 1924: »Sie ist modern in ihrem Stil, ihren Visionen und ihrem Ausdruck und in ihrer Verachtung der alten, emotionalen Ästhetik und traditioneller, plastischer Formen. Sie hat verstanden, daß ein neuer Lebensstil und eine neue Denkweise unsere Zeit prägen, daß das Maschinenzeitalter unser Wahrnehmungsvermögen verändern muß.«[7]

L'élégant *Transat* pliant de Gray s'inspirait des chaises longues de paquebot. L'architecte français Jean Badovici écrivit sur Gray dans le numéro de juin 1924 de «Wendingen», le magazine de design néerlandais: «Elle est moderne dans tous les aspects possibles de son style, de sa vision et de son expression... Elle a compris ce que notre époque, avec ses nouveaux modes de vie, nous a apporté: la nécessité de nouvelles manières de ressentir les choses et le fait que l'âge de la machine doit transformer nos sensibilités.»[7]

Eileen Gray:

Transat, reissued by Ecart

Transat, Nachbau von Ecart

Transat, copie d'Ecart

Mart Stam

1899–1986

Netherlands . Niederlande .
Pays-Bas

Side chair S33 1926
Reissued by Gebrüder Thonet,
Frankenberg

Stuhl S33 1926
Nachbau von Gebrüder Thonet,
Frankenberg

Chaise S33 1926
Copie par les Gebrüder Thonet,
Frankenberg

Lacquered, cast tubular steel
frame, internally reinforced with
solid metal rods, fabric seat and
back

Rahmen aus Gußstahlrohr,
lackiert und innen mit Rundstahl-
stäben verstärkt; Sitzfläche und
Rückenlehne aus Stoff

Structure en tubes de fonte
d'acier laquée à barres de renfort
interne en métal, siège et dossier
en tissu

**L. & C. Arnold GmbH, Schorn-
dorf, Germany (reissued by
Gebrüder Thonet, Frankenberg)**

Mart Stam:

Chair, 1926

Stuhl, 1926

Chaise, 1926

In 1926, Stam made the first prototype
chair to incorporate the cantilever
principle. Later in the same year, he
attended a meeting held in Stuttgart
for all the architects taking part in the
Deutsche Werkbund exhibition at the
Weissenhofsiedlung in 1927. At this
conference, Stam presented drawings
of the prototype to, among others,
Ludwig Mies van der Rohe, who, inspired by Stam's novel concept,
designed his own versions of the cantilevered chair.

1926 entwarf Stam den Prototyp des
ersten freitragenden Stuhls. Im gleichen Jahr nahm er teil an einem Treffen
der Architekten, die sich an der Ausstellung des Deutschen Werkbundes
in der Weißenhof-Siedlung im folgen-
den Jahr beteiligen sollten. Bei dieser
Konferenz zeigte er seine Entwurfs-
zeichnungen für den Prototyp auch
Mies van der Rohe, der – von Stams
neuem Sitzmöbeldesign inspiriert –
eine eigene Version des freitragenden
Stuhls entwarf.

En 1926, Stam réalisa le premier prototype d'un siège en porte-à-faux. Plus
tard, au cours de la même année, il
assista à une réunion organisée à
Stuttgart pour tous les architectes par-
ticipant à l'exposition du Deutsche
Werkbund, prévue pour 1927 à la
Weissenhofsiedlung. A cette conférence, il présenta les dessins de ces
prototypes à Mies van der Rohe, entre
autres, qui fasciné par la nouveauté de
l'idée de Stam dessina sa propre
version de chaise en porte-à-faux.

Ludwig Mies van der Rohe

1886–1969

Germany . Deutschland . Allemagne

Weissenhof chair, Model No. MR20 1927

Weißenhof-Stuhl, Modell Nr. MR20 1927

Chaise Weissenhof, modèle n° MR20 1927

Bent, nickel-plated tubular steel, cane, bent solid steel

Rahmen aus gebogenem Stahlrohr, nahtlos gezogen und vernickelt, Sitzfläche Rohrgeflecht

Structure, en tube d'acier cintré et nickelé, siège canné

Berliner Metallgewerbe Joseph Müller, Berlin from c. 1927–31 and Bamberg Metallwerkstätten, Berlin-Neukölln from 1931

Like Stam's earlier side chair, this more eloquent design of 1927 was first shown publicly at the Weissenhof as part of the Deutscher Werkbund "Die Wohnung" ("The Dwelling") exhibition. Mies' *Model No. MR20* armchair, was received with greater acclaim and later named after this landmark exhibition.

Genau wie ein früherer Stuhl von Stam, so wurde auch dieses gefälligere Design zum erstenmal öffentlich auf der Weißenhof-Ausstellung als Teil der Deutschen Werkbund-Ausstellung »Die Wohnung« gezeigt. Mies' Armlehnstuhl *Modell Nr. MR20* stieß dort auf breite Resonanz und wurde später nach dieser Ausstellung benannt.

Comme le fauteuil de Stam qui l'a précédé, ce design plus éloquent de 1927 a d'abord été présenté au Weissenhof en tant qu'élément de l'exposition du Deutscher Werkbund «Die Wohnung». Le fauteuil *MR20* de Mies fut plus applaudi et a ensuite reçu le nom de cette exposition marquante.

Ludwig Mies van der Rohe:

Pieces from a nine piece dining room suite, c. 1931

Elemente einer neunteiligen Kombination für ein Eßzimmer, um 1931

Elements d'un ensemble de 9 pièces pour salle à manger, vers 1931

Ludwig Mies van der Rohe:

Weissenhof *Model No. MR10* chair, 1927

Weißenhof-Sessel, *Modell Nr. MR10*, 1927

Chaise Weißenhof, *modèle n° MR10*, 1927

Marcel Breuer

1902–81

Germany . Deutschland .
Allemagne

Chair B32 1928
Armchair B64 1928

Stuhl B32 1928
Armlehnstuhl B64 1928

Chaise B32 1928
Fauteuil B64 1928

Chrome-plated, bent tubular steel
frame, bent solid beechwood seat
and back with woven cane

Stahlrohrrahmen, gezogen und
verchromt; Sitzfläche und Rückenlehne gebogenes Buchenrundholz
mit Rohrgeflecht

Structure en tubes d'acier cintrés
et chromés, siège et dossier en
hêtre massif cintré et canné

**Gebrüder Thonet, Frankenberg,
from c.1931 (reissued by
Gavina, Italy, from 1962 to 1968
and Knoll International, Inc.,
New York from 1968 to present)**

Marcel Breuer writes in "das neue
frankfurt" (1927): "One may conclude
that any object properly and practically
designed should "fit" into any room in
which it is used as would any living object, like a flower or a human being."[8]

Marcel Breuer schreibt 1927 in der
Zeitschrift »das neue frankfurt«: »man
darf annehmen, daß jedes objekt mit
einem guten und praktischen design in
jeden raum »paßt«, in dem es gebraucht wird, genau wie jedes leben-
dige objekt, sei es eine blume oder ein
menschliches wesen.«[8]

Marcel Breuer écrivit dans «das neue
frankfurt» en 1927: «On pourrait con-
clure que n'importe quel objet conçu
adéquatement et avec le sens du pratique devrait pouvoir s'adapter à n'importe quelle pièce dans laquelle il est
utilisé, comme tout objet vivant, fleur
ou être humain.»[8]

Thonet brochure, 1930/31,
cover

Thonet-Prospekt, 1930/31,
Einband

Prospectus Thonet, 1930/31,
couverture

The chaises longues described by Le Corbusier as "équipement de l'habitation"[9], are early examples of ergonomic design. The innovative movable seat section with adjustable neckrest affords a great degree of comfort to a wide range of users – a feature that has guaranteed the design's continuing appeal.

Die Chaiselongues, von Le Corbusier, als »Wohnausstattung«[9] beschrieben, sind frühe Beispiele des ergonomischen Designs. Die bewegliche Liegefläche mit der verstellbaren Kopfstütze bietet den verschiedensten Benutzern ein größeres Maß an Komfort – ein Merkmal, das die noch immer anhaltende Beliebtheit dieses Entwurfs erklärt.

Les chaises longues décrites par Le Corbusier comme un «équipement de l'habitation»[9] sont de précoces exemples de design ergonomique. Le siège réglable en inclinaison, très innovateur, et son repose-tête adaptable assurent un grand degré de confort à toutes sortes d'utilisateurs, caractéristique qui a assuré le succès continu de ce modèle.

Le Corbusier
1887–1965

Pierre Jeanneret
1896–1967

Charlotte Perriand
*1903

France . Frankreich

Chaise longue c. 1928

Chaiselongue um 1928

Chaise longue vers 1928

Black-painted metal, tubular metal framework covered in ponyskin on an elongated H-form base

Schwarz lackiertes Metall, Stahlrohrrahmen, bezogen mit Pferdefell auf einer verlängerten H-förmigen Basis

Métal laqué noir, structure en tube de métal, cuir de poney sur une base en forme de H allongé

Embru-Werke AG, Rüti, Zurich, from 1932. The hide-covered Model No. B306 version of this design was manufactured by Gebrüder Thonet, Frankenberg, from c. 1929 (reissued by Cassina, Italy, from 1965)

Le Corbusier:

Model *LC4*, reissued by Cassina, 1965

Modell *LC4*, Nachbau von Cassina, 1965

Modèle *LC4*, copie de Cassina, 1965

Le Corbusier:

Chaise longue, Model No. 2072, 1928

Chaiselongue, Modell Nr. 2072, 1928

Chaise longue, modèle n° 2072, 1928

Embru-Werke AG catalogue showing *Model No. 2072*, 1936

Embru-Werke AG, Katalog: *Modell Nr. 2072*, 1936

Embru-Werke AG, catalogue présentant le *modèle n° 2072*, 1936

Le Corbusier
1887–1965

Pierre Jeanneret
1896–1967

Charlotte Perriand
*1903

France . Frankreich

Le Corbusier collaborated with Charlotte Perriand and his cousin Pierre Jeanneret in the design of this chair, which was initially used in the interior of a villa in Ville-d'Avray and first exhibited at the 1929 Salon d'Automne, Paris. With its undeniable luxury and elegant proportions, the *Grand Confort* is quintessentially of the International Style.

Zusammen mit Charlotte Perriand und seinem Cousin Pierre Jeanneret entwarf Le Corbusier diesen Sessel als Teil der Inneneinrichtung einer Villa in Ville-d'Avray. 1929 wurde er auf dem Salon d'Automne (Paris) der breiten Öffentlichkeit vorgestellt. Der ausgesprochen luxuriöse und elegante Sessel *Grand Confort* ist geradezu eine Verkörperung des Internationalen Stils.

Le Corbusier collabora avec Charlotte Perriand et son cousin Pierre Jeanneret au dessin de ce siège qui fut placé dans une villa de Ville-d'Avray avant d'être exposé pour la première fois au Salon d'Automne (Paris) de 1929. De par son luxe indéniable et ses élégantes proportions, le *Grand Confort* représente la quintessence du style international.

**Grand Confort,
Model No. LC3** 1928

**Sessel Grand Confort,
Modell Nr. LC3** 1928

**Grand Confort,
modèle n° LC3** 1928

Chrome-plated, bent tubular steel frame with loose, leather-covered, upholstered cushions

Rahmen Stahlrohr, gezogen und verchromt; lose, lederbezogene Polsterkissen

Structure en tube d'acier cintré et chromé à coussins mobiles en cuir

Gebrüder Thonet, Vienna & Paris (reissued by Cassina, Italy, from 1965)

Le Corbusier, Pierre Jeanneret, Charlotte Perriand:

LC3 chair, 1928/29 (Cassina)

Stuhl *LC3*, 1928/29 (Cassina)

Chaise *LC3*, 1928/29 (Cassina)

Le Corbusier, Pierre Jeanneret, Charlotte Perriand:

LC2 chair, 1928/29 (Cassina)

Stuhl *LC2*, 1928/29 (Cassina)

Chaise *LC2*, 1928/29 (Cassina)

Le Corbusier, Pierre Jeanneret, Charlotte Perriand:

LC2 sofa, 1928/29 (Cassina)

Sofa *LC2*, 1928/29 (Cassina)

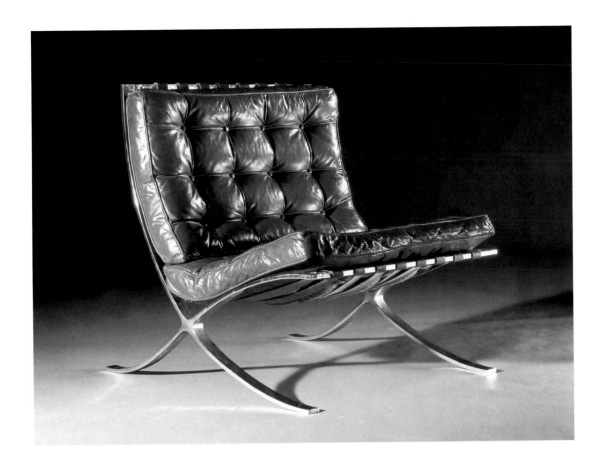

Barcelona chair, Model No. MR90 1929

Sessel Barcelona, Modell Nr. MR90 1929

Chauffeuse Barcelona, modèle n° MR90 1929

Bent, chromed flat steel with removable buttoned-leather, upholstered cushions

Rahmen gezogener Flachstahl, verchromt; lose Kissen, leder-bezogen, mit Knopfpolsterung

Acier plat cintré et chromé, acier plat chromé avec coussins amovibles en cuir capitonné

Berliner Metallgewerbe Joseph Müller, Berlin, and, slightly later, Bamberg Metallwerkstätten, Berlin-Neukölln (reissued by Knoll Associates, Inc., New York from 1948)

The *Model No. MR90* was designed for the German pavilion at the 1929 Exposición Internacional in Barcelona and for the specific use of King Alfonso XIII and his queen at the exhibition's opening ceremonies. The form of the chair was based on a folding stool of antiquity known as the "sella curulis". Although the *MR90* appears to be thoroughly modern, the methods used in its manufacture were, ironically, traditional and extremely labour-intensive.

Van der Rohe entwarf das *Modell Nr. MR90* für den Deutschen Pavillon auf der Exposición Internacional von 1929 in Barcelona. Während der Eröffnungsfeier diente es König Alfonso XIII. und der Königin von Spanien als Sitzgelegenheit. Der Sessel mit den lederbezogenen Kissen strahlt Würde und Eleganz aus; seine Form geht zurück auf den zusammenklappbaren Stuhl der Antike, die »sella curulis«. Obwohl das *Modell Nr. MR90* höchst modern wirkt, ist seine Herstellungsweise traditionell und ungewöhnlich arbeitsintensiv.

Ce modèle fut dessiné pour le Pavillon d'Allemagne de l'Exposition Internacional de Barcelone en 1929 et à l'usage exclusif du roi Alphonse XIII et de son épouse lors des cérémonies d'ouverture. De ce siège, dont la forme rappelle les anciennes chaises curules pliantes, émane un sens affirmé du luxe. Bien que le *MR90* apparaisse comme profondément moderne, ses méthodes de fabrication se révélèrent ironiquement très traditionnelles et très longues.

Ludwig Mies van der Rohe:

The German Pavilion, Barcelona International Exhibition, 1929

Der Deutsche Pavillon, Weltausstellung in Barcelona, 1929

Pavillon d'Allemagne, Exposition Internationale de Barcelone, 1929

Reconstruction of the German pavilion at the International Exhibition in Barcelona, 1929

Rekonstruktion des Deutschen Pavillons auf der internationalen Weltausstellung in Barcelona, 1929

Reconstruction du Pavillon d'Allemagne à l'Exposition Internationale de Barcelone en 1929

Alvar Aalto

1898–1976

Finland . Finnland . Finlande

**Paimio chair,
Model No. 41** 1931/32

**Sessel Paimio,
Modell Nr. 41** 1931/32

**Fauteuil Paimio,
modèle n° 41** 1931/32

Bent, laminated birch frame, solid birch, with painted, bent plywood seat

Gestell laminiertes, gebogenes Birkenholz, massiv; Sitz aus verformtem Schichtholz, lackiert

Structure en bouleau lamellé cintré, bouleau massif et siège de contreplaqué cintré et peint

Oy Huonekalu-ja Rakennust-yötehdas AB, Turku, Finland (reissued by Artek, Finland)

Subsequently known as the *Paimio* chair, the *Model No. 41* did not figure in the original interior scheme of Aalto's Paimio Sanatorium project, initiated in 1929. The design actually dates from 1932, when the sanatorium was completed. Exhibited at the Building Congress for Nordic Countries that year, the construction of the *Model No. 41* was revolutionary. Where there was a need for greater pliancy, as in the scrolls of the seat and back, Aalto thinned out the laminate by removing several layers of veneer.

Das *Modell Nr. 41*, das als *Paimio-Sessel* bekannt wurde, gehörte nicht zu der Originalausstattung des von Aalto konzipierten Sanatoriums Paimio, das 1929 eröffnet wurde. Das Modell entstand 1932, mit der Fertigstellung des Sanatoriums, und wurde im selben Jahr auf dem Baukongreß für Nordische Länder vorgestellt. Die Konstruktion war revolutionär. Um eine stärkere Krümmung einiger Teile zu erreichen, verdünnte Aalto das Schichtholz, indem er einige Lagen Furnierblatt abtrug.

Ce *modèle n° 41*, le fauteuil *Paimio*, ne figurait pas à l'origine dans le projet de décoration d'Aalto pour le Sanatorium de Paimio en 1929. Son dessin date en réalité de 1932. Présenté au Congrès de la Construction des Pays Scandinaves en 1932, il était révolutionnaire dans sa construction. Pour permettre un meilleur pliage du bois, en particulier dans les enroulements du dossier et du siège, Aalto amincit le lamellé en éliminant plusieurs couches de placage pour augmenter la souplesse du matériau.

Marcel Breuer:

Chaise longue, 1935/36

Chaiselongue, 1935/36

Alvar Aalto:

Model No. 60 stool, 1930–33

Hocker *Modell Nr. 60,* 1930–33

Tabouret *modèle n° 60,* 1930–33

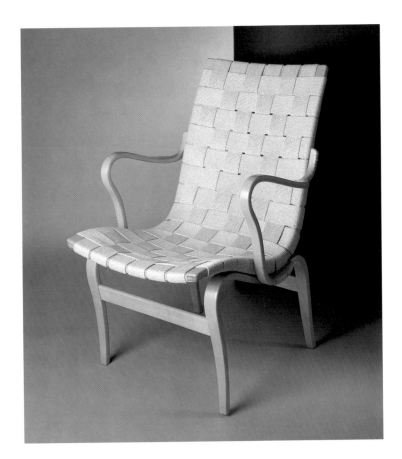

Bruno Mathsson

*1907
Sweden . Schweden . Suède

Eva chair 1934

Stuhl Eva 1934

Chaise Eva 1934

Bent plywood, solid birch and hemp webbing

Rahmen verformtes Schichtholz und Birke massiv; Sitz aus Hanfgurten

Contreplaqué cintré, bouleau massif et sangles de chanvre

Firma Karl Mathsson, Varnamo, Sweden (reissued by Dux, Sweden from 1966)

Bruno Mathsson's own summer house in Frösakull, 1961

Bruno Mathssons eigenes Sommerhaus in Frösakull, 1961

Maison de vacances de Bruno Mathsson à Frösakull, 1961

Mathsson designed the *Eva* chair as well as the later *Pernilla* chaise longue, a lounge chair and an ottoman as a functional and aesthetically pleasing furniture group. Mathsson has declared: "the business of sitting never ceases to amaze me."[10]

Mathsson entwarf den Stuhl *Eva*, die Chaiselongue *Pernilla*, einen Liegestuhl und eine Ottomane als Teile einer funktionalen und ästhetisch ansprechenden Möbelgruppe. Mathsson sagte einmal: »Das Problem des Sitzens gibt mir immer wieder Rätsel auf.«[10]

Mathsson créa cette chaise *Eva* ainsi que plus tard la chaise longue *Pernilla* et une autre chaise longue et une ottomane avec le double souci de la fonction et de l'esthétique. Il déclara un jour que «s'asseoir est un sujet qui n'a jamais cessé d'éveiller ma curiosité.»[10]

Gerrit Rietveld

1888–1964

Netherlands . Niederlande .
Pays-Bas

Zig-Zag chair 1934
Stuhl Zig-Zag 1934
Chaise Zig-Zag 1934

Painted, solid elm construction

Konstruktion aus massivem
Ulmenholz, lackiert

Orme massif peint

**G.A. van de Groenekan, De Bilt,
Netherlands (reissued by
Cassina, Italy, from 1971)**

Using only four elements joined with a system of dovetailing secured with brass nuts and bolts, the *Zig-Zag* chair's visual simplicity belies a relatively complex construction. Examples of this design were also manufactured by Metz & Co. and in 1935 the company produced several variations, including a high-backed version and an armchair. This painted *Zig-Zag* chair was made by Gerard A. van de Groenekan in 1938 for his personal use.

Der *Zig-Zag*-Stuhl, der aus nur vier Elementen besteht, wird mit Hilfe von Schwalbenschwanzverbindungen – verstärkt durch Muttern und Schrauben – zusammengebaut. Trotz der einfachen Form ist seine Konstruktion überaus komplex. Außer bei der oben genannten Firma wurde dieses Modell auch von Metz & Co. produziert, die 1935 diverse Varianten herstellten, u.a. eine Version mit hoher Lehne und einen Armlehnstuhl. Der abgebildete *Zig-Zag*-Stuhl wurde von Gerard A. van de Groenekan 1938 zum persönlichen Gebrauch angefertigt.

Avec seulement quatre éléments montés en queue d'aronde et maintenus par un boulonnage de cuivre, l'apparente simplicité de la chaise *Zig-Zag* cache en réalité une construction assez complexe. Des modèles en furent également fabriqués par Metz & Co.(Amsterdam) et, en 1935, la société produisit plusieurs variations dont une version à haut dossier et un fauteuil. Cette chaise *Zig-Zag* a été réalisée par Gerard A. van de Groenekan en 1938 pour son usage personnel.

Gerrit Rietveld:

Interior in Stoop Family House, Velp, photographed in 1950

Inneneinrichtung, Haus der Familie Stoop, Velp, 1950 fotografiert

Vue de l'intérieur de la maison Stoop, Velp, photographiée en 1950

Reissued *Zig-Zag* chairs manufactured by Cassina

Nachgebaute *Zig-Zag*-Stühle, produziert von Cassina

Réédition des chaises *Zig-Zag* par Cassina

Giuseppe Terragni

1904–43

Italy . Italien . Italie

Follia chair 1934–36
Stuhl Follia 1934–36
Chaise Follia 1934–36

Solid wood seat and back, painted black, connected with a stainless steel backrest-support spring

Sitzfläche und Rückenlehne aus massivem Holz, schwarz lackiert; eine elastische Stütze aus rostfreiem Stahl verbindet Sitz und Rückenlehne

Siège et dossier en bois massif peint en noir, réunis par un support de dossier en acier inoxydable souple

Reissued under licence by Zanotta, Italy, from 1971

The *Follia* chair was designed for the Casa del Fascio, the Italian Fascist party headquarters in Como. Modernist architecture and designs such as the *Follia*, the *Lariana* and the *Sant'Elia* chairs were viewed favourably by the Italian Fascists until the late 1930s, when the prevailing Rationalism was generally superseded by the state-promoted neo-Classical Novecento style.

Der *Follia*-Stuhl wurde speziell für die Casa del Fascio, das Hauptquartier der Italienischen Faschistischen Partei in Como, entworfen. Die zeitgenössische, moderne Architektur und das moderne Design, z.B. der Stühle *Follia*, *Lariana* und *Sant'Elia*, wurden von den italienischen Faschisten bis gegen Ende der dreißiger Jahre favorisiert; dann wurde der vorherrschende Rationalismus europaweit vom Neoklassizismus des 20. Jahrhunderts verdrängt, dem nun auch die staatlichen Organe Italiens den Vorzug gaben.

La chaise *Follia* a été spécialement créée pour la Casa del Fascio, siège du parti fasciste à Côme. Il est intéressant de noter que l'architecture moderniste et des modèles comme, par exemple, les chaises *Follia*, *Lariana* et *Sant'Elia* furent appréciées par les fascistes italiens jusqu'à la fin des années 30 quand le rationalisme prévalant fut généralement remplacé par un style néo-classique approuvé par l'Etat.

Giuseppe Terragni:

Casa del Fascio, Como, 1932–36

Giuseppe Terragni:

Lariana chair, 1935/36

Stuhl *Lariana*, 1935/36

Chaise *Lariana*, 1935/36

Giuseppe Terragni:

Sant'Elia chair, 1936

Stuhl *Sant'Elia*, 1936

Chaise *Sant'Elia*, 1936

Jorge Ferrari-Hardoy
1913–75

Juan Kurchan
unknown

Antonio Bonet
unknown

Argentina . Argentinien . Argentine

**Butterfly chair,
Model No. 198** 1938

**Stuhl Butterfly,
Modell Nr. 198** 1938

**Chaise Butterfly,
modèle n° 198** 1938

Tubular steel frame with leather
sling seat

Stahlrohrrahmen mit locker
befestigtem Lederpolster

Structure tubulaire en acier, siège
de cuir suspendu

**Knoll Associates, Inc., New York
from c.1950 to c.1975 (reissued
by Stöhr Import-Export GmbH,
Germany, from 1982 to present)**

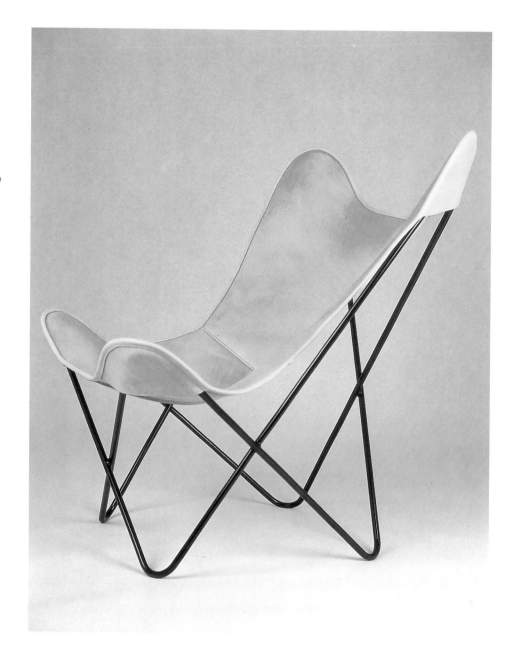

"Hardoy characterised this chair as 'an improvement on previous designs' which he and his colleagues had made for their own offices, little dreaming it would ever become so popular."[11] The *Butterfly* chair was initially produced by Artek-Pascoe and approximately 1,500 were sold. After the Second World War, Knoll took over production. A lawsuit later ensued regarding copyright infringement, which Knoll eventually lost. Consequently, the *Model No. 198* became one of the most copied chair designs in recent history.

»Hardoy beschrieb den Sessel als »Verbesserung früherer Entwürfe«, die er und seine Kollegen ausgeführt hatten, wobei sie nicht im Traum daran gedacht hatten, daß dieses Modell einmal so beliebt werden würde.«[11] Der *Butterfly*-Sessel wurde zunächst von Artek-Pascoe produziert; verkauft wurden etwa 1.500 Stück. Nach dem Zweiten Weltkrieg übernahm Knoll die Produktion. Einen Rechtsstreit wegen Verletzung des Copyrights verlor Knoll. In der Folge wurde das *Modell Nr. 198* zum meistkopierten Stuhl der jüngeren Designgeschichte.

«Hardoy considérait cette chaise comme «une amélioration de projets antérieurs» que lui et ses collègues avaient réalisés pour leurs propres bureaux, n'imaginant pas qu'ils puisssent connaître le succès.»[11] La chaise *Butterfly* fut initialement produite par Artek-Pascoe qui en vendit environ 1.500 exemplaires. Après la Seconde Guerre mondiale, Knoll reprit la production. Plus tard, un procès eut lieu sur le non-respect de ces droits que Knoll perdit. Ce modèle devint l'un des sièges les plus copiés de l'histoire récente du design.

Interior designed by Knoll International showing *Butterfly Model No. 198* chair, c.1960

Inneneinrichtung von Knoll International, zu sehen ist der *Butterfly*-Sessel, *Modell Nr. 198*, um 1960

Intérieur conçu par Knoll International, chaise *Butterfly*, modèle n° 198, vers 1960

Hans Coray

*1906

Switzerland . Schweiz . Suisse

Landi stacking chair
1939

Stapelstuhl Landi
1939

Chaise empilable Landi
1939

Bent and pressed aluminium

Aluminium, gepreßt und verformt

Aluminium embouti et cintré

Blattmann Metallwarenfabrik AG, Wädenswil, Switzerland (reissued by Zanotta, Italy, from 1970)

This 'proto-High Tech' design was commissioned by Hans Fischli for the grounds of the "Landesaustellung" (Swiss National Exhibition) held in Zurich in 1939. Weighing just over three kg, the Landi stacking chair was designed for both interior and exterior use. It was not marketed internationally until the 1950s, when it was widely acclaimed for its strength and durability.

Dieses »Proto-High-Tech«-Design wurde von Hans Fischli für das Gelände der Landesausstellung in Zürich 1939 in Auftrag gegeben. Der Landi-Stuhl wog gut drei Kilogramm und war für den Gebrauch in Innen- und Außenräumen konzipiert. International wurde er erst in den 50er Jahren vermarktet, nachdem man in weiten Kreisen seine Stärke und Haltbarkeit erkannt hatte.

Ce modèle proto-High-Tech fut commandé par Hans Fischli pour les abords de la «Landesausstellung» (Exposition Nationale Suisse) de Zurich, en 1939. Ne pesant qu'un peu plus de trois kilos, cette chaise empilable était conçue aussi bien pour un usage extérieur qu'intérieur. Elle ne fut pas commercialisée internationalement avant les années 50 et fut alors saluée pour sa solidité et sa durabilité.

"Landesausstellung" (Swiss National Exhibition), Zurich, 1939

»Landesausstellung« (Schweizer Nationalausstellung), Zürich, 1939

«Landesausstellung» (Exposition Nationale Suisse), Zurich, 1939

Carlo Mollino

1905 – 73

Italy . Italien . Italie

Side Chair designed for Lisa and Gio Ponti 1940

Stuhl, entworfen für Lisa und Gio Ponti 1940

Chaise dessinée pour Lisa et Gio Ponti 1940

Polished brass frame with Resinflex upholstered bifurcated seat and back

Messingrahmen mit Resinflex-Politur; Sitzpolster und Rückenlehne zweigeteilt

Structure de cuivre poli, siège et dossier rembourrés de Resinflex

Probably Apelli & Varesio, Turin, Italy

Carlo Mollino:

Bent wood and laminated *10-ply Ash* Side chair, 1949

10-ply Ash-Stuhl (Bugholz, gebeizt), 1949

Chaise *10-ply Ash* (bois cintré), 1949

Mollino's life and work were dictated by his firm belief that everything was "permissible as long as it is fantastic". Certainly, his life-long interest in occultism is reflected in the form of this chair, which is clearly based on a cloven hoof. The chair was designed for Lisa and Gio Ponti.

Mollinos Leben und Arbeit standen unter dem Motto »alles ist erlaubt, vorausgesetzt, es ist phantastisch«. Vorbild für die Form des Stuhls, die zweifellos sein lebenslanges Interesse am Okkultismus reflektiert, war offensichtlich ein gespaltener Huf. Der Stuhl war ein Entwurf für Lisa und Gio Ponti.

La vie et l'œuvre de Mollino furent dictées par sa croyance définitive que tout était «autorisé à condition d'être fantastique». L'intérêt qu'il témoigna sa vie durant à l'occultisme se retrouve dans la forme de cette chaise qui évoque à l'évidence un pied fourchu. Cette chaise a été dessinée pour Lisa et Gio Ponti.

Carlo Mollino:

Armchair with curved armrest, 1952

Sessel mit gebogener Armlehne, 1952

Chaise avec accoudoir incurvé, 1952

Carlo Mollino:

Chair for the Casa di Agra, 1955

Stuhl für die Casa di Agra, 1955

Chaise pour Casa di Agra, 1955

Carlo Mollino

1905–73

Italy . Italien . Italie

Armchair for Minola House
1944

Sessel für das Minola-Haus
1944

**Fauteuil pour la maison
Minola** 1944

Ebonised wood frame with velvet-
covered upholstery

Holzrahmen, schwarz gebeizt;
Polsterung mit Samt bezogen

Structure de bois noirci, rembourrage recouvert de velours

**Probably Apelli & Varesio, Turin,
Italy**

Carlo Mollino: "The best explanation
of one's work is contained in its silent
ostentation."[12] This armchair was designed for the house of Ada and Cesare Minola in Turin, Italy.

Carlo Mollino: »Die beste Erklärung
für die Arbeit, die man tut, gibt ihre
stumme Prahlerei.«[12] Der Sessel wurde für das Haus von Ada und Cesare
Minola in Turin, Italien, entworfen.

Carlo Mollino: «La meilleure explication
du travail de quelqu'un est toute en-
tière contenue dans sa présence silen-
cieuse.»[12] Ce fauteuil a été dessiné
pour la maison de Ada et Cesare
Minola à Turin, Italie.

Living room in the house of Ada
and Cesare Minola in Turin, 1944

Wohnraum im Haus von Ada und
Cesare Minola in Turin, 1944

Salle de séjour de la villa de Ada
et Cesare Minola à Turin, 1944

Charles & Ray Eames

1907–78 & 1913–88

USA . Etats-Unis

LCM (Lounge Chair Metal)
1945/46

Sessel, Modell LCM
1945/46

Chaise LCM 1945/46

Slunkskin (animal hide) covered, moulded plywood seat and back, attached with rubber shock-mounts to a chrome-plated bent tubular steel frame with self-levelling feet

Sitzschale und Rückenlehne aus mit Fell bezogenem verformtem Schichtholz, mit elastischen Gummischeiben am Rahmen befestigt; Rahmen aus gezogenem, verchromtem Stahlrohr mit selbsttätig höhenausgleichenden Beinen

Siège et dossier en contreplaqué moulé recouverts de veau mort-né, reliés par des blocs de caoutchouc à un cadre de tube d'acier cintré et chromé avec piètement à hauteur réglable

Evans Products Company, Venice, California from 1946 to 1949 and Herman Miller Inc., Zeeland, Michigan, from 1949 (Slunkskin version manufactured 1948–53)

The *LCM* forms part of the moulded plywood group of chairs, the prototypes of which were first shown in New York in December 1945. Impressed by what he saw there, Eliot Noyes, director of Industrial Design at the Museum of Modern Art, gave Charles Eames the museum's first one-man show in 1946. As a result, George Nelson introduced the Eameses to D.J. De Pree, the managing director of Herman Miller, Inc., – and so began one of the most fruitful collaborations between manufacturer and designer ever recorded.

Der Sessel *LCM* ist Teil einer Kollektion von Sitzmöbeln aus verformtem, schichtverleimtem Sperrholz, die Ende 1945 in New York vorgestellt wurde. Den Direktor der Abteilung Industrial Design des Museum of Modern Art, Eliot Noyes, beeindruckte die Präsentation, und er ermöglichte Charles Eames 1946 die erste One-man-show des Museums. George Nelson war begeistert und stellte die Eames dem Generaldirektor von Herman Miller, Inc., D.J. De Pree, vor. So begann eine äußerst fruchtbare Zusammenarbeit.

La *LCM* fait partie du groupe de sièges en «contreplaqué moulé» dont les prototypes furent à l'origine présentés à New York en 1945. Eliot Noyes, directeur du Design Industriel au Museum of Modern Art, offrit à Eames la première exposition personnelle jamais consacrée par le musée à un designer (1946). A la suite de cette exposition, George Nelson présenta les Eames à D.J. De Pree, directeur-gérant d'Herman Miller, Inc. C'est ainsi que commença l'une des collaborations les plus fructueuses qui aient jamais existé entre fabricant et créateur.

Charles & Ray Eames:
LCW, 1946

Charles & Ray Eames:
DCM, 1946

Charles & Ray Eames:
LCW, 1946

In his pursuit of a unified and organic form of design, Saarinen's principal concern was with human anatomy and its relationship to furniture. He said that the design of the *Womb* chair represented an "attempt to achieve psychological comfort by providing a great big cup-like shell into which you can curl up and pull up your legs (something that women seem especially to like to do)".[13]

Saarinen strebte ein ganzheitliches, organisches Design an und orientierte sich dabei vor allem an der menschlichen Anatomie und ihrer Relation zum Möbel. Er sagte, der Sessel *Womb* sei ein »Versuch, das Gefühl von Behaglichkeit zu erzeugen – und zwar indem man eine große schalenförmige Muschel wählte, in die man sich mit angezogenen Beinen schmiegen kann (was Frauen anscheinend besonders gern tun).«[13]

Le principal souci de Saarinen, dans sa recherche d'une forme de design organique et unifié, était l'anatomie et ses relations avec le mobilier. Il déclara que le dessin de ce siège représentait «une tentative de parvenir à un confort psychologique en offrant une sorte de grande coque dans laquelle vous pouvez vous blottir et ramener vos jambes (ce que les femmes aiment particulièrement faire).»[13]

Eero Saarinen

1910–61

USA . Etats-Unis

**Womb chair,
Model No. 70** 1946

**Sessel Womb,
Modell Nr. 70** 1946

**Fauteuil Womb,
modèle n° 70** 1946

Fabric-covered, upholstered, moulded fibreglass seat shell, with loose latex-foam cushions, supported on a bent tubular steel frame with nylon swivel glides

Formgepreßte, mit Latexschaum gepolsterte Sitzschale aus glasfaserverstärktem Kunststoff auf Stahlrohrgestell mit schwenkbaren Gleitrollen aus Nylon. Stoffbezug. Lose Kissen mit Latexschaum-Füllung

Coque de siège en fibre de verre moulée, rembourrée et recouverte de tissu avec coussins amovibles en mousse de latex sur cadre en tubes d'acier cintrés et glissières de pivotement en nylon

Knoll Associates, Inc., New York, from 1948 to present

Eero Saarinen:

Three models from a 1948 collection

Drei Modelle aus einer Kollektion von 1948

Trois modèles d'une collection de 1948

Herbert Matter:

Knoll advertisement for *Womb* chair, c.1950

Knoll-Werbung für den Sessel *Womb*, um 1950

Publicité de Knoll pour le fauteuil *Womb*, vers 1950

Hans Wegner

*1914

Denmark . Dänemark . Danemark

Classic armchair 1949
Armlehnstuhl Classic 1949
Fauteuil Classic 1949

Solid teak construction with woven cane seat

Rahmen Teakholz massiv; Sitzfläche aus Rohrgeflecht

Teak massif et siège canné

Johannes Hansen, Denmark (reissued by PP Møbler, Allerørd, Denmark from 1992)

"Wegner's original title for the *Classic* chair was the *Round* chair... but the name *Classic* chair soon caught on and was advocated by its admirers, who often referred to it as The Chair. Wegner designed this classic when he was only thirty-five years old and tended to be a little reticent in accepting the honour of having designed The Chair, believing that he had not at that point reached the height of his creative powers and was therefore not deserving of such an honour."[14]

»Wegner wollte den Stuhl ursprünglich *Round Chair* nennen..., aber die Bezeichnung *Classic* bürgerte sich schnell ein und wurde auch von den Anhängern Wegners befürwortet, die ihn häufig als Der Stuhl bezeichneten. Wegner entwarf das Modell *Classic*, als er fünfunddreißig Jahre alt war, und reagierte immer ein wenig zurückhaltend, wenn man ihm die Ehre antrug, den Stuhl entworfen zu haben, denn er glaubte, den Höhepunkt seines Schaffens noch nicht erreicht zu haben und daher eine solche Ehre nicht zu verdienen.«[14]

«Le nom donné originellement par Wegner à ce fauteuil *Classic* était *Round Chair*, mais le terme de *Classic* fut préféré et défendu par ses admirateurs qui souvent l'appelaient La Chaise. Wegner dessina ce modèle alors qu'il n'avait que vingt-cinq ans et montrait quelques réticences à accepter l'honneur de l'avoir dessiné, pensant qu'il était encore loin d'avoir atteint le sommet de sa puissance créative et qu'il ne méritait donc pas un tel honneur.»[14]

Hans Wegner:

Chinese chair, 1944

Chinesischer Stuhl, 1944

Chaise chinoise, 1944

Hans Wegner:

Peacock chair, 1947

Stuhl *Peacock*, 1947

Chaise *Peacock*, 1947

Hans Wegner:

Stacking chairs, 1949

Stapelstühle, 1949

Chaises empilables, 1949

In 1948, Marco Zanuso was commissioned by the Pirelli Company to investigate the potential of latex foam as a material suitable for upholstery. Later, in March 1950, the company established the Arflex firm to manufacture Zanuso's and other designers' foam-upholstered furniture. The *Antropus* was the first chair produced by Arflex and it is a tribute to Zanuso's unquestionable genius that it remains in production today.

1948 wurde Marco Zanuso von der Pirelli Company beauftragt, die Möglichkeiten von Latexschaumstoff als Polstermaterial zu untersuchen. Im März 1950 gründete Pirelli die Firma Arflex, um die schaumstoffgepolsterten Sitzmöbel von Zanuso und anderen Designern zu produzieren. *Antropus* war der erste Stuhl, den Arflex herstellte, und es ist Zanusos großem Können zuzuschreiben, daß sein Stuhl noch heute produziert wird.

En 1948, Pirelli demanda à Marco Zanuso d'explorer les possibilités de la mousse de latex dans le domaine du garnissage. Plus tard, en mars 1950, Pirelli créa Arflex pour réaliser les projets de Zanuso et d'autres designers de meubles recouverts de mousse de latex. L'*Antropus* fut le premier siège produit par Arflex et le fait qu'il soit toujours en production aujourd'hui est en soi un hommage au génie incontesté de Zanuso.

Marco Zanuso

*1916

Italy . Italien . Italie

Antropus chair 1949
Stuhl Antropus 1949
Fauteuil Antropus 1949

Fabric-covered, latex foam upholstered, moulded plywood

Verformtes, schichtverleimtes Sperrholz; Polsterung aus Latexschaum, mit Stoff bezogen

Contreplaqué moulé garni de mousse de latex et recouvert de tissu

Arflex, Italy, from 1950 to present

Marco Zanuso:
Lady armchair, 1951
Armlehnstuhl *Lady*, 1951
Fauteuil *Lady*, 1951

Franco Albini:
Fiorenza chair, 1952
Stuhl *Fiorenza*, 1952
Chaise *Fiorenza*, 1952

Ernest Race

1913 – 64

Great Britain . Großbritannien .
Grande-Bretagne

**Antelope chair with
matching table** 1950

**Armlehnstuhl Antelope mit
dazugehörigem Tisch** 1950

**Chaise Antelope avec table
assortie** 1950

Painted, bent steel rod frame with
painted, moulded plywood seat

Rahmen und Rückenlehne
gebogener Rundstahl, lackiert;
Sitzfläche verformtes, schichtverleimtes Sperrholz

Structure en acier cintré peint
et siège en contreplaqué moulé
peint

**Ernest Race Ltd., UK, from
1950 to present (table 1950
to c. 1955)**

The *Antelope* chair was designed for the Royal Festival Hall's outdoor terraces at the year-long Festival of Britain exhibition of 1951. Designed to comply with the constraints of national rationing, the *Antelope* chair's spindly legs terminating on ball feet echoed the new imagery of nuclear physics and molecular chemistry.

Der *Antelope*-Stuhl war anläßlich der Ausstellung Festival of Britain von 1951, die ein Jahr lang dauerte, speziell für die Außenterrassen der Royal Festival Hall entworfen worden; er entsprach den restriktiven Bedingungen der nationalen Rationierungsmaßnahmen. Seine staksigen Beine endeten in kugelförmigen Füßen – ein Motiv, das das zunehmende Publikumsinteresse an Nuklearphysik und Molekularbiologie widerspiegelte.

La chaise *Antelope* fut créée pour les terrasses en plein air du Royal Festival Hall à l'occasion de l'exposition du Festival de Grande-Bretagne qui dura toute l'année 1951. Dessinés en pensant aux contraintes du rationnement d'après-guerre, ses maigres pieds se terminant par des boules reflétaient l'intérêt grandissant du public pour la physique nucléaire et la chimie moléculaire.

Antelope chairs and tables in the Café of the Homes and Gardens Pavilion, Festival of Britain, 1951

Stühle und Tische aus der *Antelope*-Serie im Café des Homes and Gardens Pavillon, Festival of Britain, 1951

Chaises et tables *Antelope* dans le Café du Pavillon Homes and Gardens, Festival of Britain, 1951

Antelope chairs outside the Lion and Unicorn Pavilion, Festival of Britain, 1951

Antelope-Stühle vor dem Lion and Unicorn Pavillon, Festival of Britain, 1951

Chaises *Antelope* devant le Lion and Unicorn pavillon, Festival of Britain, 1951

Advertising leaflet showing designs by Jean Prouvé, Steph Simon, Paris, 1950s

Werbebroschüre mit Entwürfen von Jean Prouvé, Steph Simon, Paris, 50er Jahre

Pospectus montrant des créations de Jean Prouvé, Steph Simon, années 50

Jean Prouvé

1901–84
France . Frankreich

Antony chair 1950
Sessel Antony 1950
Chaise Antony 1950

Bent and painted tubular steel and flat steel frame, with moulded plywood seat

Rahmen Stahlrohr und Flachstahl, gezogen, Sitzschale verformtes, schichtverleimtes Sperrholz

Structure en tube d'acier cintré peint et acier plat, siège en contreplaqué moulé

Les Ateliers Jean Prouvé S.A., Maxéville, France, from 1950 to 1954

Originally designed for use at the University of Strasbourg, the *Antony* chair was manufactured by Prouvé's own company, founded in 1931, and was distributed by Steph Simon, Paris. Prouvé gave up furniture design when he left his company in 1953.

Der *Antony*-Sessel war ein Entwurf für die Ausstattung der Universität von Straßburg. Er wurde in Prouvés eigener, 1931 gegründeter Firma hergestellt und von Steph Simon, Paris, vertrieben. Prouvé gab seine Tätigkeit als Möbeldesigner auf, nachdem er seine Firma 1953 verlassen hatte.

Conçue à l'origine pour l'Université de Strasbourg, cette chaise fut fabriquée par l'usine que Prouvé avait ouverte en 1931 et distribuée par Steph Simon, Paris. Prouvé abandonna la création de mobilier lorsqu'il quitta sa société en 1953.

Harry Bertoia

1915–78

USA . Etats-Unis

Diamond chair 1950–52
Sessel Diamond 1950–52
Fauteuil Diamond 1950–52

Bent and welded steel rod construction, either chrome-plated or
vinyl-coated finish

Konstruktion aus gebogenem
Rundstahl, geschweißt und
verchromt oder vinylbeschichtet

Construction en tiges de fer cin-
trées et soudées, chromées ou
gainées de vinyl

Knoll International, Inc., New
York, from c.1953 to present

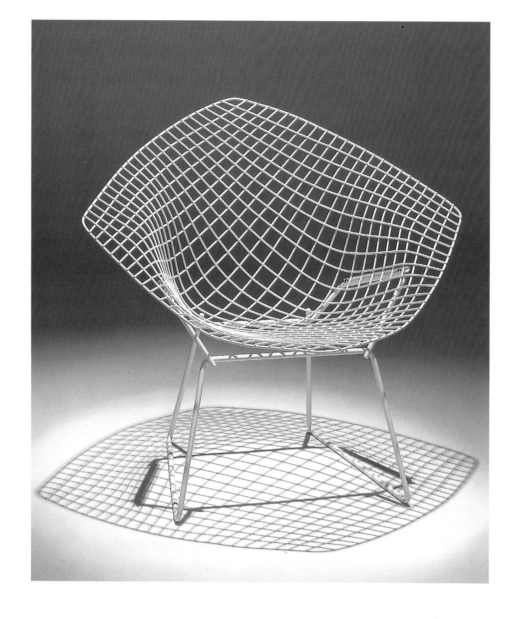

Harry Bertoia:

The Bertoia Collection, 1951

"In sculpture, I am concerned primarily with space, form and the character-istics of metal. In the chairs, many func-tional problems have to be satisfied first... but when you get right down to it, the chairs are studies in space, form and metal too. If you will look at them, you will find they are mostly made of air, just like sculpture. Space passes right through them."[15]

»Bei der Skulptur interessiert mich vor allem das Verhältnis von Form und Raum und die Eigenschaften des Me-talls. Bei den Stühlen muß man zuerst viele funktionale Probleme lösen... aber genaugenommen sind Stühle auch Studien in Raum, Form und Metall. Wenn man genau hinschaut, wird ei-nem klar, daß sie hauptsächlich aus Luft bestehen, genau wie die Skulptur. Der Raum geht direkt durch sie hindurch.«[15]

«En sculpture, je m'intéresse essen-tiellement à la forme spatiale et aux caractéristiques du métal. En matière de sièges, de nombreux problèmes fonctionnels doivent d'abord être ré-solus… mais lorsque vous allez au fond des choses, vous vous apercevez qu'un siège est une étude de l'espace, de la forme et également du métal. Si vous le regardez, vous constaterez qu'il est surtout fait d'air, comme une sculp-ture. L'espace circule à travers lui.»[15]

Charles & Ray Eames:

Rocking-chair *RAR 1*, 1950

Schaukelstuhl *RAR 1*, 1950

Chaise à bascule *RAR 1*, 1950

Charles & Ray Eames

1907–78 & 1913–88

USA . Etats-Unis

DAR (Dining Armchair Rod)
1950–53

Moulded, fibreglass-reinforced, polyester seat shell connected to a metal rod base with rubber shock-mounts

Sitzschale fiberglasverstärktes Polyester; Untergestell aus Metallstangen, durch flexible Hartgummischeiben mit der Sitzschale verbunden

Coque de siège en fibre de verre moulée et polyester renforcé, réunie au piètement de métal par des blocs de caoutchouc

Zenith Plastics, Gardena, California, for Herman Miller, Inc. from 1950 to c. 1953 and Herman Miller, Inc., Zeeland, Michigan, from c. 1953 to c. 1972

Charles & Ray Eames:
La Chaise, 1948

The *DAR* forms part of the Eameses' revolutionary Plastic Shell group of chairs. This was the culmination of ideas explored by Charles Eames and Eero Saarinen in prototype chairs for the Museum of Modern Art's "Organic Design in Home Furnishings" competition in 1940. Having submitted a number of designs with stamped metal seat shells to MoMA's "International Competition for Low Cost Furniture" in 1948, the Eameses developed the chairs in fibreglass in collaboration with Herman Miller, Inc., UCLA and Zenith Plastics.

Der Sessel *DAR* gehört zu der Plastic-Shell-Stuhlkollektion von Charles und Ray Eames, die Charles Eames und Eero Saarinen erstmalig 1940 für den Wettbewerb »Organic Design in Home Furnishings« des Museum of Modern Art verwirklicht hatten. 1948 reichten die Eames' preisgekrönte Prototypen mit Sitzschalen aus gepreßtem Metall für die »International Competition for Low Cost Furniture« des MoMA ein. Mit Herman Miller, der UCLA und der Firma Zenith entwickelten sie Fiberglas-Kunststoffstühle.

Ce *DAR* fait partie du groupe de sièges révolutionnaires Plastic Shell des Eames. Il peut être considéré comme le point d'aboutissement logique des idées explorées antérieurement par Charles Eames et Eero Saarinen dans leur série de sièges prototypes. Après le MoMA «International Competition for Low Cost Furniture» de 1948, les Eames reçurent une bourse et furent parrainés par Herman Miller, Inc. pour mettre au point leurs sièges plastiques (fibre de verre) en collaboration avec l'Université UCLA et Zenith Plastics.

William Katavolos
*1924

Ross Littell
*1924

Douglas Kelley
*1928

USA . Etats-Unis

T chair, Model No. 3LC
1952

T-Stuhl, Modell Nr. 3LC
1952

Chaise T, modèle n° 3LC
1952

Chrome-plated tubular steel and enamelled steel frame with leather sling

Rahmen aus verchromtem Stahlrohr und emailliertem Stahl; Sitzfläche und Rückenlehne Lederbespannung

Structure en tube d'acier chromé et acier émaillé, siège suspendu en cuir

Laverne Originals, New York
(reissued by Cadsana, Italy,
from c. 1988)

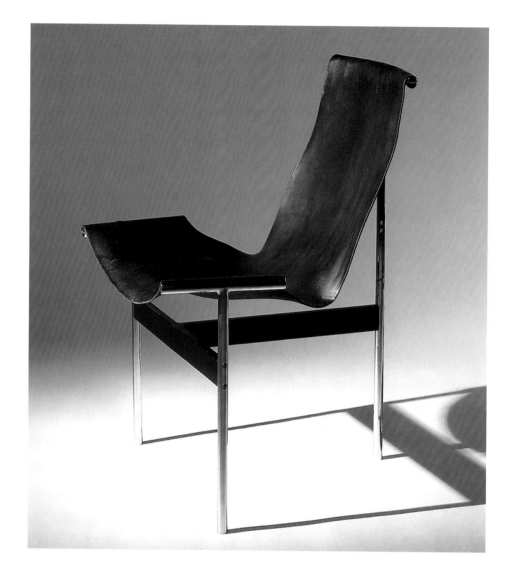

Continuing the tradition of Modern Movement geometric formalism, Katavolos, Littell & Kelley aimed "to work through to a way of beauty usefully conceived in essential structure, intrinsically materialized and appropriately performed".[16] The *3LC* uses a system of concealed screws to secure the sling seat onto the frame, predating by six years a solution utilised by Charles Eames on his Aluminium Group of chairs. The *3LC* was later dubbed "the T chair" by the art critic Clement Greenberg.

Katavolos, Littell und Kelley setzten den geometrischen Formalismus der Moderne fort, sie sahen »die Schönheit in der aufs Wesentliche beschränkten Form, in der angemessenen, materialgerechten Gestaltung und in der sauberen Verarbeitung«.[16] Beim Modell *3LC* verwandte man verdeckte Schrauben, um die Lederbespannung am Rahmen zu befestigen – damit hatte man eine Lösung vorweggenommen, ähnlich derjenigen, die Charles Eames für seine Aluminiumstühle fand. Modell *3LC* wurde vom Kunstkritiker Clement Greenberg später »T-Stuhl« getauft.

Poursuivant la tradition du formalisme géométrique du Mouvement moderniste, Katavolos, Littell & Kelley avaient pour but «d'aboutir à une forme de beauté conçue, pour sa structure essentielle, dans un esprit d'utilité, faisant appel à des matériaux évidents et mis en œuvre avec à-propos.»[16] La *3LC* utilise un système d'écrous dissimulés pour fixer le siège suspendu au cadre, devançant de six ans la solution que retiendra Charles Eames pour ses sièges en aluminium. Elle fut surnommée «chaise T» par le critique d'art Clement Greenberg.

William Katavolos, Ross Littell &
Douglas Kelley:
New York sofas, 1952
Sofas *New York*, 1952

"A machine for sitting, of the greatest sophistication, it has a retractable foot rest, and its elements can be adjusted to take up to *486* positions. The rubber arms, lined with a steel spring, and forming a parabolic curve, are a particularly notable feature."[17]

»Der Liegesessel ist eine Sitzmaschine von größter Einfachheit und Eleganz; er ist mit einer einklappbarer Fußstütze ausgerüstet, und die diversen Bestandteile können in *486* Positionen gebracht werden. Die parabolisch gekrümmten Armstützen sind durch eine Stahlfeder verstärkt und mit Gummi überzogen; sie sind ein besonders interessantes Konstruktionselement.«[17]

«Machine pour s'asseoir, de la plus grande sophistication, elle possède un repose-pieds rétractable et ses éléments peuvent prendre jusqu'à *486* positions différentes. Les accoudoirs de caoutchouc, armés d'un ressort d'acier plat, forment une courbe parabolique et sont particulièrement originaux.»[17]

Osvaldo Borsani

*1911

Italy . Italien . Italie

**Chaise-longue,
Model No. P40** 1954

**Chaiselongue,
Modell Nr. P40** 1954

**Chaise longue,
modèle n° P40** 1954

Pressed steel frame with latex foam upholstery and rubber-covered steel spring arms

Preßstahl-Gestell mit Latexschaum-Polsterung und gummiüberzogenen Stahlfeder-Armstützen

Structure en acier embouti avec rembourrage en mousse de latex et accoudoirs en acier souple recouvert de caoutchouc

**Tecno, Italy, from 1954
to present**

Tecno promotional photograph of the *Model No. P40*

Tecno-Werbung für den Sessel *Modell Nr. P40*

Tecno-Publicité de Tecno pour le fauteuil *modèle n° P40*

Arne Jacobsen

1902–71

Denmark . Dänemark . Danemark

3107 chair 1955
Stuhl 3107 1955
Chaise 3107 1955

Teak veneer, moulded plywood seat with chrome-plated, bent tubular steel base

Sitzschale verformtes Schichtholz mit Teakholzfurnier; Stahlrohr-gestell, verchromt

Siège en contreplaqué plaqué de teak sur piètement en tube d'acier cintré et chromé

Fritz Hansen, Denmark, from 1955 to present

Arne Jacobsen:

3107 & 3207, 1955

Arne Jacobsen:

3100 Ant chairs with *B413* table, 1952

3100-Ant-Stühle mit *B413*-Tisch, 1952

Chaises *3100 Ant* avec table *B413*, 1952

The *Series* 7 group of chairs, which includes the *3107*, was awarded a Grand Prix at the 1957 Milan Triennale. Initially available only in wood-veneer finishes, coloured versions were later introduced. Jacobsen's approach to the complex moulding of the seat and back out of one piece of plywood was clearly influenced by the earlier work of Charles and Ray Eames.

Die *Serie 7*, zu der auch der Stuhl Nr. *3107* gehört, gewann 1957 auf der Mailänder Triennale einen Grand Prix. Anfangs war die Serie nur furniert zu haben, später wurden farbige Versio-nen hergestellt. Zweifellos war Jacob-sen durch die frühen Arbeiten von Charles und Ray Eames zu der kompli-zierten Verformung von Sitzschale und Rückenlehne aus einem einzigen Stück Schichtholz angeregt worden.

Les chaises de la Série 7, qui com-prend la *3107*, reçurent un Grand Prix à la Triennale de Milan de 1957. Uni-quement disponibles à l'origine en placage de bois, ses versions en cou-leur furent introduites un peu plus tard. L'approche de Jacobsen des pro-blèmes complexes de moulage de cette chaise réalisée en un seul mor-ceau de contreplaqué fut clairement influencée par les travaux antérieurs de Charles et Ray Eames.

Arne Jacobsen:

Variants of the *3100 & 3107* chairs, 1952–55

Varianten der Stühle *3100 & 3107*, 1952–55

Variantes des chaises *3100 & 3107*, 1952–55

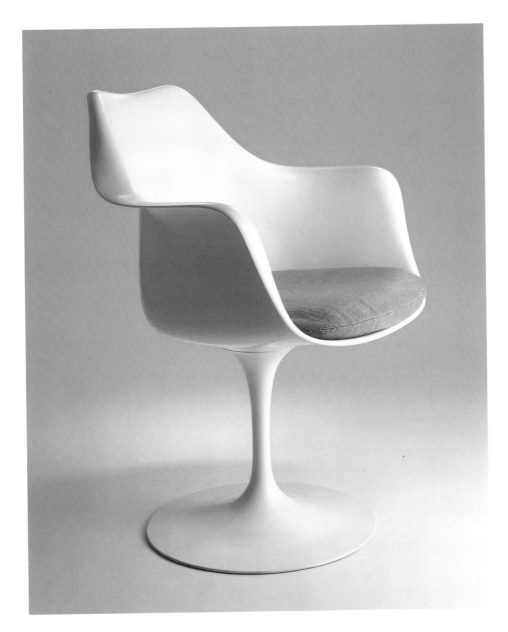

Eero Saarinen

1910–61

USA . Etats-Unis

Tulip chair 1955–57
Stuhl Tulip 1955–57
Chaise Tulipe 1955–57

Plastic-coated, cast-aluminium base, supporting a moulded fibreglass seat shell with loose, fabric-covered, foam-filled cushion

Piedestalfuß aus Gußaluminium, kunststoffbeschichtet; Sitzschale fiberglasverstärkter Kunststoff; loses Sitzkissen aus Schaumstoff, mit Stoff bezogen

Piètement en aluminium moulé recouvert de plastique supportant une coque de siège en fibre de verre moulée. Coussin amovible en mousse recouverte de tissu

Knoll International, Inc., New York, from 1957 to present

Eero Saarinen:

Pedestal Group, 1957

Saarinen strove for an organic unity of design. The *Pedestal* group, though visually unified, was a disappointment to Saarinen, as he was unable to achieve material unity – plastics technology did not allow for a single-moulded pedestal chair form. Instead, a cast-aluminium base had to be integrated with the fibreglass seat-shell. The use of a pedestal base, however, did fulfil one of Saarinen's intentions – to clean up the "slum of legs". He later said, "Modern chairs, with shell shapes and cages of little sticks below… became a sort of metal plumbing".[18]

In seinem Design hat Saarinen stets die Einheit von Form und Material angestrebt. Die *Pedestal*-Gruppe war eine Enttäuschung für ihn, weil es ihm wegen der Unzulänglichkeit der Kunststoffindustrie nicht gelungen war, die Stühle aus einem einzigen Material herzustellen. Statt dessen verband man die Sitzschale aus fiberglasverstärktem Kunststoff mit einem Fuß aus Gußaluminium. Später sagte er: »Diese Stühle mit ihren schalenförmigen Sitzen und den käfigartigen Gestellen aus Metallstäben darunter… glichen immer eher Klempnerarbeiten.«[18]

Tout au long de sa carrière, Saarinen s'efforça d'atteindre une unité organique de conception. Ce groupe de sièges sur piètement, bien que d'une grande homogénéité visuelle, fut une déception pour lui car la technologie des plastiques n'était pas encore assez avancée pour permettre de réaliser en une seule pièce ce type de forme. Il fallut ajouter à la coque de fibre de verre une base d'aluminium moulé. Il déclara: «Ces sièges, avec leurs formes en coque et leurs cages de petits bâtons par dessous, devenaient une sorte d'exercice de plomberie.»[18]

Knoll International advertising shot showing *Pedestal* Group in outside setting, c. 1960

Werbespot der Firma Knoll International, auf der die *Pedestal*-Gruppe im Freien zu sehen ist, um 1960

Publicité de Knoll International montrant le groupe de sièges *Pedestal* à l'air libre, vers 1960

Gio Ponti

1891–1979

Italy . Italien . Italie

**Superleggera chair,
Model No. 699** 1955–57

**Stuhl Superleggera,
Modell Nr. 699** 1955–57

**Chaise Superleggera,
modèle n° 699** 1955–57

Solid ash frame with ebonised or
natural finish, rush seat

Rahmen Esche massiv, natur-
farben oder schwarz gebeizt;
Sitzfläche aus Binsengeflecht

Structure de frêne massif, finition
naturelle ou noire, siège paillé

**Cassina, Italy, from 1957
to present**

Extremely light in weight, the *Superleggera* was based on a traditional
chair produced in the fishing village of
Chiavari, Italy. The evolution of this
vernacular precedent would have appealed to Ponti, who attempted to design furniture (in his words) "without
adjectives".

Der extrem leichte Stuhl *Superleggera*
ging auf einen traditionellen Stuhl zurück, der in dem italienischen Fischer-
dorf Chiavari hergestellt wurde. Dieser
bodenständige Vorläufer mußte Ponti,
der (nach seinen eigenen Worten) Möbel »ohne Eigenschaften« entwerfen
wollte, allein schon aus diesem Grund
gefallen.

D'un poids extrêmement léger, la
Superleggera s'inspire des chaises
traditionnelles du village de pêcheurs
de Chiavari, en Italie. Ce précédent
régional attira l'attention de Ponti qui
s'efforçait de créer des meubles –
selon ses propres mots – «sans
adjectifs».

Alessandro Mendini:

Gio Ponti's *Superleggera*,
redesigned 1978

Gio Pontis *Superleggera*,
Redesign von 1978

Chaise *Superleggera* de Gio
Ponti, redessinée en 1978

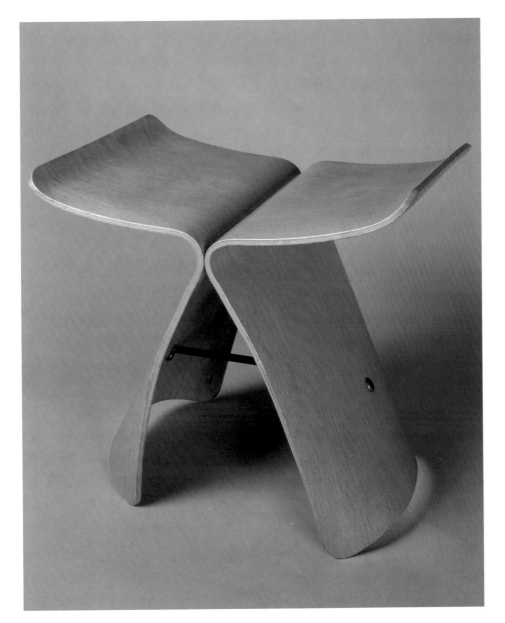

Sori Yanagi

*1915

Japan . Japon

Butterfly stool 1956

Stuhl Butterfly 1956

Tabouret Butterfly 1956

Moulded plywood with metal stretcher

Verformtes Schichtholz mit Metallsteg

Contreplaqué moulé et traverse de métal

Tendo Mokko, Japan

The *Butterfly* stool can be seen as a delicate and harmonious synthesis of Eastern and Western culture. Highly favoured in America during the 1950s, it was easy to dismantle and transport.

Den *Butterfly*-Stuhl kann man als gefällige, ausgewogene Synthese östlicher und westlicher Kultur betrachten. Er war in den 50er Jahren in den Vereinigten Staaten sehr beliebt; man konnte ihn leicht zerlegen und transportieren.

Le tabouret *Butterfly* peut être vu comme une synthèse délicate et harmonieuse des cultures occidentale et orientale. Très apprécié aux Etats-Unis pendant les années 50, il était facile à démonter et à transporter.

Poul Kjaerholm

*1929

Denmark . Dänemark . Danemark

Chair, Model No. PK22 1956

Stuhl, Modell Nr. PK22 1956

Chaise basse, modèle n° PK22 1956

Chrome-plated steel frame with leather seat and back

Stahlrahmen verchromt; Sitzfläche und Rückenlehne mit Leder bezogen

Structure en acier inoxydable, siège canné

E. Kold Christensen A/S, Denmark, from c. 1956 to c. 1970 and Fritz Hansen, Denmark, from c. 1970 to present

Kjaerholm's elegant designs owe much to the designers of the Modern Movement. The *PK22* chair is reminiscent of Mies van der Rohe's *Barcelona* chair of 1929 and the ancestry of Kjaerholm's remarkable *Hammock* chaise longue, Model No. *PK24*, can be traced to Le Corbusier's chaise longue of 1928.

Kjaerholms elegante Entwürfe sind dem Design der Klassischen Moderne sehr verpflichtet. Der Stuhl *PK22* erinnert an Mies van der Rohes *Barcelona*-Sessel von 1929, und die elegante Chaiselongue *Hammock*, Modell Nr. *PK24*, geht auf Le Corbusiers Chaiselongue von 1928 zurück.

Les élégantes créations de Kjaerholm doivent beaucoup aux dessinateurs du Mouvement moderniste. La chaise *PK22* rappelle la *Barcelona* chair de Mies van der Rohe (1929) et l'ancêtre de la remarquable chaise longue *Hammock* de Kjaerholm, le modèle n° *PK24*, n'est pas sans évoquer la chaise longue de 1928 de Le Corbusier.

Poul Kjaerholm:

PK22 chairs, *PK31* sofa and *PK24* chaise longue, c. 1956, 1958 & 1965

Stühle *PK22*, Sofa *PK31* und Chaiselongue *PK24*, um 1956, 1958 & 1965

Chaises *PK22*, sofa *PK31* et chaise longue *PK24*, vers 1956, 1958 & 1965

Poul Kjaerholm:

Hammock chaise longue PK24, 1965

Chaiselongue *Hammock* PK24, 1965

Chaise longue *Hammock* PK24, 1965

Although visually light in weight, with its wedge-like form seemingly hovering in space, the *Coconut* chair is in fact extremely heavy, owing to the considerable amount of steel used in its construction. The chair's unique shape, as its name suggests, was inspired by a cracked section of coconut.

Der Sessel *Coconut* scheint mit seiner keilartigen Sitzschale geradezu zu schweben, aber in Wirklichkeit macht ihn die große Menge Stahl, die die Konstruktion des Untergestells erfordert, ungewöhnlich schwer. Wie der Name suggeriert, ähnelt der Stuhl einem Stück einer Kokosnuß.

Bien qu'apparemment légère, avec sa forme d'aile flottant dans l'espace, cette chauffeuse est en fait extrêmement lourde du fait de l'énorme quantité d'acier utilisée pour sa fabrication. Sa forme unique, comme son nom le suggère, fut inspirée par un morceau de noix de coco brisée.

George Nelson

1907–86
USA . Etats-Unis

Coconut chair 1956
Sessel Coconut 1956
Chauffeuse Coconut 1956

Fabric-covered, foam-upholstered, steel shell, supported on chrome plated steel legs

Schaumstoffgepolsterte Sitzschale aus Stahl, mit Stoff bezogen; Untergestell aus Rundstahl, verchromt

Coque d'acier rembourrée de mousse recouverte de tissu sur piètement d'acier chromé

Herman Miller, Inc., USA, from 1956 to c. 1975 (reissued by Vitra GmbH, Germany, from 1988)

George Nelson:
Marshmallow sofa, 1952
Sofa *Marshmallow*, 1952

George Nelson:
Kangaroo chair, 1956
Stuhl *Kangaroo*, 1956
Chaise *Kangaroo*, 1956

Charles &
Ray Eames

1907–78 & 1913–88

USA . Etats-Unis

**Lounge chair and footstool,
Model Nos. 670 & 671**
1956/57

**Sessel mit Hocker,
Modell Nr. 670 & Nr. 671**
1956/57

**Chaise longue et
repose-pieds,
modèles n° 670 & 671**
1956/57

The *Model No. 670* was the Eameses first design for the luxury end of the furniture market, retailing at \$634 in 1957. Originally conceived as a birthday gift for the film director Billy Wilder, the Lounge chair is unashamedly masculine, exuding a sense of executive power and comfort through its generous proportions and use of high-quality materials.

Mit dem *Modell Nr. 670* hatten Charles und Ray Eames ihr erstes Möbelstück der Luxusklasse entworfen, 1957 betrug der Einzelhandelspreis 634 Dollar. Der Sessel, als Geburtstagsgeschenk für Filmregisseur Billy Wilder entworfen, war unverhohlen maskulin in seiner Ausstrahlung und signalisierte durch seine großzügigen Abmessungen und die erstklassige Qualität des Materials Macht und Reichtum.

Ce *modèle n° 670* fut le premier dessin des Eames pour le haut du marché. Il était vendu 634 \$ en 1957. Conçue au départ comme un cadeau d'anniversaire pour le metteur en scène Billy Wilder, cette chaise longue affirme sa masculinité et, à travers ses généreuses proportions et l'utilisation de matériaux de haute qualité, affiche aussi bien son grand confort qu'un certain sens du pouvoir.

Rosewood veneer, moulded plywood seat-shells with leather-covered, foam-and-down-filled cushions, on swivelling cast-aluminium base

Sitzschale verformtes Schichtholz mit Rosenholzfurnier, Schaumstoffpolster mit Lederbezug, lederbezogene Daunenkissen; drehbarer Säulenfuß aus Gußaluminium

Plaqué de bois de rose, coques de sièges en contreplaqué moulé avec coussins rembourrés de mousse et de plume recouverts de cuir, sur socle pivotant d'aluminium moulé

**Herman Miller Inc., Zeeland,
Michigan, from 1957 to present**

Charles Kratka:

Exploded drawings of
Model No. 670, showing
components

Skizzen des *Modells Nr. 670,* auf
denen die Einzelkomponenten des
Stuhls zu erkennen sind

Dessins explosés du
modèle n° 670 montrant
la composition du siège

Top: The lounge chair at the Eames House. A ... chair components by Charles Kratka (with F ... ...xploded drawing of lounge ...ettering by Sister Corita Kent
of Immaculate Heart College)

George Nelson Associates:

Laminated wood chair, known as *Pretzel* chair, 1952

Schichtholz-Sessel, bekannt unter der Bezeichnung *Pretzel*-Sessel, 1952

Fauteuil en bois lamellé, connu sous le nom *Pretzel*, 1952

Paul Goldman

*1912

USA . Etats-Unis

Cherner chair 1957
Armlehnstuhl Cherner 1957
Fauteuil Cherner 1957

Walnut veneer moulded plywood

Verformtes Schichtholz mit Nußbaumfurnier

Contreplaqué moulé plaqué de noyer

Plycraft, Inc., Massachusetts, from 1957 to present

This extremely elegant chair evolved from the earlier *Pretzel* armchair of 1952 by George Nelson Associates, the latter's design in turn having been inspired by Gebrüder Thonet's *Model No. 9* chair of c.1904. The design of the *Cherner* chair, with its sinuous armrest and single moulded seat and back, was originally ascribed to Norman Cherner and, on other occasions, to George Mulhauser. This was a marketing ploy conceived by Paul Goldman, the designer of the chair and owner of the manufacturing company.

Dieser elegante Stuhl ging auf den älteren *Pretzel*-Sessel von 1952 von George Nelson Associates zurück, dessen Form wiederum vom *Modell Nr. 9* der Gebrüder Thonet von 1904 inspiriert worden war. Der Entwurf des *Cherner*-Armlehnstuhls mit seinen geschwungenen Armstützen und der aus einem Stück geformten Sitz- und Rückenschale wurde Norman Cherner zugeschrieben und ein andermal George Mulhauser – ein Marketingmanöver, das sich Paul Goldman, der Designer des Stuhls und Inhaber der Herstellerfirma, ausgedacht hatte.

Ce très élégant fauteuil est inspiré d'un précédent modèle *Pretzel* de George Nelson Associates (1952) dont le dessin rappelait à son tour le *modèle n° 9* des Gebrüder Thonet (1904). Avec ses accoudoirs sinueux et son siège et son dossier en une seule pièce, il fut à l'origine attribué à Norman Cherner et même à George Mulhauser. C'était une sorte d'astuce de marketing de Paul Goldman, son créateur et en même temps propriétaire de l'usine de fabrication.

Paul Goldman:
Cherner side chair, 1957
Stuhl *Cherner*, 1957
Chaise *Cherner*, 1957

Achille &
Pier Giacomo
Castiglioni

*1918 & 1913–68

Italy . Italien . Italie

Mezzadro stool 1957

Hocker Mezzadro 1957

Tabouret Mezzadro 1957

Tractor seat on chrome plated, bent flat steel stem with wing-nut, solid beech footrest

Traktorsitz auf einer Stütze aus gezogenem Flachstahl, verchromt, mit Flügelmutter; Fußstütze massives Buchenholz

Siège de tracteur sur support d'acier plat cintré avec écrou papillon, repose-pied en hêtre massif

Zanotta, Italy, from 1970 to present

Exploiting Marcel Duchamp's concept of the "ready-made" in furniture design, the *Mezzadro* (Sharecropper) stool was deemed too radical to be put into production until thirteen years after its original date of design. Interestingly, a similar design incorporating a tractor seat in its construction, by Baldwin and Machado, is illustrated in George Nelson's book "Chairs" of 1953.

Der Hocker *Mezzadro*, mit dem sich Achille und Pier Castiglioni Marcel Duchamps Konzept des »Ready-made« für das Möbeldesign zunutze machten, wurde für so avantgardistisch gehalten, daß er erst dreizehn Jahre nach Erscheinen des Entwurfs in Serie ging. Ein ähnlicher Entwurf von Baldwin und Machado, ebenfalls mit einem Traktorsitz, ist in George Nelsons Buch »Chairs« von 1953 abgebildet.

Appliquant le concept des «ready-made» de Marcel Duchamp à la conception du meuble, ce tabouret *Mezzadro* (Métayer) fut jugé tellement radical qu'il ne fut produit que treize ans après sa date de conception. Il est intéressant de noter qu'un modèle similaire à un siège de tracteur, de Baldwin et Machado, est illustré dans le livre de George Nelson «Chairs» de 1953.

Achille Castiglioni:

Primate, 1970

**Achille &
Pier Giacomo
Castiglioni:**

Sella, 1957

**Achille &
Pier Giacomo
Castiglioni:**

Allunaggio, 1965

These highly organic and materially unified designs formed part of the *Invisible Group*, which also included the *Buttercup* and *Lily* chairs as well as the better-known *Champagne* dining chair. The Lavernes later licensed to other manufacturers their innovative process of moulding perspex which had been developed for the production of these chairs.

Diese durch und durch organischen, aus einem einzigen Material gestalteten Entwürfe gehören zu der *Invisible Group*, zu der auch die Stühle *Buttercup* und *Lily* so wie der noch bekanntere Speisezimmerstuhl *Champagne* zählen. Später vergaben Erwine und Estelle Laverne die Lizenz für ihre innovative Technologie, die speziell für die Herstellung dieser Plexiglasstühle entwickelt worden war, an andere Firmen.

Ces modèles très organiques et réalisés avec un seul matériau font partie du *Invisible Group* qui comprenait également les fauteuils *Buttercup* et *Lily* ainsi que la chaise *Champagne* encore plus connue. Les Laverne cédèrent ensuite les licences de fabrication du procédé de moulage du perspex qu'ils avaient mis au point.

Erwine & Estelle Laverne

*1909 & *1915

USA . Etats-Unis

Daffodil and Jonquil chairs
1957

Sessel Daffodil und Jonquil
1957

Fauteuils Daffodil et Jonquil
1957

Moulded perspex seat shell and base with loose fabric-covered foam-filled cushion

Sitzschale und Sockel aus verformtem Perspex; loses, schaumstoffgefülltes Sitzkissen mit Stoffbezug

Coque et pied de siège en perspex moulé avec coussin amovible en mousse recouvert de tissu

**Laverne Originals, New York
from 1957 to c. 1972**

Erwine & Estelle Laverne:
Lotus Chair, 1958
Stuhl *Lotus*, 1958
Chaise *Lotus*, 1958

Arne Jacobsen

1902–71

Denmark . Dänemark . Danemark

Egg chair,
Model No. 3316 1957

Sessel Egg,
Modell Nr. 3316 1957

Fauteuil Egg,
modèle n° 3316 1957

Fabric covered, foam-upholstered, moulded fibreglass seat shell on a swivelling cast-aluminium base, with loose seat cushion

Drehbarer Säulenfuß aus Gußaluminium. Formgepreßte Sitzschale aus glasfaserverstärktem Kunststoff mit Schaumstoffpolsterung und Stoffbezug, loses Sitzkissen

Coque de fibre de verre rembourrée de mousse et recouverte de tissu, sur socle d'aluminium pivotant, avec coussin de siège amovible

Fritz Hansen, Denmark, from 1958 to present

The *Egg* chair was originally designed for one of Jacobsen's major architectural projects, the Royal SAS Hotel in Copenhagen. He designed not only the building, its interior and furniture, but also the light fixtures, carpets, cutlery and even the ashtrays – effecting a meticulously detailed and refined unity of design.

Den *Egg*-Sessel hat Jacobsen ursprünglich für eines seiner wichtigsten Architekturprojekte, das Royal SAS Hotel in Kopenhagen, konzipiert. Er entwarf nicht nur das Gebäude, die Innenausstattung und die Möbel, sondern auch die Beleuchtungskörper, die Teppiche, das Besteck und sogar die Aschenbecher – wobei ihm eine subtile, bis ins kleinste Detail gehende Einheitlichkeit seines Designs gelang.

Ce fauteuil fut conçu au départ pour l'un des plus importants chantiers architecturaux de Jacobsen, le Royal SAS Hotel, à Copenhague. Il réalisa non seulement le bâtiment, sa décoration intérieure et son mobilier, mais également les luminaires, les tapis, la coutellerie et même les cendriers, atteignant une unité de conception méticuleusement raffinée et détaillée.

Arne Jacobsen:

Swan chair, 1957

Sessel *Swan*, 1957

Fauteuil *Swan*, 1957

Interior of Fritz Hansen Showroom showing *Egg* chairs

Inneneinrichtung des Fritz-Hansen-Ausstellungsraums, in dem die *Egg*-Stühle zu sehen sind

Salle d'exposition de Fritz Hansen, vue intérieure avec fauteuils *Egg*

George Nelson

1907–86

USA . Etats-Unis

MAA chair 1958

Stuhl MAA 1958

Chaise MAA 1958

Moulded fibreglass seat and back with stainless steel fittings and rubber sockets, on a bent tubular steel base

Sitz- und Rückenschale fiberglasverstärkter Kunststoff; Kugelgelenk aus rostfreiem Stahl und Hartgummischeiben; Untergestell gezogenes Stahlrohr

Siège et dossier en fibre de verre moulée avec accessoires en acier inoxydable et emboîtements de caoutchouc, sur base en tube d'acier cintré

Herman Miller, Inc., Zeeland, Michigan

Part of the *Swagged-leg* group of chairs, the *MAA* was only produced for one year before it was withdrawn, owing to an inherent design flaw. The rubber sockets, which are welded to the back of the chair and connect with a system of pivoting ball pins allowing the back section to articulate through 90°, degrade under stress. Once the critical ball-and-socket joint is weakened, the back disconnects from the rest of the chair. Despite this, the concept of an independently articulating moulded-plastic back element was exceptionally innovative.

Der zur *Swagged-leg*-Gruppe gehörende *MAA*-Stuhl wurde nur ein Jahr hergestellt, bevor man die Produktion einstellte. Bei starker Beanspruchung nutzten sich die an die Rückenlehne geschweißten Kugelgelenke ab, die mit drehbaren Kugelgelenkstiften verbunden waren, wodurch sich die Rückenlehne um 90° schwenken ließ. Ist das Gelenk erst einmal geschwächt, löst sich die Rückenlehne vom Stuhl. Trotzdem war die Idee einer vom Untergestell unabhängig beweglichen Rückenlehne aus Kunststoff innovativ.

Faisant partie de la série *Swagged-leg*, la *MAA* ne fut produite qu'une année seulement avant d'être retirée pour défaut de conception. Après un certain temps, le dossier se décrochait car les emboîtements de caoutchouc s'abîmaient. Ils étaient électroniquement soudés au dos du siège et connectés par un double système de roulements à bille pivotant permettant au dossier de pivoter sur 90°. Malgré ce défaut essentiellement technique, le concept d'un dossier articulé indépendant en plastique apportait une innovation majeure.

George Nelson:

DAF chair, 1958

DAF-Stuhl, 1958

Chaise *DAF*, 1958

Charles & Ray Eames

1907 – 78 & 1913 – 88
USA . Etats-Unis

Aluminium Group side chair, Model No. EA105
1958

Stuhl aus der Aluminium Group, Modell Nr. EA105
1958

Chaise du groupe Aluminium, modèle n° EA105 1958

Aluminium frame with leather or vinyl upholstered sling seat

Aluminiumrahmen mit gebogener Sitzschale; Leder- oder Vinyl-polsterung

Cadre en aluminium, siège en coque incurvé, recouvert de cuir ou de vinyl

Herman Miller, Inc., Zeeland, Michigan, from 1958 to present

The *Aluminium Group* of chairs and tables was first produced as a special project for Alessandro Girard and Eero Saarinen's Irwin Miller House in Columbus, Indiana. The brief submitted to the Eameses described a series of chairs that could be used indoors or outdoors. During the development stage, this furniture was often referred to as the "leisure group". Ironically, it is now almost exclusively used within the office environment.

Die *Aluminium Group*, zu der Stühle und Tische gehörten, war ein spezielles Projekt für das Irwin-Miller-Haus in Columbus, Indiana, das Alessandro Girard und Eero Saarinen entworfen hatten. In der Kurzbeschreibung, die Charles und Ray Eames erhielten, war hauptsächlich die Rede von einer Serie von Stühlen, verwendbar für Innen- wie für Außenräume. Während der Versuchsphase wurden die Möbel häufig als »leisure group« bezeichnet – paradoxerweise werden sie heute fast ausschließlich in Büros verwendet.

Le groupe de sièges et de tables *Aluminium* fut au départ un projet spécialement conçu par Alessandro Girard et Eero Saarinen pour la maison d'Irwin Miller à Colombus, Indiana. Le cahier des charges soumis aux Eames décrivait principalement une série de sièges à utiliser aussi bien à l'intérieur qu'à l'extérieur. Pendant la phase de mise au point, cet ensemble fut souvent baptisé le groupe loisirs ce qui me manque pas d'ironie quand on sait que ces sièges sont aujourd'hui presque toujours utilisés dans des bureaux.

Charles & Ray Eames:

Lounge armchairs, *Model No. 682*, shown in outside setting, 1958

Armlehnsessel, *Modell Nr. 682*, im Freien, 1958

Chaises longues *modèle n° 682*, à l'air libre, 1958

Charles & Ray Eames:
Aluminium Group, 1958

Highly futuristic, Panton's upholstered *Cone* chair and slightly later wire *Cone* and *Heart* chairs were the result of a conscious decision to divorce himself from any preconceived notions of how a chair should be designed. When conceptualising a design, Panton concerned himself primarily with the inherent potential of new materials and their application in generating new forms.

Pantons ausgesprochen avantgardistischer *Cone*-Stuhl und seine späteren *Cone*- und *Heart*-Stühle sind Resultate seiner bewußten Abkehr von bestehenden Vorstellungen, wie ein Stuhl auszusehen habe. Wenn Panton einen neuen Entwurf konzipierte, befaßte er sich vor allem mit dem Potential neuer Materialien und deren Verwendbarkeit für die Gestaltung neuer Formen.

Très futuriste, cette chaise *Cone* rembourrée est légèrement postérieure aux modèles en fil d'acier *Cone* et *Heart*, qui avaient pour point de départ l'abandon de toute idée préconçue sur les principes de construction d'un siège. En conceptualisant son idée, Panton s'intéressa principalement au potentiel de nouveaux matériaux et de leur application dans la génération de formes nouvelles.

Verner Panton

*1926

Denmark . Dänemark . Danemark

Upholstered Cone chair
1958

Stuhl Cone, gepolstert
1958

Chaise Cone rembourrée
1958

Fabric-covered, foam upholstered, bent sheet metal construction on a chrome-plated base

Konstruktion aus verformten Metallblechen, schaumstoffgepolstert und mit Stoff bezogen; Säulenfuß aus verchromtem Metall

Construction en tôle de métal cintrée, rembourrage de mousse recouverte de tissu, sur piètement chromé

Plus-linje, Denmark, from 1959 to c. 1966

Verner Panton sitting in *Heart* chair, 1959

Verner Panton in seinem *Heart*-Stuhl, 1959

Verner Panton assis sur la chaise *Heart*, 1959

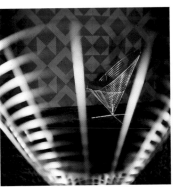

Verner Panton:

Wire Cone chair, 1959

Wire-Cone-Stuhl, 1959

Chaise *Wire Cone*, 1959

Advertisement for the *Wire Cone* chair

Werbefoto für den Stuhl *Wire Cone*

Publicité pour la chaise *Wire Cone*

Achille & Pier Giacomo Castiglioni

*1918 & 1913–68
Italy . Italien . Italie

Sanluca armchair 1959
Sessel Sanluca 1959
Fauteuil Sanluca 1959

Leather-covered, polyurethane foam-upholstered frame on rosewood legs

Rahmen mit Leder bezogen und mit Polyurethanschaum gepolstert; Beine aus Rosenholz

Structure rembourrée de mousse de polyuréthane, recouverte de cuir, sur piètement en bois de rose

Gavina, Italy (later Simon International, Italy), from 1960 to 1990, and Bernini, Italy, from 1990 to present

Dino Gavina, Achille & Pier Giacomo Castiglioni photographed with the *Sanluca* armchair in the San Luca portico, Bologna, 1960

Dino Gavina, Achille & Pier Giacomo Castiglioni, fotografiert mit dem Armlehnsessel *Sanluca* in San Luca, Bologna, 1960

Dino Gavina, Achille & Pier Giacomo Castiglioni photographiés avec *Sanluca* sous le portique de San Luca, Bologne, 1960

Although designed for industrial production, the *Sanluca* chair was manufactured by hand. "In (this) chair the convergence of the architect's brilliance and the commercial indifference of the manufacturer (who is first and foremost an aesthetic operator) is the basis for the remarkable construction of a figurative language, with powerful architectural intonations, which have nothing to do with stylistic conventions." Carlo Scarpa said of this design: "this is an armchair for which a formalist like myself would gladly take credit."[19]

Der *Sanluca* war zwar für die Massenproduktion konzipiert, wurde aber in Handarbeit hergestellt. »Hier ist die Verschmelzung der Ideen des Designers mit der kommerziellen Gleichgültigkeit des Herstellers (der in erster Linie vom ästhetischen Standpunkt her operiert) Voraussetzung für das Zustandekommen einer figurativen Sprache mit architektonischen Anklängen, die nichts mit stilistischen Konventionen zu tun hat.« Carlo Scarpa bemerkte: »Das Verdienst, einen solchen Sessel geschaffen zu haben, würde ich mir, als Formalist, gern anrechnen lassen.«[19]

Bien que destiné à la production industrielle, ce fauteuil fut fabriqué à la main. «Dans ce fauteuil, la convergence du brio de l'architecte et de l'indifférence aux contingences commerciales du fabricant (qui est d'abord et avant tout un opérateur esthétique) est à la base de cette remarquable construction d'un langage figuratif, aux puissantes intonations architecturales, étranger au concept et à la pratique de style.» Carlo Scarpa déclara de cette création: «Voici un fauteuil dont un formaliste comme moi aimerait à être crédité.»[19]

Studio Simon:

Sforzesca chair, 1986 (designed as a homage to the Castiglioni brothers)

Stuhl *Sforzesca*, 1986 (entworfen als Hommage an die Brüder Castiglioni)

Chaise *Sforzesca*, 1986 (dessinée en hommage aux frères Castiglioni)

The first single-form, materially unified chair design in plastic, the *Stacking* chair was not put into full-scale manufacture until 1968. Originally prototyped in GFK Polyester (fibreglass-reinforced plastic), early production models were produced in moulded "Baydur" (PU-hardfoam) and then lacquered. In 1970 the material was changed to "Luran-S", an injection-moulded non-reinforced thermoplastic.[20] Panton writes, "I attempt to make good designs with new materials. My pieces try to be versatile and accessible to all classes of buyer."[21]

Als erster aus einem einzigen Material und in einem einzigen Guß hergestellter Stuhl gelangte der *Stapelstuhl* erst 1968 zur Serienreife. Der Prototyp wurde aus GFK-Polyester (fiberglasverstärkter Kunststoff), die ersten in Serie produzierten Exemplare aus verformtem, später lackiertem »Baydur« (PU-Hartschaumstoff) hergestellt. Seit 1970 verwendet man »Luran-S«, einen nicht fiberglasverstärkten, durch Erwärmung im Spritzgußverfahren formbaren Kunststoff.[20] Panton schreibt: »Ich versuche mit neuen Materialien gutes Design zu machen. Meine Stücke sollen vielseitig verwendbar und erschwinglich sein.«[21]

Premier siège réalisé avec un seul matériau plastique, cette chaise ne fut pas réellement produite en série avant 1968. Le premier prototype fut réalisé en polyester GFK (plastique renforcé de fibre de verre) et les premiers modèles produits en «Baydur» moulé (Mousse dure PU) puis laqués. En 1970, ce matériau fut abandonné pour le «Luran-S», un thermoplastique moulé par injection et non renforcé.[20] Panton écrivit: «Je tente de faire de bons projets avec des matériaux nouveaux. Mes œuvres essayent d'être polyvalentes et accessibles.»[21]

Verner Panton

*1926

Denmark . Dänemark . Danemark

Stacking chair
c. 1960 – 67

Stapelstuhl
um 1960 – 67

Chaise empilable
vers 1960 – 67

Injection-moulded Luran-S thermoplastic

Konstruktion aus Luran-S-Kunststoff, im Spritzgußverfahren hergestellt

Thermoplastique Luran-S moulé par injection

Vitra GmbH, Germany, for Herman Miller, Inc., New York, from 1968 to 1979, and Herman Miller, Inc., New York, from 1973 to 1975

Verner Panton:
Living Tower, 1969

Cesare Leonardi & Franca Stagi

*1935 & *1937

Italy . Italien . Italie

**Ribbon chair,
Model No. CL9** 1961

**Stuhl Ribbon,
Modell Nr. CL9** 1961

**Chaise Ribbon,
modèle n° CL9** 1961

Chrome-plated, bent tubular steel
base with moulded fibreglass seat
section

Formgepreßte Sitzschale aus
glasfaserverstärktem Kunststoff
auf verchromten Gestell aus
gezogenem Stahlrohr

Piètement en tube d'acier cintré
et chromé, siège en fibre de verre
moulée

**Bernini, Italy, from 1961 to
1969, and Elco, Italy, from 1969**

The continuous band of moulded fibre-glass forming the sculptural seat section of this remarkable design is attached to the tubular steel base by means of rubber shock-mounts. This construction allows the cantilevered CL9 an inherent degree of springiness.

Die skulptural gestaltete Sitzfläche, ein durchgehendes Band aus fiberglasverstärktem Kunststoff, ist durch elastische Gummipuffer mit dem Stahlrohrgestell verbunden. Diese Konstruktion verleiht dem freitragenden Stuhl CL9 seine federnde Elastizität.

La bande continue en fibre de verre moulée qui forme le siège de ce modèle très sculptural est fixée au piètement tubulaire au moyen de blocs de caoutchouc. Cette construction confère à ce siège en porte-à-faux un certain degré de flexibilité.

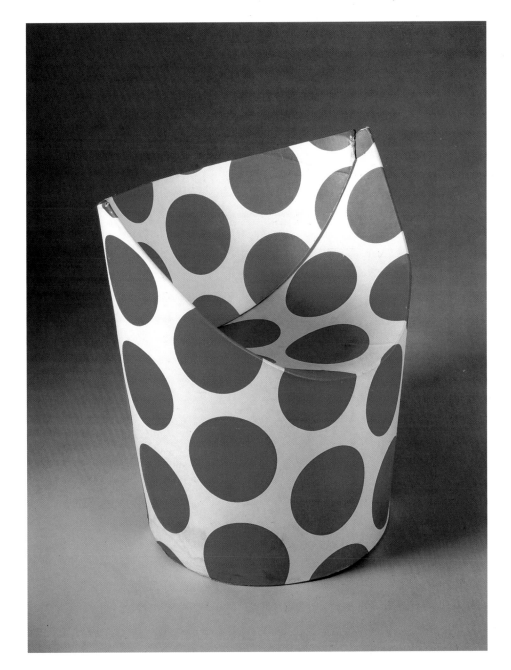

Peter Murdoch

*1940

Great Britain . Großbritannien .
Grande-Bretagne

Child's chair 1963

Kinderstuhl 1963

Chaise d'enfant 1963

Polyethylene-coated, laminated
paperboard

Mit Polyäthylen überzogener,
schichtverleimter Karton

Carton lamellé enduit de
polyéthylène

**International Paper, USA, from
1964 to 1965**

Peter Murdoch:

Those Things table, 1967

Tisch *Those Things*, 1967

Table *Those Things*, 1967

Designed while Murdoch was studying
at the Royal College of Art in London,
the polka-dotted *Child's chair* is an
icon of the Pop era. Its low production
costs and inherent disposability were
ideally suited to the demands of the
mass consumer market in the 1960s.
Later, in 1967, Murdoch designed the
similarly constructed *Those Things*
chair, table and stool, for which he
received a Council of Industrial
Design award.

Der *Kinderstuhl* mit dem auffallenden
Punktmuster ist eine Ikone der Popära.
Murdoch entwarf ihn während seiner
Studienzeit am Royal College of Art in
London. Seine niedrigen Herstellungs-
kosten und seine materialbedingte
Kurzlebigkeit machten den Stuhl zu
einem idealen Produkt des Massen-
konsums der 60er Jahre. 1967 entwarf
Murdoch die ähnlich konstruierte Grup-
pe *Those Things*, bestehend aus Stuhl,
Tisch und Hocker, für die er mit dem
Preis des Council of Industrial Design
ausgezeichnet wurde.

Conçue alors que Murdoch étudiait
encore au Royal College of Art, Lon-
dres, cette *Chaise d'enfant* à pois est
devenue une véritable icône de la
période Pop. Ses faibles coûts de
production et son caractère jetable,
par nature, correspondaient idéalement
aux attentes du marché de la grande
consommation des années 60. En
1967, Murdoch dessina une chaise,
une table et un tabouret *Those Things*,
de principe similaire, pour lesquels il
reçut une distinction du Council of
Industrial Design.

Robin Day

*1915

Great Britain . Großbritannien .
Grande-Bretagne

Polyprop chair 1962/63
Stuhl Polyprop 1962/63
Chaise Polyprop 1962/63

Injection-moulded, polypropylene
seat shell on chrome-plated, bent
tubular steel base

Sitzschale Polypropylen, im
Spritzgußverfahren hergestellt;
Untergestell Stahlrohr, verchromt

Coque de siège en polypropylène
moulé par injection sur piètement
de tube d'acier cintré et chromé

**S. Hille & Co. Ltd, UK (later to
become Hille International, UK),
from 1963 to present**

Polyprop chair under test at FIRA

Polyprop-Stuhl im Test, bei FIRA

Chaise *Polyprop* testée chez FIRA

The *Polyprop* is one of the most successful contract chairs ever produced.
A single tool can produce 4,000 seat
shells per week and from 1963 to the
present over 14 million chairs have
been sold in twenty-three countries.
Day writes: "Designers have respon-
sibilities other than the profit motive,
and must be increasingly concerned
with conservation and the sensible use
of the planet's resources... I am less
interested in fashion than in a synthesis
of good construction, good function
and aesthetics."[22]

Der *Polyprop* war ein erfolgreicher, nur
in großen Stückzahlen vermarkteter
Stuhl. Eine einzige Maschine kann
4.000 Sitzschalen pro Woche produzieren. Von 1963 bis heute wurden 14
Millionen Stühle verkauft. Day schreibt:
»Designer haben andere Motive als die
Gewinnmaximierung, sie sind in zuneh-
mendem Maße verantwortlich für die
Erhaltung und die vernünftige Verwendung der Ressourcen dieses Plane-
ten... Ich bin weniger an Mode interessiert als an der Synthese von guter
Konstruktion, guter Funktion und
Ästhetik.«[22]

Le *Polyprop* est l'un des sièges les
plus vendus au monde. De 1963 à nos
jours, plus de 14 millions d'exemplaires
ont été commercialisés dans vingt-trois
pays. Day écrit: «Les designers ont des
responsabilités qui ne se limitent pas à
la seule recherche du profit et doivent
se sentir de plus en plus concernés
par la protection et l'utilisation intelli-
gente des ressources de la planète...
Je suis moins intéressé à la mode qu'à
une synthèse de bonne construction,
de bonne fonction et d'esthétique.»[22]

Robin Day:

Stacked *Polyprops*

Polyprops gestapelt

Polyprops empilées

Robin Day:

Polyprop chairs, 1963–67

Polyprop-Stühle, 1963–67

Chaises *Polyprop*, 1963–67

Eero Aarnio

*1932

Finland . Finnland . Finlande

Ball or Globe chair
1963 – 65

Ball- oder Globe-Sessel
1963 – 65

Fauteuil Ball ou Globe
1963 – 65

Fabric-covered, foam-upholstered, moulded, glass-reinforced poly-ester seat shell with painted aluminium base

Kugelförmige Sitzschale aus fiber-glasverstärktem Polyester, innen mit Schaumstoff gepolstert und mit Stoff bezogen; Säulenfuß aus Aluminium, lackiert

Coque de siège en polyester moulé renforcé de fibre de verre, rembourrée de mousse recou-verte de tissu, sur base d'alumi-nium peint

Asko Oy, Finland, from 1966 to c. 1980 and from c. 1983 to 1987 (reissued by Adelta Finland from 1992)

Eero Aarnio designed the *Ball*, *Pastille* (*Gyro*), *Tomato* and *Bubble* series of chairs as a complete departure from traditional forms of seating. Employing state-of-the-art manufacturing technol-ogy, Aarnio's designs express the icon-oclasm of the 1960s. Both materially and in terms of their production, how-ever, these chairs were of a high qual-ity and did not embrace Pop culture's aesthetic of disposability.

Zu Eero Aarnios Entwürfen zählen die Stuhlserien *Ball*, *Pastille* (*Gyro*), *To-mato* und *Bubble*, mit denen er eine vollkommene Abkehr von der her-kömmlichen Sitzmöbelform vollzog. Aarnio machte sich die neuesten Erkenntnisse moderner Herstellungs-technologien zunutze; seine Entwürfe waren Ausdruck der bilderstürmeri-schen Ideen der sechziger Jahre. Was Material und Produktionstechnik be-trifft, waren die Stühle von bester Qualität und entsprachen nicht der Wegwerfmentalität der Popkultur.

Eero Aarnio conçut les gammes de sièges *Ball*, *Pastille* ou *Gyro*, *Tomato* et *Bubble* en rupture complète avec les formes traditionnelles de sièges. Faisant appel à une technologie de fabrication d'avant-garde, ses dessins expriment l'esprit iconoclaste des années 60. Cependant, que ce soit en termes de matériaux ou de fabrication, il s'agissait de sièges de haute qualité qui ne participaient ni de l'esthétique ni de la recherche du "jetable" de la culture Pop.

Eero Aarnio:

Mustangs, c. 1970

Mustangs, um 1967

Mustangs, vers 1967

Eero Aarnio:

Bubble chair, c. 1967

Stuhl *Bubble*, um 1967

Chaise *Bubble*, vers 1967

Joe Colombo

1930–71

Italy . Italien . Italie

**Universale chair,
Model No. 4867** 1965

**Stuhl Universale,
Modell Nr. 4867** 1965

**Chaise Universale,
modèle n° 4867** 1965

Injection-moulded "Cycolac"
ABS plastic (1974 to 75 PA6
nylon and 1975 to present polypropylene)

Stuhl aus verformtem »Cycolac«-
ABS-Kunststoff (von 1974 bis
1975 aus PA6-Nylon, von 1975
bis heute aus Polypropylen)

Plastique ABS «Cycolac», moulé
par injection (de 1974 à 1975,
nylon PA6 et de 1975 à ce jour,
polypropylène)

**Kartell, Italy, from 1967
to present**

Joe Colombo:

Armchair *4801/5*, 1964/65

Armlehnstuhl *4801/5*, 1964/65

Fauteuil *4801/5*, 1964/65

"Visiona" exhibition at Bayer AG,
Leverkusen, 1969

Ausstellung »Visiona« bei der
Bayer AG, Leverkusen, 1969

Exposition «Visiona», Bayer AG,
Leverkusen, 1969

The first full-scale chair to be injection-
moulded, the *4867* had interchange-
able legs of two heights and could be
stacked into sets of three. Originally
known as the *4860*, the model number
changed in 1974 when the materials
used and the shape of the seat profile
were altered. Colombo said: "All the
objects needed in a house should be
integrated with the usable spaces;
hence they no longer ought to be
called furnishings but equipment."[23]

Der Universale *Nr. 4867* war der erste
im Spritzgußverfahren hergestellte
Stuhl; er hatte auswechselbare Beine
in zwei verschiedenen Höhen und ließ
sich bis zu drei Exemplaren stapeln.
Die ursprüngliche Bezeichnung
Nr. 4860 wurde 1974 geändert; man
wählte damals ein anderes Material
und veränderte die Form der Sitzfläche. Colombo: »Alle in einem Haus-
halt benötigten Gegenstände sollten in
die entsprechenden Räume integriert
werden; man sollte sie daher nicht
mehr als Möbel, sondern als Ausstattung bezeichnen.«[23]

Première chaise à être moulée par injection, la *4867* possédait des pieds
interchangeables de deux hauteurs différentes et pouvait s'empiler par trois
unités. Identifiée à l'origine comme la
4860, son numéro changea en 1974
lorsque d'autres matériaux furent utilisés et que la forme du siège fut mo-
difiée. Colombo écrivit: «Tous les
objets dont a besoin une maison devraient être intégrés dans les espaces
utilitaires; ils ne devraient donc plus
être appelés meubles mais
équipements.»[23]

Used in Stanley Kubrick's film "2001: A Space Odyssey", the *Djinn* series derived its title from a spirit in Islamic mythology that can assume human or animal form and control men with its supernatural powers. During the 1960s, the emerging popular interest in Eastern mysticism influenced the decorative arts in Europe and America.

Die *Djinn*-Serie, die in Stanley Kubricks Film »2001: Odyssee im Weltraum« zu sehen war, ist nach einer Gestalt aus der islamischen Mythologie benannt. Sie erscheint als Mensch oder Tier und kann den Menschen mit ihren übernatürlichen Kräften beherrschen. Während der 60er Jahre beeinflußte das allgemein wachsende Interesse am Mystizismus östlicher Kulturen die angewandte Kunst in Europa und den USA.

Utilisée dans le film de Stanley Kubrick «2001: Odyssée de l'espace», la série *Djinn* doit son nom à un esprit qui, en pays musulman, peut prendre forme humaine ou animale et dominer l'homme grâce à des pouvoirs surnaturels. Pendant les années 60, l'intérêt de plus en plus grand pour le mysticisme oriental influença les arts décoratifs en Europe et en Amérique. Les couleurs franches des jerseys utilisés au départ pour cette série étaient safran, écarlate, vert olive, tous coloris de sensibilité orientale.

Olivier Mourgue

*1939

France . Frankreich . France

Djinn chair and stool
1965

Stuhl und Hocker Djinn
1965

Siège et tabouret Djinn
1965

Stretch fabric-covered, polyurethane foam-upholstered, bent tubular steel frame

Rahmen gezogenes Stahlrohr; Polsterung aus Polyurethanschaum, mit Stretchstoff bezogen

Structure en tube d'acier cintré rembourrée de mousse de polyuréthane, recouverte de jersey extensible

Airborne International, France, from 1963 to 1976

Still from Stanley Kubrick's Film "2001: A Space Odyssey", showing Space Station

Standfoto aus Stanley Kubricks Film »2001 : Odyssee im Weltraum«, auf dem die Raumstation zu sehen ist

Image du Film de Stanley Kubrick «2001 : Odyssée de l'espace» montrant une station spatiale

Olivier Mourgue:

Djinn chaise longue, 1963

Djinn-Chaiselongue, 1963

Chaise longue *Djinn*, 1963

Kazuhide Takahama

*1930

Japan . Japon

Suzanne seat 1965
Sitzmöbel Suzanne 1965
Siège Suzanne 1965

Fabric-covered, polyurethane foam-upholstered, tubular steel frame with chrome-plated steel fittings

Stahlrohrrahmen mit Beschlägen aus verchromtem Stahl; Polsterung aus Polyurethanschaum, mit Stoff bezogen

Structure en tube d'acier rembourrée de mousse de polyuréthane et recouverte de tissu, accessoires en acier chromé

Gavina, Italy, from 1965 to 1968, and Knoll International, Inc., New York, from 1968 to 1989

Utilising large block constructions of polyurethane foam, Takahama designed the *Marcel*, *Raymond* and *Suzanne* modular seating units for Dino Gavina in 1965. "All three were ideas generated in the laboratory of manufacturing and aesthetic experimentation, specific to the culture in question."[24]

Bei Takahamas aus Modulen zusammengesetzten Sitzmöbel *Marcel*, *Raymond* und *Suzanne*, die er 1965 für Dino Gavina entwarf, handelt es sich um blockartige Konstruktionen aus Polyurethanschaum. »Alle drei waren Ideen, die im Versuchslabor für Produktionsmethoden und ästhetische Gestaltung geboren wurden und für die betreffende Kultur charakteristisch sind.«[24]

A partir de gros blocs de mousse polyuréthane, Takahama créa les sièges modulaires *Marcel*, *Raymond* et *Suzanne* pour Dino Gavina en 1965. «Tous trois étaient nés d'idées issues du laboratoire du fabricant et d'expérimentations esthétiques, spécifiques à la culture en question.»[24]

Warren Platner explains: "I felt there was room for the kind of decorative, gentle, graceful kind of design that appeared in a period style like Louis XV… It is important that if you design a chair you produce something that enhances the person in it."[25]

Warren Platner sagt über seine Entwürfe: »Ich fand, daß es an der Zeit war für ein dekoratives, weich fließendes, elegantes Design von der Art des Louis-XV-Stils… Wenn man einen Stuhl entwirft, ist es wichtig, daß man etwas kreiert, das die Person, die darin Platz nimmt, aufwertet.«[25]

«Je sentais qu'il y avait une place pour le type de dessin décoratif, agréable et gracieux qui apparut dans une période stylistique comme celle de Louis XV… Il est important, lorsque vous dessinez un siège, de produire quelque chose qui mette en valeur la personne qui s'y asseoit.» Warren Platner.[25]

Warren Platner

*1919

USA . Etats-Unis

Platner chair, Model No. 1725A 1966

Platner-Stuhl, Modell Nr. 1725A 1966

Fauteuil Platner, modèle n° 1725A 1966

Nickel-plated steel construction with fabric-covered, foam-rubber upholstery

Rahmen Stahl vernickelt; Schaumstoffpolsterung, mit Stoff bezogen

Construction en acier nickelé, rembourrage en mousse de caoutchouc recouverte de tissu

Knoll International, Inc., New York, from 1966 to present

Warren Platner:

Platner Collection, 1966

Warren Platner:

Platner Collection, 1966

Archizoom
Associati

1966 – 74

Italy . Italien . Italie

Superonda 1966

Sofa Superonda 1966

Système Superonda 1966

Vinyl-covered polyurethane foam

Polyurethanschaum, mit Vinyl
bezogen

Mousse de polyuréthane recouverte de vinyl

**Poltronova, Italy, from 1966
to present**

Cut from a single block of polyurethane foam, the *Superonda* is exceptionally lightweight and easy to move. It can be configured in several ways – either as a chaise longue, sofa or divan – and is a highly interactive design, functioning more as a plaything than as a serious seating solution.

Das Sofa *Superonda* ist aus einem einzigen Block Polyurethanschaum geschnitten; es ist extrem leicht und bequem zu bewegen. Man kann es als Sofa oder Chaiselongue benutzen, je nachdem, wie man es hinlegt – ein Design, das zu Verwandlungen auffordert, aber eher eine Spielerei als ein ernstzunehmender Entwurf.

Taillée dans un bloc de mousse de polyuréthane, la *Superonda* est extrêmement légère et se déplace donc facilement. Elle peut servir à plusieurs usages, chaise longue, sofa ou divan. C'est un concept hautement convivial, plus ludique que réellement fonctionnel.

Archizoom Associati:

Mies chair, 1969

Mies-Stuhl, 1969

Chaise *Mies*, 1969

Archizoom Associati:

Superonda sofa (detail), 1966

Sofa *Superonda* (Detail), 1966

Système *Superonda* (détail), 1966

Roberto Matta

*1911

Chile . Chili

Malitte seating system
1966

Wohnlandschaft Malitte
1966

Système Malitte
1966

Fabric-covered polyurethane foam

Polyurethanschaum, mit Stoff
bezogen

Mousse de polyuréthane recouverte de tissu

Gavina, Italy, from 1966 to 1968,
and Knoll International, Inc.,
New York, from 1968 to 1974

Roberto Matta, best known as a Sur-
realist painter, confidently exploited the
potential of polyurethane foam in creating this sculptural seating system.
Although seen at the time as highly
whimsical, the *Malitte* was an extremely
innovative and functional design, rationally conceived for high-volume production. It was particularly well suited to
the less formal and minimalist interiors
that were becoming increasingly
popular in the late 1960s.

Roberto Matta, der vor allem als surrealistischer Maler bekannt ist, schöpf-
te mit dem Entwurf seiner skulpturalen
Wohnlandschaft sehr kühn die Möglichkeiten von Polyurethanschaum aus.
Obwohl das Design damals als schrul-
lig galt, war es ungewöhnlich innovativ
und funktional. Nicht zuletzt handelte
es sich um einen rationalen Entwurf,
der auf die Produktion von großen
Stückzahlen abzielte. Besonders gut
eignete sich der Entwurf für unkonventionelle, minimalistische Interieurs, die
in den 60er Jahren immer beliebter
wurden.

Roberto Matta, plus connu comme
peintre surréaliste, exploita sans hési-
tation le potentiel de la mousse de
polyuréthane pour créer ce concept de
siège-sculpture. Bien que considéré à
l'époque comme un objet hautement
bizarre, le *Malitte* était une création
extrêmement innovatrice et fonction-
nelle, conçue pour une production en
série. Elle correspondait particulièrement bien aux intérieurs moins forma-
listes et moins minimalistes devenant à
la mode à la fin des années 60.

Günter Belzig

*1941

Germany . Deutschland . Allemagne

Floris chair 1967
Stuhl Floris 1967
Chaise Floris 1967

Moulded, fibreglass-reinforced polyester

Verformter, fiberglasverstärkter Polyester

Polyester moulé renforcé de fibre de verre

Brüder Belzig Design, Germany, from 1968 (reissued limited edition by Galerie Objekte, Munich, from 1992)

This extraordinary anthropomorphic chair, produced by Günter, Berthold and Ernst Belzig, was first shown at the Cologne Furniture Fair in 1968. Intended as a totally weather-resistant stacking chair, only fifty examples were originally manufactured, as its hand laid-up, two-part construction proved too complicated for efficient industrial production.

Dieser außergewöhnlich anthropomorphe Stuhl, den die Brüder Günter, Berthold und Ernst Belzig herstellten, wurde auf der Kölner Möbelmesse von 1968 vorgestellt. Er wurde als wetterbeständiger Stapelstuhl konzipiert, dennoch wurden anfangs nur fünfzig Exemplare hergestellt, denn die zweiteilige Konstruktion, die teilweise Handarbeit erforderte, war für eine effiziente Massenproduktion zu kompliziert.

Cet extraordinaire siège anthropomorphique produit par Günter, Berthold et Ernst Belzig fut tout d'abord présenté au Salon du Meuble de Cologne en 1968. Modèles empilables résistant aux intempéries, seuls cinquante exemplaires en furent fabriqués au départ, car la construction en deux parties se révéla trop complexe pour une production industrielle rentable.

Günter Belzig with his range of children's furniture

Günter Belzig mit seinen Kindermöbeln

Günter Belzig et ses meubles pour enfants

Pierre Paulin:

Ribbon chair, *Model No. 582*, 1965

Sessel *Ribbon*, *Modell Nr. 582*, 1965

Fauteuil *Ribbon*, *modèle n° 582*, 1965

Pierre Paulin

*1927

France . Frankreich

Chair, Model No. 577
1967

Sessel, Modell Nr. 577
1967

Chauffeuse, modèle n° 577
1967

Fabric-covered, foam-upholstered, tubular steel frame

Stahlrohrgestell; Schaumstoffpolsterung, mit Jersey bezogen

Structure en tube d'acier rembourrée de mousse et recouverte de tissu

Artifort, Netherlands, from 1967 to present

Pierre Paulin:

Chair, *Model No. 560*, 1963

Stuhl, *Modell Nr. 560*, 1963

Chaise, *modèle n° 560*, 1963

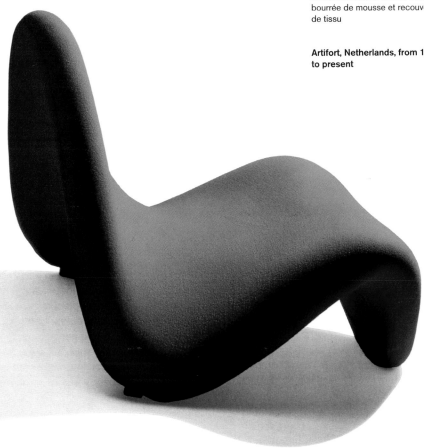

The *577* chair, which rests directly on the floor, allows the user to assume a relaxed and informal posture. Through his use of visually unified, abstracted sculptural forms, combined with an understanding of ergonomics and the degree to which his designs afford the sitter freedom of movement, Paulin's chairs are not only beautiful to look at but also extremely comfortable to use.

Der Sessel *Nr. 577* hat weder Beine noch Untergestell; er liegt direkt auf dem Boden. So kann der Benutzer eine entspannte, unkonventionelle Haltung einnehmen, die dem saloppen Lebensstil der Zeit entsprach. Paulin verbindet ganzheitliche, ungegenständlich-skulpturale Formen mit einer individuellen Auslegung ergonomischer Prinzipien und gestattet dem Benutzer seiner Sitzmöbel viel Bewegungsfreiheit. Daher sind sie nicht nur schön anzusehen, sondern auch äußerst bequem.

La chauffeuse *n° 577*, qui repose directement sur le sol, permet à son utilisateur de trouver une position détendue et informelle, ce qui était tout à fait dans l'air du temps de cette période. A travers leurs formes sculpturales abstraites, simples et lisses, combinant une sensibilité réelle à l'ergonomie et à la recherche de liberté de mouvement, les sièges de Paulin ne sont pas seulement beaux mais extrêmement confortables.

Pierre Paulin:

Chair, *Model No. 598*, 1972

Sessel, *Modell Nr. 598*, 1972

Fauteuil, *modèle n° 598*, 1972

Jonathan De Pas
Donato D'Urbino
Paolo Lomazzi
Carla Scolari

all born in the 1930s

alle in den dreißiger Jahren
geboren

nés au cours des années 30

Italy . Italien . Italie

Blow chair 1967
Blow-Sessel 1967
Fauteuil Blow 1967

Radio frequency welded PVC
(Polyvinylchloride)

PVC (Polyvinylchlorid), mit
Hochfrequenz geschweißt

PVC (Polyvinylchlorid) soudé
électroniquement

**Zanotta, Italy, from 1967
to 1991**

The *Blow* chair, the first inflatable chair successfully mass-produced in Italy, is an icon of 1960s popular culture. Inexpensive to manufacture, it possessed an intrinsic expendability that dismissed the traditional associations of high cost and permanence with chair design. Only recently taken out of production, the *Blow* chair could be used in an interior or exterior context and was even suitable for use in swimming pools.

Der *Blow*-Sessel, das erste aufblasbare Sitzmöbel, in Italien mit großem Erfolg in Serie produziert, ist eine Ikone der Popkultur der Sechziger. Seine geringen Herstellungskosten machten ihn zu einer Art Konsumgegenstand und veränderten grundlegend die bisherigen Vorstellungen von hohen Produktionskosten und Haltbarkeit. Der *Blow*-Sessel konnte in Innen- und Außenräumen verwendet werden; er eignete sich sogar für die Benutzung im Swimmingpool. Seine Produktion wurde erst vor kurzem eingestellt.

Le fauteuil *Blow*, premier siège gonflable produit avec succès en Italie, est devenu une icône de la culture populaire des années 60. Economique à fabriquer, il présentait des caractères intrinsèques de produit «consommable» qui niaient les idées reçues traditionnelles sur le coût élevé et la permanence. Retiré de la production récemment seulement, il pouvait servir aussi bien à l'extérieur qu'à l'intérieur, et même au bord d'une piscine.

**De Pas, D'Urbino, Lomazzi &
Scolari:**

Zanotta stand at Eurodomus 3,
Turin

Stand der Firma Zanotta auf der
Eurodomus 3, Turin

Stand de la firme Zanotta à
l'Eurodomus 3, Turin

**De Pas, D'Urbino,
Lomazzi & Scolari:**

Blow chairs

Blow-Sessel

Chaises *Blow*

From a range of cardboard furniture pieces that included modular seating, storage units and tables, the *Papp* chair was one of the first designs to explore the possibilities of cardboard seating and as such can be seen as an important precursor of Frank Gehry's *Easy Edges* series of 1972. The *Papp* chair's form, however, is reminiscent of a plywood cut-out chaise-longue designed in 1953 by Vittorio Gregotti, Lodovico Meneghetti and Giotto Stoppino.

Der *Papp*-Stuhl war Teil einer Gruppe von Möbeln aus Karton: Sitzmodule, Anbauschränke und Tische. Er gehörte zu den ersten Entwürfen, die Einsatzmöglichkeiten von Pappmöbeln erprobte und daher als wichtiger Vorläufer von Frank Gehrys Entwurf *Easy Edges* von 1972 angesehen werden kann. Die Form des *Papp*-Stuhls erinnert an die Chaiselongue aus schichtverleimtem Sperrholz, die Vittorio Gregotti, Lodovico Meneghetti und Giotto Stoppino 1953 entworfen hatten.

Faisant partie d'une gamme de mobilier comprenant des sièges modulaires, des rangements et des tables, la chaise *Papp* fut l'une des premières chaises à explorer les possibilités du carton et peut être considérée à ce titre comme un important précurseur de la gamme *Easy Edges* de Frank Gehry (1972). Sa forme rappelle néanmoins une chaise longue en contreplaqué découpé dessinée en 1953 par Vittorio Gregotti, Lodovico Meneghetti et Giotto Stoppino.

Peter Raacke

*1928

Germany . Deutschland . Allemagne

Papp chair 1967
Papp-Stuhl 1967
Chaise Papp 1967

Cardboard

Karton

Carton

Faltmöbel Ellen Raacke, Germany, from 1967 to present

Joe Colombo

1930–71

Italy . Italien . Italie

Additional Living System
1967/68

Tubular iron frame upholstered in fabric-covered polyurethane foam, with metal clamps

Stahlrohrrahmen mit stoffüberzogener Polyurethanschaum-Polsterung und Metallklammern

Cadre en tube de fer garni de mousse polyuréthane recouverte de tissu, pinces métalliques

Sormani, Italy, from 1968 to 1971

This extraordinary seating system is convertible into several combinations. Equally ingenious and innovative was Colombo's *Visiona* habitat, a space-age living cell, designed in 1969 for Bayer. Colombo explained: "Today the problem lies in offering furnishing which is purely autonomous, independent of architectural considerations and flexible and programmable enough that it suits every present and future room set-up."

Dieses außergewöhnliche Sitzmöbelsystem läßt sich zu verschiedenen Einheiten zusammensetzen. Genauso ausgefallen und innovativ war Colombos 1969 für die Bayer AG entworfene *Visiona*-Ausstattung, eine Wohnzelle wie in einer Raumstation. Colombo erklärte sein Design wie folgt: »Heutzutage muß man eine Einrichtung anbieten können, die von architektonischen Vorgaben unabhängig ist. Sie muß so flexibel und integrationsfähig sein, daß sie sowohl gegenwärtigen als auch zukünftigen Raumkonzepten genügt.«

Ce système de fauteuils tout à fait extraordinaire peut être combiné de diverses façons. L'ensemble *Visiona* que Colombo avait réalisé en 1969 pour Bayer était lui aussi étonnant et innovatif. Il s'agissait d'une cellule habitable ressemblant à une station spatiale. Colombo fournissait l'explication suivante: «Aujourd'hui, nous devons proposer des meubles autonomes, ne se rattachant en rien à des considérations architectoniques. Ils doivent être flexibles et programmables afin de pouvoir s'adapter à toute installation intérieure, présente et future.»

Joe Colombo:
Additional Living System, 1967/68

Joe Colombo:
Elda chair, 1965
Stuhl *Elda*, 1965
Chaise *Elda*, 1965

Joe Colombo:
Roto Living Unit, 1969

The *Pastille*, or as it is sometimes known, the *Gyro*, is a novel approach to the traditional rocking-chair format. A singular chair design intended for interior and exterior use, it won an AID award in 1968. "Aarnio is always ahead of his time. Although perhaps the most international of Finnish designers of furniture, he is nevertheless intensely individual. Not a follower of any school, but conceivably the founder of one."[26]

Der *Pastille*- oder *Gyro*-Sessel, wie er auch genannt wird, ist Ausdruck einer völlig neuen Auffassung von der Konstruktion eines Schaukelstuhls, wie man ihn bisher kannte. Dieser einzigartige Stuhl, der für die Verwendung drinnen und draußen konzipiert wurde, gewann 1968 den AID-Award. »Aarnio ist seiner Zeit immer voraus. Er ist vielleicht der internationalste aller finnischen Designer, ist aber dennoch durch und durch Individualist. Er gehört keiner Schule an, ist aber offensichtlich Gründer einer Schule.«[26]

Le *Pastille*, connu aussi sous le nom de *Gyro*, marque une approche très nouvelle du siège à bascule. Conçu pour l'intérieur ou l'extérieur, ce modèle remporta un prix AID en 1968. «Aarnio est toujours en avance sur son temps. Bien qu'il soit peut-être le plus international des créateurs de meubles finlandais, il possède néanmoins une très forte personnalité. Ce n'est pas un suiveur d'une quelconque école, mais sans doute le fondateur d'un nouveau mouvement.»[26]

Eero Aarnio

*1932

Finland . Finnland . Finlande

Pastille or Gyro chair
1968

Sessel Pastille oder Gyro
1968

Fauteuil Pastille ou Gyro
1968

Moulded, glass-reinforced polyester

Fiberglasverstärkter, verformter Polyester

Polyester moulé, renforcé de fibre de verre

Asko Oy, Finland, from 1968 to c. 1980 (reissued from 1991 to present)

Stendig promotional photograph of *Gyro* chairs, c. 1970

Werbefoto von Stendig: *Gyro*-Stühle, um 1970

Photographie publicitaire de Stendig montrant les chaises *Gyro*, vers 1970

Piero Gatti
*1940

Cesare Paolini
1937–83

Franco Teodoro
*1939

Italy . Italien . Italie

Sacco chair 1968

Stuhl Sacco 1968

Siège Sacco 1968

Vinyl bag containing semi-expanded polystyrene pellets

Vinylsack, gefüllt mit halbauf-geschäumten Styroporkugeln

Sac de vinyl rempli de billes de polystyrène semi-expansé

Zanotta, Italy, from 1968 to present

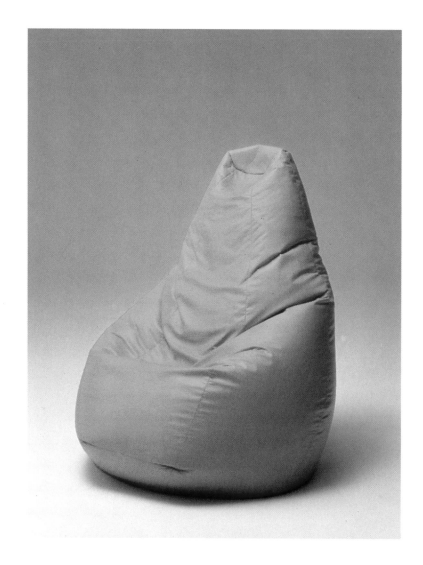

The first commercially produced bean-bag seat, the *Sacco* easily adapts to whatever position the sitter assumes. The designers originally proposed a fluid-filled transparent envelope but the excessive weight and complications of filling it eventually led to the inspired choice of semi-expanded polystyrene beads. It was claimed by Zanotta to be "The Chair of 1001 Nights (1000 positions by day, one position by night, marvellously comfortable)."[27]

Der erste kommerziell hergestellte Sitz-sack, der *Sacco*, verändert seine Form, je nachdem welche Position man ein-nimmt. Die Designer hatten ursprüng-lich eine mit Flüssigkeit gefüllte, trans-parente Hülle vorgeschlagen, sich aber wegen des ungeheuren Gewichts und der Schwierigkeiten beim Einfüllen schließlich für halbaufgeschäumte Sty-roporkügelchen entschieden. Zanotta meinte, es sei »der Stuhl von 1001 Nacht (1000 Positionen am Tag, eine bei Nacht, herrlich bequem)«.[27]

Premier siège-sac commercialisé, le *Sacco* s'adapte immédiatement à n'im-porte quelle position. Ses designers avaient au départ proposé une enve-loppe transparente emplie de liquide, mais le poids et les complications du remplissage conduisirent à ce choix inspiré de petites billes de polystyrène semi-expansé. Zanotta le présenta comme «le siège des mille et une nuits – 1000 positions pour le jour, une pour la nuit, merveilleusement confortable».[27]

Piero Gatti photographed with a prototype of the *Sacco*

Piero Gatti, fotografiert mit einem *Sacco*-Prototyp

Photographie de Piero Gatti avec un prototype du *Sacco*

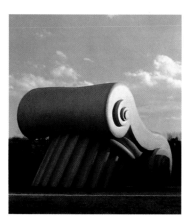

Gatti, Paolini & Teodoro:

Capitello chair, 1971

Stuhl *Capitello*, 1971

Siège *Capitello*, 1971

Compressed and vacuum-packed in a PVC wrapper, the *Up 5* chair literally bounced into life when unwrapped. Pesce described his *Up* Series as "transformation" furniture, intended to turn the act of purchasing into a "happening". With specific reference to *Up 5*, Pesce declared: "In that design I was expressing my own view of women: they have always been, against their own wills, prisoners of themselves. So I felt like giving this armchair the shape of a woman with a ball on her feet, which is indeed the traditional image of the prisoner."[28]

Der *Up-5*-Sessel, der vakuumverpackt in PVC-Folie geliefert wurde, sprang buchstäblich ins Leben. Pesce nannte seine exzentrischen *Up*-Serien »Verwandlungsmöbel«. Der Akt des Kaufens wurde zum Happening. In bezug auf die *Up-5*-Serie erklärte Pesce: »In diesem Design habe ich meine persönliche Sicht der Frauen ausgedrückt: sie sind stets Gefangene ihres Wesens. Deshalb wollte ich diesem Sessel die Gestalt einer Frau mit einer Kugel an den Füßen geben – einer Gestalt, die dem traditionellen Bild eines Strafgefangenen entspricht.«[28]

Comprimé et livré sous emballage sous vide, le fauteuil *Up 5* éclosait littéralement à la vie lorsque l'enveloppe de plastique était déchirée. Gaetano Pesce décrivit cette gamme *Up* comme un mobilier «à transformation». Se référant spécifiquement au *Up 5*, Pesce déclara: «A travers ce fauteuil, j'exprimais mes vues personnelles sur les femmes. C'est pourquoi j'ai eu envie de donner à ce fauteuil la forme d'une femme avec une boule attachée à ses pieds, ce qui est en fait l'image traditionnelle du prisonnier.»[28]

Gaetano Pesce

*1939
Italy . Italien . Italie

Up 5 (Donna) 1969
Sessel Up 5 (Donna) 1969
Fauteuil Up 5 (Donna) 1969

Stretch fabric-covered, moulded polyurethane foam

Verformter Polyurethanschaum, mit Stretchstoff bezogen

Mousse de polyuréthane moulée, recouverte de tissu élastique

C&B Italia (later to become known as B&B Italia), Italy, from 1969 to 1976

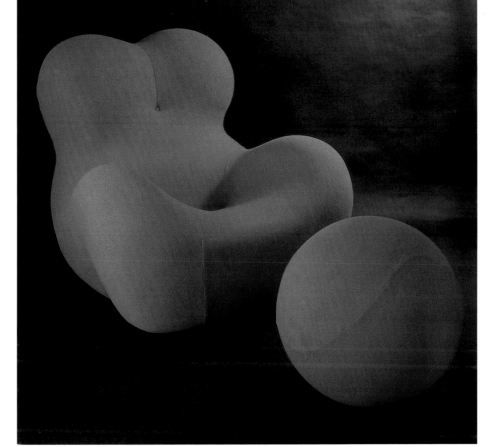

A photo by Zaugg for a C&B Italia advertising campaign for the *Up* series, c. 1970

Ein Foto von Zaugg für die C&B-Italia-Werbekampagne der *Up*-Serien, um 1970

Une photographie de Zaugg pour une campagne publicitaire de C&B Italia pour les séries *Up*, vers 1970

Gaetano Pesce:

Up Series, 1969

Up 5 Donna bouncing into life

Up 5 Donna springt ins Leben

Up 5 Donna en pleine éclosion

Giancarlo Piretti:

Plia chairs with *Plano* table, 1969

Plia-Stühle mit *Plano*-Tisch, 1969

Chaises *Plia* et table *Plano*, 1969

Giancarlo Piretti

*1940

Italy . Italien . Italie

Plia chair 1969

Stuhl Plia 1969

Chaise Plia 1969

Chrome-plated steel frame with moulded perspex seat and back

Rahmen aus verchromtem Stahl; Sitz- und Rückenschale aus verformtem Perspex

Structure d'acier chromé, siège et dossier en perspex moulé

Castelli, Italy, from 1969 to present

The *Plia* chair is an efficient modern reworking of the traditional wooden folding chair. When collapsed, the *Plia* is only an inch in depth, excluding the central hub. Piretti also designed a similar folding armchair, the *Plona*, in 1970, followed in 1971 by a matching desk, the *Plano*. The *Plia* has won several prizes, including the Bundespreis "Gute Form" in 1973.

Der Armlehnstuhl *Plia* ist eine moderne Version des traditionellen Klappstuhls aus Holz. Zusammengefaltet ist er etwa 2,5 cm dick, die Nabe in der Mitte ausgenommen. 1970 entwarf Piretti einen ähnlichen zusammenklappbaren Armlehnstuhl, das Modell *Plona*, und 1971 einen dazugehörigen Schreibtisch *Plano*. Der Armlehnstuhl *Plia* wurde mit mehreren Preisen ausgezeichnet, u.a. mit dem Bundespreis für »Gute Form« von 1973.

Le siège *Plia* est une réinterprétation moderne convaincante de la traditionnelle chaise pliante en bois. Repliée, la *Plia* ne mesure que 4 cm d'épaisseur, hors moyeu central. Piretti dessina également un fauteuil pliant similaire, le *Plona*, en 1970 et un bureau assorti, le *Plano* en 1971. La *Plia* a remporté plusieurs distinctions dont le prix fédéral «Gute Form», en 1973.

Vico Magistretti:

Gaudí chair, 1970

Stuhl *Gaudí*, 1970

Chaise *Gaudí*, 1970

Aiming to create a single-piece chair in compression-moulded plastic with a traditional four-legged form, Magistretti brilliantly resolved the technical difficulties associated with the strength of the legs by configuring them in an "S" shape. He based this solution on the leg design of his earlier injection-moulded *Stadio* table of 1966. The *Gaudí* and *Vicario* armchairs, both designed in 1970, are similarly constructed and equally restrained.

Die Schwierigkeiten mit der Stärke des Materials bei der Konstruktion eines Kunststoffstuhls mit den herkömmlichen vier Beinen, die im Kompressionsverfahren aus einem Stück hergestellt werden, löste Magistretti auf brillante Art und Weise, er gab ihnen eine S-förmige Gestalt. Diese Idee ging auf das innovative Design der Beine seines Tisches *Stadio* von 1966 zurück, der ebenfalls im Spritzgußverfahren hergestellt wurde. Auch die Modelle *Gaudí* und *Vicario* von 1970 sind ähnlich konstruiert und ausgewogen.

Afin de réaliser une chaise à quatre pieds en un seul élément de plastique moulé par compression, Magistretti résolut brillamment les difficultés techniques posées par la solidité des pieds en leur donnant une forme en S. Cette solution venait de sa table *Stadio*, créée en 1966. De même que la *Selene*, les fauteuils *Gaudí* et *Vicario*, tous deux dessinés en 1970 et de construction similaire et tout aussi sobre, traduisent le classicisme de la philosophie de Magistretti.

Vico Magistretti

*1920

Italy . Italien . Italie

Selene chair 1969

Stuhl Selene 1969

Chaise Selene 1969

Compression-moulded 'Reglar' fibreglass-reinforced polyester

Fiberglasverstärktes Kunstharz, im Spritzgußverfahren hergestellt

Résine renforcée moulée par injection

Artemide, Italy, from 1969 to present

Wendell Castle

*1932

USA . Etats-Unis

Molar sofa 1969/70

Sofa Molar 1969/70

Canapé Molar 1969/70

Moulded glass-reinforced polyester

Verformter, fiberglasverstärkter Polyester

Polyester moulé renforcé de fibre de verre

Beylerian Limited, USA, from 1970 to c. 1975

Best known for his superbly crafted wooden furniture, Castle translated his highly organic forms into plastic. The surrealistic *Molar* sofa and matching *Molar* chair were based on the shape of large back teeth. Not intended for high-volume production, the *Molar* group and the similar *Castle* series of chairs were exclusively distributed by Stendig, New York.

Castle, der in erster Linie für seine hervorragend gearbeiteten Holzmöbel bekannt ist, übersetzte seine organischen Formen in Kunststoff. Das surrealistisch anmutende Sofa *Molar* und der dazugehörige Stuhl hatten die Form von riesigen Backenzähnen. Die Gruppe *Molar* und die ähnliche Sitzmöbelgruppe *Castle* waren nicht für die Massenproduktion vorgesehen; sie wurden exklusiv von der Firma Stendig, New York, vertrieben.

Plus connu pour ses meubles en bois superbement exécutés, Castle traduisit ses formes organiques en plastique. Ce canapé surréaliste et son fauteuil assorti s'inspiraient de la forme d'une molaire. Non conçues pour être produites en grande série, la gamme *Molar* et celle de sièges similaires de Castle étaient distribuées en exclusivité par Stendig, New York.

Wendell Castle:

Castle Chair, 1970

Stuhl *Castle*, 1970

Chaise *Castle*, 1970

Jonathan De Pas
Donato D'Urbino
Paolo Lomazzi

all born in the 1930s

alle in den dreißiger Jahren
geboren

nés au cours des années 30

Italy . Italien . Italie

Joe chair 1970

Sessel Joe 1970

Fauteuil Joe 1970

Leather-covered, moulded
polyurethane foam

Verformter Polyurethanschaum,
mit Leder bezogen

Mousse de polyuréthane moulée,
recouverte de cuir

**Poltronova, Italy, from 1971
to present**

Named after the baseball legend Joe
DiMaggio, the design of this gigantic
glove was inspired by the oversized
and out-of-context sculptures of Claes
Oldenburg. The form of the *Joe* chair
can also be seen as an ironic comment
on the proliferation of reissued Bauhaus furniture covered with high-priced
glove leather.

Dieser Entwurf, der nach dem legen-
dären Baseballspieler Joe DiMaggio
benannt war und einen riesigen Hand-
schuh darstellte, war inspiriert von
Claes Oldenburgs überlebensgroßen
Skulpturen verfremdeter Alltagsgegen-
stände. Der Sessel *Joe* kann auch als
ironischer Kommentar zur verschwen-
derischen Gestaltung neu aufgelegter
Bauhaus-Möbel verstanden werden,
die mit teurem Handschuhleder bezogen waren.

Nommé d'après le célèbre joueur de
base-ball, Joe DiMaggio, cet énorme
gant doit son inspiration aux sculptures
surdimensionnées d'objets sortis de
leur contexte, de Claes Oldenburg. La
forme de ce fauteuil peut également
être vue comme un commentaire ironique sur la prolifération des rééditions
de meubles du Bauhaus recouverts de
coûteuses pausseries de gant.

111

Rodney Kinsman

*1943

Great Britain . Großbritannien . Grande-Bretagne

Omkstak chair 1971
Stuhl Omkstak 1971
Chaise Omkstak 1971

Tubular steel frame with epoxy-coated pressed sheet-steel seat and back

Stahlrohrrahmen; Sitz und Rückenlehne aus gepreßtem Stahlblech, mit Epoxyharz (emailleähnliches Kunstharz) überzogen

Cadre en tube d'acier, siège et dossier en tôle d'acier emboutie traitée époxy

Bieffeplast, Italy, from 1972 to present

The *Omkstak* chair epitomises the High-Tech style of the mid-1970s. It is a highly rational design that was intended for interior and exterior use. Kinsman notes: "It is irresponsible to design things that don't last visually. I don't believe that products should have such an ephemeral form that they will be out of date long before they should be."[29]

Der *Omkstak*-Stuhl, ein Höhepunkt des rationalen High-Tech-Designs der 70er Jahre, war für die Verwendung für drinnen und draußen gedacht. Kinsman sagte dazu: »Es ist unverantwortlich, Dinge zu entwerfen, an denen man sich schnell satt sieht. Ich bin nicht der Meinung, Produkte sollten eine so kurzlebige Gestalt haben, daß sie aus der Mode kommen, lange bevor es an der Zeit wäre.«[29]

La chaise *Omkstak* représente le sommet du style High-Tech du milieu des années 70. C'est un modèle rationnel conçu aussi bien pour l'intérieur que l'extérieur. Kinsman note: «C'est faire preuve d'irresponsabilité que de dessiner des objets qui ne possèdent pas une certaine durée de vie visuelle. Je ne crois pas que les produits doivent avoir une forme tellement éphémère qu'ils se trouvent dépassés avant la date à laquelle ils devraient normalement l'être.»[29]

This chair and table form part of the *Easy Edges* series, which comprised seventeen pieces in cardboard. To increase the strength and resilience of the construction, the layers of cardboard were laminated at right angles to one another. Originally conceived as low-cost furniture, *Easy Edges* was so immediately successful that Gehry withdrew the series from production after only three months, fearing that his ascendancy as a popular furniture designer would distract him from realising his potential as an architect.

Der Stuhl und der Tisch sind Teile der Serie *Easy Edges*, die siebzehn Stücke aus Pappe umfaßte. Um die Festigkeit und die Elastizität zu steigern, wurden die einzelnen Schichten jeweils in einem Winkel von 90° übereinandergelegt. Die Stücke der Kollektion *Easy Edges* wurden als Niedrigpreismöbel konzipiert und waren derart erfolgreich, daß Gehry die Produktion nach drei Monaten stoppte, weil er befürchtete, daß sein Aufstieg als populärer Möbeldesigner ihn daran hindern würde, sein Können als Architekt zu beweisen.

Cette chaise et cette table font partie de la gamme *Easy Edges* qui comprenait dix-sept éléments en carton. Pour accroître la solidité et la résistance du montage, les couches de carton étaient lamellées selon un angle de 90°. Conçu à l'origine comme un mobilier économique, *Easy Edges* connut immédiatement un tel succès que Gehry retira sa gamme de production après trois mois seulement, craignant que cette réussite de dessinateur de meubles bon marché ne l'empêche de poursuivre ses ambitions d'architecte.

Frank O. Gehry

*1929
USA . Etats-Unis

Easy Edges collection 1972
Kollektion Easy Edges 1972
Gamme Easy Edges 1972

Laminated corrugated cardboard
Schichtverleimte Wellpappe
Carton ondulé laqué

Jack Brogan, USA (some models reissued by Vitra GmbH, Germany, from 1992)

Frank O. Gehry:
Experimental Edges: *Little Beaver, Carumba & Bubbles*, 1987

Mario Bellini

*1935

Italy . Italien . Italie

Cab chair 1977
Stuhl Cab 1977
Chaise Cab 1977

Enamelled steel frame with zip-fastened saddle-stitched leather covering

Emaillierter Stahlrahmen; gepolstert, Lederbezug mit Reißverschluß

Structure d'acier émaillé recouverte de cuir cousu point sellier et zippé

Cassina, Italy, from 1977 to present

This elegant chair helped maintain Italy's reputation in the 1970s for high-quality, innovative design. The leather upholstery of the *Cab* chair zips directly onto the skeletal steel frame and functions as a supporting material. Bellini also designed the similarly constructed *Cab* armchair and sofa. All remain in production and are available with either white, tan or black leather covers.

Dieser elegante Stuhl trug in den 70er Jahren dazu bei, Italiens Ruf als Land für hochwertiges, innovatives Design zu festigen. Das Lederpolster ist durch den Reißverschluß direkt mit dem Rahmen des Stuhls verbunden, der sozusagen das Skelett der Konstruktion bildet. Bellini entwarf noch ein weiteres Sofa und einen Armlehnstuhl *Cab* im gleichen Design – alle Stücke werden noch heute hergestellt und sind in Weiß, Natur und Schwarz erhältlich.

Cette chaise élégante contribua à maintenir, au cours des années 70, la réputation italienne de créations innovatrices de haute qualité. Le cuir est directement fixé sur la structure par une fermeture à glissière et fonctionne comme un matériau de soutien. Dans cette série, Bellini dessina également un fauteuil *Cab* et un sofa, proposés en cuir blanc, marron clair ou noir, et toujours fabriqués aujourd'hui.

Mario Bellini:

Cab sofa, 1987

Sofa *Cab*, 1987

Believing "good design" (Modernism) to be dead, Mendini "redesigned" furniture in an attempt to demonstrate, among other things, that the intellectual content of a design can be derived solely from decorative embellishment. Andrea Branzi further explained: "Operations of redesign consisted of touching-up found objects or famous products of design to illustrate the impossibility of designing something new in respect to what has already been designed."[30]

Mendini war der Meinung, »gutes Design« sei tot, und begnügte sich mit dem »Re-Design« von Möbeln. Damit wollte er unter anderem demonstrieren, daß man den geistigen Gehalt eines Designs allein an der dekorativen Verzierung ablesen könne. Andrea Branzi bemerkte dazu: »Redesign besteht darin, daß man Fundstücke oder Entwürfe berühmter Designer aufpeppt, um zu zeigen, daß es absolut unmöglich ist, etwas Neues zu entwerfen, was nicht schon entworfen worden ist.«[30]

Croyant à la mort du «bon design», Mendini repensait le mobilier pour tenter de montrer, entre autres, que le contenu intellectuel d'une création peut ne venir que d'embellissements décoratifs. Andrea Branzi expliqua plus tard que: «Les opérations de re-design consistent à retoucher des objets trouvés ou des créations célèbres du design pour illustrer l'impossibilité de dessiner quelque chose de nouveau.»[30]

Alessandro Mendini

*1931

Italy . Italien . Italie

Proust's armchair 1978
Prousts Sessel 1978
Le fauteuil de Proust 1978

Existing chair with hand-painted decoration

Bereits existierender Sessel mit handgemalter Verzierung

Fauteuil existant peint à la main

Studio Alchimia, Italy (out of production)

Alessandro Mendini:

Dorifora chair, redesigned 1984

Dorifora-Stuhl, nachgebaut 1984

Chaise *Dorifora*, redessinée en 1984

Alessandro Mendini:

Joe Colombo's 4860, redesigned 1978

Joe Colombos 4860, nachgebaut 1978

Joe Colombo's 4860, redessinée en 1978

Ron Arad

*1951

Great Britain . Großbritannien . Grande-Bretagne

Rover chair 1981

Sessel Rover 1981

Chauffeuse Rover 1981

Tubular steel frame supporting a salvaged Rover 2000 car seat

Stahlrohrrahmen, darauf ein ausgeschlachteter Autositz aus einem Rover 2000

Cadre de tube d'acier, siège de Rover 2000

One Off Ltd, UK, from 1981 to 1991

During the early 1980s, the work of the British avant-garde was characterised by the inclusion of found objects in their furniture designs. These rough and ready pieces gave way to more materially sophisticated work in the mid-1980s, such as Arad's *Well Tempered* chair. Also available as a two-seater, the *Rover* chair, born out of the High-Tech style, bears a striking yet unintentional similarity to Jean Prouvé's adjustable armchair prototype of 1924.

Die Verwendung gebrauchter Gegenstände für ihr Design charakterisierte die Arbeiten der britischen Avantgarde. Die ersten, recht groben Ready-mades wurden Mitte der 80er Jahre in bezug auf Material und Ausführung von anspruchsvolleren Arbeiten abgelöst – ein Beispiel dafür war Arads Sessel *Well Tempered*. Der Sessel *Rover* war auch als Zweisitzer erhältlich. Das Modell, das seinen Ursprung im High-Tech-Design hatte, war dem Prototyp des verstellbaren Sessels von Jean Prouvé von 1924 sehr ähnlich – wenn auch unbeabsichtigt.

Au début des années 80, les travaux de l'avant-garde britannique se caractérisaient par l'inclusion d'objets trouvés dans ses créations de meubles. Vers le milieu des années 80, ces éléments bruts ouvrirent la voie, dans certains cas, à des créations mieux finies et plus sophistiquées, comme, par exemple, le fauteuil *Well Tempered* d'Arad. Egalement proposée en version deux places, la chauffeuse *Rover*, enfant du High-Tech, présente une similarité frappante, bien que non voulue, avec le prototype de fauteuil réglable de Jean Prouvé (1924).

Ron Arad:
Well Tempered chair, 1986/87
Sessel *Well-Tempered*, 1986/87
Fauteuil *Well Tempered*, 1986/87

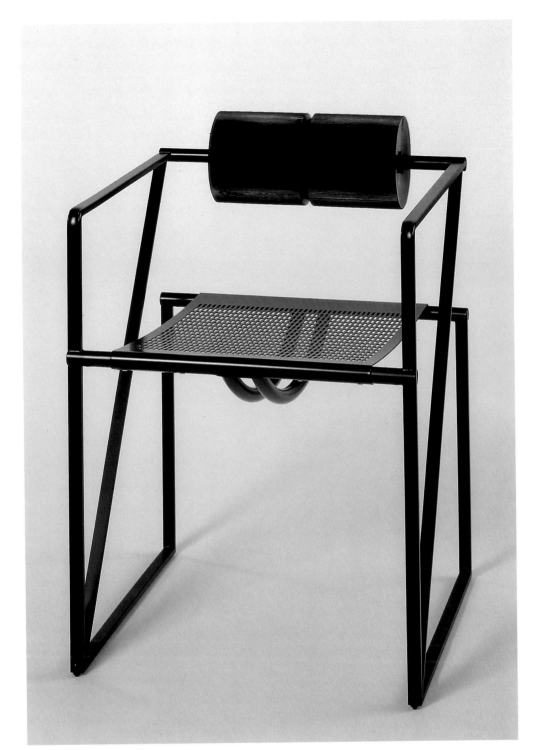

Mario Botta

*1943
Switzerland . Schweiz . Suisse

Seconda chair 1982
Stuhl Seconda 1982
Chaise Seconda 1982

Steel frame with epoxy-coated, perforated sheet steel seat and expanded polyurethane back rest

Stahlrahmen; Sitzfläche aus perforiertem Stahlblech, mit Epoxyharz überzogen; Rücken-lehne aus Polyurethan

Structure d'acier traité époxy, siège en acier perforé et dossier en polyuréthane expansé

Alias, Italy, from 1982 to present

Mario Botta:
Quinta chairs, 1985
Stühle *Quinta*, 1985
Chaises *Quinta*, 1985

Mario Botta:
Seconda chairs, 1982
Seconda-Stühle, 1982
Chaises *Seconda*, 1982

Evolving stylistically from 1970s High-Tech, the *Seconda* chair epitomises the "Matt Black" style of the 1980s. Arising in part as a rejection of the decorative excesses of design movements such as Memphis, "Matt Black" seat furniture is frequently uncomfortable and uncompromising in expressing its hard-edged "rational" aesthetic. For this reason, designs such as the *Seconda* chair are best described as Post-Modern rather than Modern.

Der Stuhl *Seconda*, Höhepunkt des »Matt-Black«-Stils der 80er Jahre, hatte sich aus dem High-Tech-Design der 70er Jahre entwickelt. Die »Matt-Black«-Sitzmöbel, die man zum Teil als Gegenbewegung zu den dekorativen Exzessen von Designbewegungen wie z.B. Memphis deuten kann, sind meist unbequem und stellen kompromißlos ihre rationale, kantige Ästhetik zur Schau. Daher gehören Entwürfe wie der *Seconda* eher zur Moderne als zur Postmoderne.

Venue du style High-Tech des années 70, la chaise *Seconda* incarne le style «Matt Black» (noir mat) des années 80. Nés du rejet des excès décoratifs de mouvements comme Memphis, les meubles «Matt Black» sont souvent in-confortables et sans concessions dans l'expression de leur rigueur esthétique «rationnelle». Pour cette raison, des créations comme la *Seconda* peuvent davantage être qualifiées de post-modernes que de modernes.

Philippe Starck

*1949

France . Frankreich

Costes chair 1982
Sessel Costes 1982
Fauteuil Costes 1982

Painted tubular steel frame with
bent mahogany plywood back and
leather-covered, foam-upholstered
seat

Stahlrohrrahmen, lackiert;
Rückenlehne aus verformtem
Mahagonischichtholz; Sitzfläche
mit Schaumstoff gepolstert und
mit Leder bezogen

Cadre de tube d'acier peint avec
dossier en contreplaqué d'acajou
cintré, siège garni de mousse et
recouvert de cuir

**Driade, Italy, from 1985
to present**

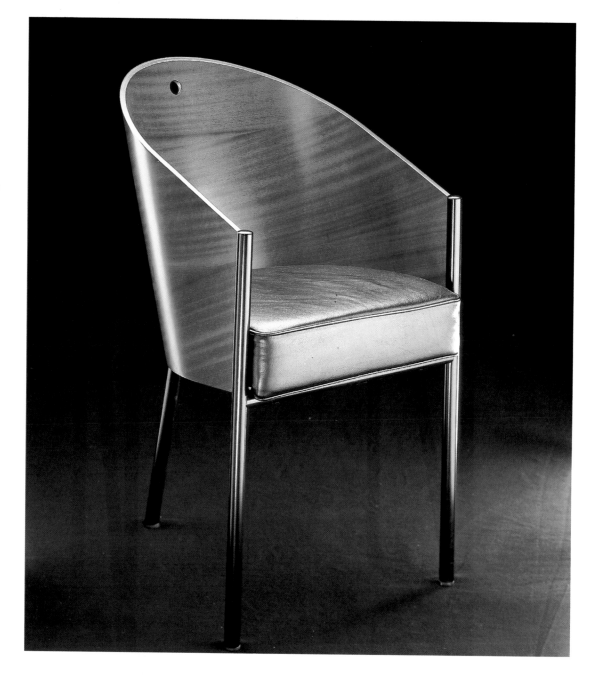

Perhaps Philippe Starck's best-known
chair design, the *Costes* was originally
designed for the Café Costes in Paris.
He has explained that the chair was
designed with three legs so that the
waiters at the café would trip up only
half as much as is usual. The *Pratfall*,
a lower lounge-chair version of the
Costes, was designed the same year.

Der *Costes*-Sessel ist Starcks bekann-
tester Stuhl, er hat ihn ursprünglich für
das Café Costes in Paris entworfen.
Starck erklärte, daß er dem Sessel drei
Beine gegeben habe, damit die Kellner
des Cafés nur halb soviel stolperten
wie gewöhnlich. Der *Pratfall*, eine nie-
drige Liegesesselversion des *Costes*-
Sessels, entstand im gleichen Jahr.

Le siège sans doute le plus célèbre de
Starck, ce modèle *Costes*, fut spécialement dessiné pour le Café
Costes, à Paris. Starck expliqua que le
fauteuil n'avait que trois pieds pour
que les serveurs aient moins de pas à
faire en tournant autour. Le modèle
Pratfall, version chauffeuse du *Costes*,
fut dessiné la même année.

Philippe Starck:
Café Costes, 1982

At the launch of the first Memphis Collection, Ettore Sottsass wrote: "All that walking through realms of uncertainty... all that talking with metaphors and utopia... all that getting away from it all... has given us a certain experience; we've become good explorers. Maybe we can navigate dangerous rivers, penetrate jungles where no-one has ever been. There's no reason for getting worked up. We can finally make our way with ease; the worst is over."31

Die erste öffentliche Präsentation der Memphis-Kollektion kommentierte Ettore Sottsass: »Dieser endlose Marsch durch Sphären der Ungewißheit... dieses endlose Gerede voller Seifenblasen... diese endlosen Versuche, davon wegzukommen... all das hat uns ein gewisses Maß an Erfahrung gebracht. Vielleicht können wir in gefährlichen Gewässern navigieren, den unentdeckten Dschungel durchdringen. Es gibt keinen Grund, sich aufzuregen. Wir können unseren Weg ganz gelassen zu Ende gehen; das Schlimmste ist vorbei.«31

Lors du lancement de la première collection Memphis, Ettore Sottsass écrivit: «Tout ces mouvements dans l'univers de l'incertitude... tout ces discours de métaphores et d'utopie... tous ces rejets de tout... nous ont donné une certaine expérience; nous sommes devenus de bons explorateurs. Peut-être voguerons-nous sur des rivières dangereuses, pénétrerons-nous des jungles où personne n'a jamais mis le pied. Il n'y a aucune raison d'avoir peur. Nous pourrons finalement trouver notre voie sans trop de peine; le pire est derrière nous.»31

Michele De Lucchi

*1951
Italy . Italien . Italie

First chair 1983
Stuhl First 1983
Chaise First 1983

Epoxy-coated, tubular metal frame with painted wood elements

Metallrohrrahmen, mit Epoxy (emailleähnliches Kunstharz) überzogen; farbig lackierte Holzelemente

Cadre de tubes métalliques traités époxy, éléments de bois peint

Memphis, Italy, from 1983 to c. 1987

119

Stiletto Studios

*1959

Germany . Deutschland . Allemagne

Consumer's Rest 1983

Zinc-plated, cut and bent supermarket trolley

Supermarkt-Einkaufswagen, verzinkt, geschnitten und gebogen

Chariot de supermarché coupé et cintré, zingué

Brüder Siegel GmbH & Co. KG, Berlin, from 1983

The *Consumer's Rest* is a "ready-made" design which has been produced as an edition of 100. There is a smaller version for children, *Short Rest*, available in a colour choice of red, yellow and blue. The first example of the *Consumer's Rest* was presented in 1983 by Christian Borngräber to Dr. Wolfgang Schepers for the design collection at The Museum of Art, Düsseldorf.

Der Einkaufswagen *Consumer's Rest* ist ein Ready-made, das in einer Auflage von 100 Stück produziert wurde. Die kleinere Version für Kinder, *Short Rest*, ist in Rot, Gelb und Blau erhältlich. Das erste Exemplar des *Consumer's Rest* übergab Christian Borngräber 1983 an Dr. Wolfgang Schepers für die Designkollektion des Kunstmuseums der Stadt Düsseldorf.

Ce *Consumer's Rest* est un «ready-made» produit en 100 exemplaires. Il en existe une version plus petite pour enfants, *Short Rest*, disponible en rouge, bleu et jaune. Le premier exemplaire fut offert par Christian Borngräber au Dr. Wolfgang Schepers pour la collection de design du Musée d'Art de Düsseldorf.

Stiletto Studios:

Consumer's Rest & Short Rest, 1983

Danny Lane:
Dwarf chairs, 1988
Dwarf-Stühle, 1988
Chaises *Dwarf*, 1988

Lane's *Etruscan* chair is perhaps one of his more rational designs, yet it is still highly expressive, appearing spontaneously composed. Lane does not attempt to turn design into art but enjoys working on the murky edges of both disciplines. Only one of his designs is industrially produced, the *Atlas* table by the Italian company, Fiam, from 1988. More recently, Lane has been devoting his attentions to large-scale sculpture commissions.

Lanes *Etruscan*-Stuhl gehört zu seinen eher rationalen Entwürfen, dennoch wirkt er äußerst expressiv und spontan. Lane will Design nicht zur Kunst machen, fischt aber gern in den trüben Wassern am äußersten Rand beider Disziplinen. Nur einer seiner Entwürfe ging in die Massenproduktion; es war der *Atlas*-Tisch, den die italienische Firma Fiam seit 1988 produziert. In der letzten Zeit hat Lane sich auf Auftragsarbeiten für großformatige Skulpturen konzentriert.

Cette chaise *Etruscan* est sans doute l'un des projets les plus rationalistes de Lane, tout en restant extrêmement expressive dans sa composition faussement spontanée. Lane ne confond pas art et design, mais aime travailler aux limites des deux disciplines. Une seule de ses créations, la table *Atlas*, a été produite industriellement par la société italienne Fiam, à partir de 1988. Plus récemment, il s'est consacré à des commandes de sculptures de grandes dimensions.

Danny Lane

*1955

Great Britain . Großbritannien . Grande-Bretagne

Etruscan chair 1984
Stuhl Etruscan 1984
Chaise Etruscan 1984

Glass, forged mild steel and carved marble

Glas, geschmiedeter Flußstahl und behauener Marmor

Verre, acier doux et marbre taillé

Danny Lane, UK

Danny Lane:
Angaraib, 1987

Shiro Kuramata

1934–91

Japan . Japon

How High the Moon
1986/87

Sessel How High the Moon
1986/87

**Fauteuil How High
the Moon** 1986/87

Nickel-plated, wire-mesh construction

Konstruktion aus vernickeltem Stahlgitter

Construction en grillage nickelé

**Vitra GmbH, Germany, from
1986 to present**

Shiro Kuramata:

*Begin the Beguine – Homage to
Josef Hoffmann*, 1985

Hommage an Hoffmann, 1985

Hommage à Hoffmann, 1985

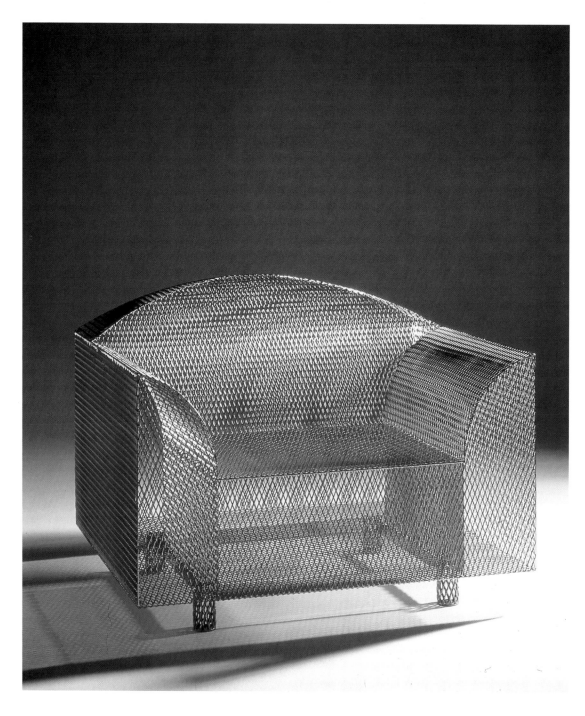

Through his intriguing choice of materials and graceful use of proportions, Kuramata's *How High the Moon* expresses a highly refined sense of lightness and space. Peter Dormer writes, "His art lies in the ease with which his materials do his work. There is no stress in Kuramata's imagery – hence they present themselves gently."[32]

In der provokativen Wahl des Materials und der Ausgewogenheit der Proportionen des Sessels *How High the Moon* erkennt man Kuramatas feines Gespür für Leichtigkeit und Raumaufteilung. Peter Dormer schreibt: »Seine Kunst liegt in der Ungezwungenheit, mit der seine Materialien für ihn arbeiten. In Kuramatas Erfindungen gibt es nichts Angespanntes – sie präsentieren sich mit natürlicher Anmut.«[32]

A travers le choix d'un matériau étrange et des proportions pleines de grâce, ce fauteuil de Kuramata exprime un sens très raffiné de la légèreté et de l'espace. Peter Dormer écrit: «Son art (de Kuramata) réside dans l'aisance avec lesquels ses matériaux font leur travail. Il n'y a pas de tension dans l'imagerie de Kuramata – ces matériaux peuvent donc s'offrir au regard en toute sérénité.»[32]

Jasper Morrison

*1959

Great Britain . Großbritannien .
Grande-Bretagne

Thinking Man's chair 1987
Thinking-Man's-Stuhl 1987
Chaise Thinking Man's 1987

Painted, bent tubular steel and flat
steel bars

Gezogenes Stahlrohr und Flachstahl, farbig lackiert

Tube d'acier cintré peint et barres
d'acier plat

Cappellini, Italy, from 1988
to present

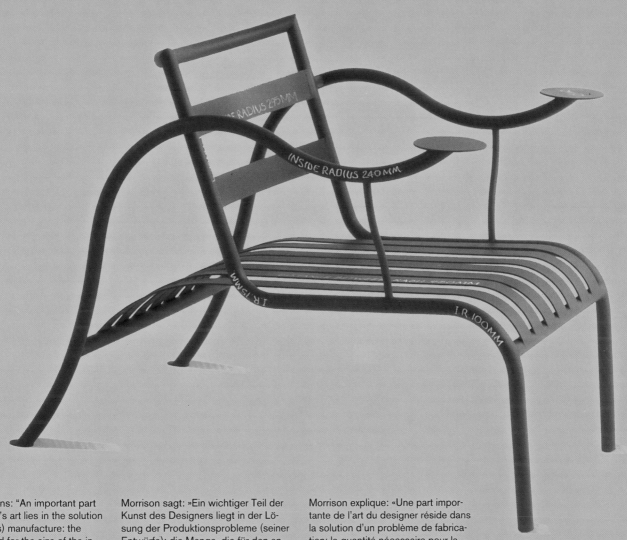

Morrison explains: "An important part
of the designer's art lies in the solution
of (the design's) manufacture: the
quantity needed for the size of the intended market, and the costs involved.
The balance of these variables is every
bit as important to the art of design as
its sculptural content. Indeed, the two
aspects are interwoven, and to ignore
either in pursuit of the other is to miss
the point of designing."[33]

Morrison sagt: »Ein wichtiger Teil der
Kunst des Designers liegt in der Lösung der Produktionsprobleme (seiner
Entwürfe): die Menge, die für den an-
gepeilten Markt erforderlich ist, und die
anfallenden Kosten. Das Gleichge-
wicht dieser Variablen ist nicht einen
Deut weniger wichtig für die Designkunst als deren plastischer Gehalt.
Diese beiden Aspekte gehören in der
Tat eng zusammen, und einen von beiden zugunsten des anderen zu ver-
nachlässigen bedeutet, daß man das
Ziel der Designkunst verfehlt hat.«[33]

Morrison explique: «Une part importante de l'art du designer réside dans
la solution d'un problème de fabrication: la quantité nécessaire pour la
taille du marché visé et les coûts.
L'équilibre de ces variables est tout
aussi important pour l'art du design
que le contenu sculptural. En fait, ces
deux aspects sont liés et ignorer l'un
pour atteindre l'autre serait passer à
côté de l'essence même du design.»[33]

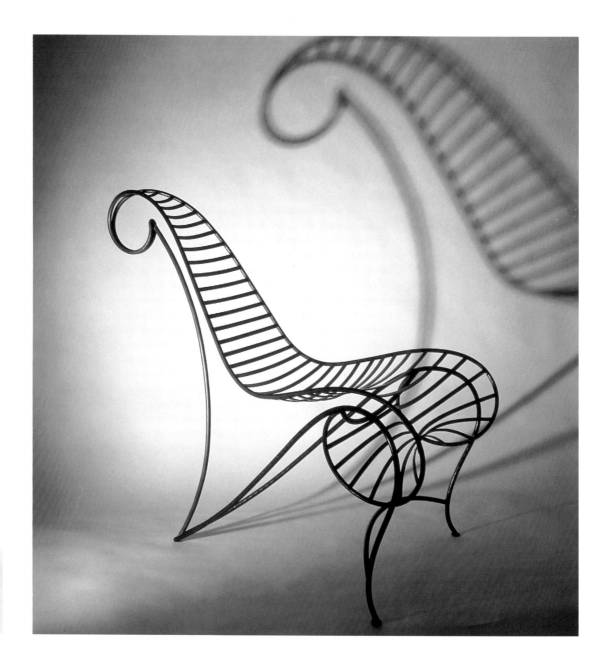

André Dubreuil:

Paris chair, 1988

Stuhl *Paris*, 1988

Chaise *Paris*, 1988

André Dubreuil

*1951

France . Frankreich

Spine chair 1988

Stuhl Spine 1988

Chaise Spine 1988

Bent and welded mild steel

Weichstahl, gebogen und geschweißt

Acier doux, cintré et soudé

A.D. Decorative Arts Ltd., France (originally UK), from 1988 to present

Alluding to previous decorative styles, the *Spine* chair is hand-forged by a blacksmith in the Dordogne region of France. Because Dubreuil's designs depend on such labour-intensive production methods, his furniture is produced only in small quantities. Like many avant-garde designers, Dubreuil prefers the flexibility and scope for personal creativity that exclusive and small-scale methods of operation provide.

Der *Spine*-Stuhl orientiert sich an Stilarten vergangener Epochen; er wird von einem Schmied in der Dordogne, Frankreich, von Hand gefertigt. Da Dubreuils Entwürfe diese und ähnliche arbeitsintensive Produktionsmethoden erfordern, werden seine Möbel nur in geringen Mengen hergestellt. Wie viele Avantgarde-Designer legt er Wert auf die Flexibilität und die größeren Entfaltungsmöglichkeiten seiner Kreativität, die ihm exklusive Herstellungsmethoden mit kleinen Stückzahlen bieten.

Faisant allusion à des styles décoratifs historiques, cette chaise est forgée à la main par un forgeron traditionnel en Dordogne. Parce que les créations de Dubreuil dépendent de méthodes de production coûteuses en heures de travail, ses meubles ne sont produits qu'en petites quantités. Comme de nombreux designers d'avant-garde, Dubreuil attache beaucoup de prix à la souplesse et à la liberté créative que permet une production exclusive et à petite échelle.

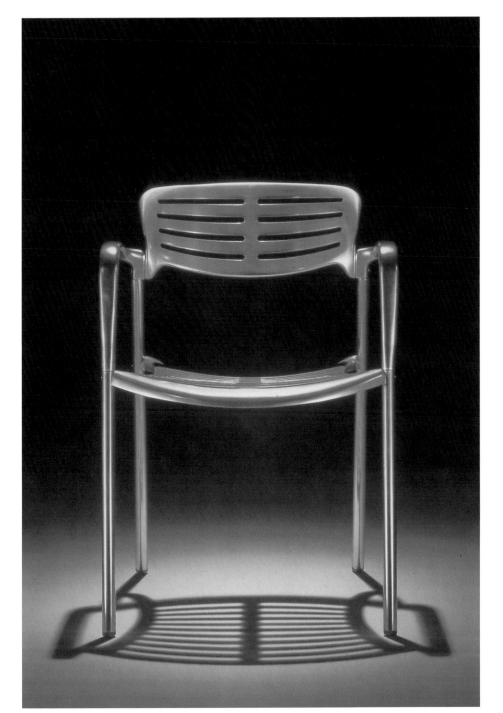

Jorge Pensi

*1946

Spain . Spanien . Espagne

**Toledo chair,
Model No. 2604** 1988

**Stuhl Toledo,
Modell No. 2604** 1988

**Siège Toledo,
modèle n° 2604** 1988

Cast aluminium

Gußaluminium

Fonte d'aluminium

**Amat s.a., Spain, from 1988
to present**

The *Toledo* is a reworking of earlier chair designs intended for use in Spanish open-air cafés. This highly functional chair recalls Gio Ponti's appeal for "furniture without adjectives".

Der *Toledo*-Stuhl ist eine Neubearbeitung älterer Stuhlentwürfe, die für die Terrassen in spanischen Straßencafés gedacht waren. Dieser ausgesprochen funktionale Stuhl läßt an Gio Pontis Forderung nach »Möbeln ohne Eigenschaften« denken.

Le *Toledo* est une réinterprétation d'un précédent modèle conçu pour les terrasses de café. Ce siège très fonctionnel rappelle le goût de Gio Ponti pour un «mobilier sans adjectifs».

Ron Arad

*1951

Great Britain . Großbritannien .
Grande-Bretagne

Big Easy Volume 2
1988

Sessel Big Easy Volume 2
1988

Siège Big Easy Volume 2
1988

Blackened sheet steel with
welded and polished stainless
steel

Geschwärztes Stahlblech und
polierter, geschweißter Edelstahl

Tôle d'acier noirci, soudures en
acier inoxydable poli

**One Off Ltd., UK, from 1988
to present**

The individual elements of Arad's *Volume* series chairs are cut from a pattern and then welded together. Each chair, therefore, varies slightly as a result of the welding process and can be seen as unique. The polished stainless steel welds stand out against the blackened steel construction and are intended to be read as a freehand line drawing. An upholstered version of this chair is currently produced by Moroso, Italy.

Die einzelnen Elemente von Arads *Volume*-Serie werden nach Vorlagen ausgeschnitten und zusammengeschweißt. Durch das Schweißen weicht jeder Stuhl ein wenig von der Norm ab und kann als Unikat bezeichnet werden. Die polierten Schweißnähte des Edelstahls heben sich von der Konstruktion aus geschwärztem Stahlblech ab und sollen als freihändig gezogene Linien gelesen werden. Zur Zeit wird in Moroso, Italien, eine gepolsterte Version dieses Sessels hergestellt.

Les divers éléments des sièges de la série *Volume* d'Arad sont coupés d'après un modèle, puis soudés ensemble. Du fait du procédé de soudure, aucun siège n'est donc strictement identique à l'autre et peut être considéré comme une pièce unique. Les soudures en acier inoxydable poli ressortent sur le fond noir et se lisent comme un dessin à main levée. Une version rembourrée de ce siège est actuellement produite par Moroso, Italie.

Ron Arad:
A.Y.O.R., 1990

Tom Dixon:

Upholstered *Bird*
chaise longue, 1992

Gepolsterter
Bird-Liegesessel, 1992

Chaise longue *Bird*
rembourrée, 1992

Tom Dixon

*1959

Great Britain . Großbritannien .
Grande-Bretagne

S chair 1988

Stuhl S 1988

Chaise S 1988

Welded mild steel frame with
woven wicker, raffia or latex
rubber

Rahmen aus Weichstahl,
geschweißt, Bast- und Binsengeflecht oder Latexüberzug

Cadre en acier doux soudé, siège
tissé en raphia ou en caoutchouc

Cappellini, Italy, from 1992

Tom Dixon:

S chair, 1988

Stuhl *S*, 1988

Chaise *S*, 1988

Tom Dixon's woven wicker and raffia *S* chairs of 1988 have recently been adapted for production in full upholstery. Celebrated throughout the 1980s by the international design press, the poetic and emotionally charged work of the British avant-garde is now being taken seriously by established manufacturers. Firms such as Vitra, Cappellini and Moroso have all begun either limited or full-scale production of this expressive furniture aimed primarily at the domestic market.

Dixons *S*-Stühle von 1988 mit Raffia- oder Binsengeflecht werden seit kurzem mit Polsterung hergestellt. Das poetische und emotional aufgeladene Design der britischen Avantgarde, das internationale Designpublikationen in 80ern priesen, wird heute von etablierten Herstellern ernst genommen. Firmen wie Vitra, Cappellini und Moroso haben entweder mit limitierten Auflagen begonnen oder die Produktion dieser ausdrucksvollen – hauptsächlich für den jeweiligen heimischen Markt bestimmten – Möbel voll anlaufen lassen.

Les chaises *S* de jonc et de raffia tressé de 1988 ont récemment été adaptées pour être produites en version rembourrée. Célébrée tout au long des années 80 par la presse internationale du design, l'œuvre poétique et émotionnellement chargée de l'avant-garde britannique est maintenant prise au sérieux par les grands fabricants. Des firmes comme Vitra, Cappellini et Moroso ont toutes commencé à produire en série limitée ou à grande échelle ces meubles expressifs qui étaient à l'origine destinés au seul marché domestique.

Shiro Kuramata

1934–91

Japan . Japon

Miss Blanche chair 1989
Stuhl Miss Blanche 1989
Fauteuil Miss Blanche 1989

Paper flowers cast in acrylic resin
with tubular aluminium legs

Papierblumen, in Acryl gegossen;
Beine aus Aluminiumrohr

Fleurs de papier incluses dans
une résine acrylique, piètement
en tube d'aluminium

Kokuyo Co., Japan

Conceived for limited production, *Miss Blanche* is a visually delicate chair with its fall of red paper roses suggesting, perhaps, the frailty of love. Kuramata combines unusual forms and materials in a masterly fashion to produce minimalistic designs that run counter to preconceived notions of what furniture can look like or be made from.

Der Stuhl *Miss Blanche*, ein graziles Möbel, das mit seinen fallenden roten Papierrosen die Zerbrechlichkeit der Liebe anzudeuten scheint, wurde für eine limitierte Auflage konzipiert. Kuramata kombiniert auf meisterliche Art und Weise ungewöhnliche Formen und Materialien zu einem minimalistischen Design, das den herkömmlichen Vorstellungen, wie Möbel aussehen und aus welchen Materialien sie sein sollten, zuwiderläuft.

Conçu pour une production limitée, *Miss Blanche* et ses roses de papier rouge qui suggèrent, peut-être, la fragilité de l'amour, est un fauteuil d'aspect délicat. Kuramata combine en maître formes et matériaux inhabituels pour produire des dessins minimalistes qui vont à l'encontre des notions préconçues sur l'aspect et la fabrication d'un meuble.

Shiro Kuramata:

Armchair *Miss Blanche*, 1989

Sessel *Miss Blanche*, 1989

Fauteuil *Miss Blanche*, 1989

128

Morita's creations are luxury objects for the feelings, aiming to offer more than mere functionality. His preference for basic materials such as stone, steel and glass, together with his occasionally zoomorphic shapes, show a strong sense of Nature, for all his abstraction. He sees bright colours as artificial, and prefers dark shades.

Morita kreiert Luxusobjekte für die Gefühle. Sie wollen mehr bieten als bloße Funktionalität. Seine Vorliebe für elementare Materialien wie Stein, Stahl und Glas und seine zuweilen zoomorphen Formen haben bei aller Abstraktion einen starken Bezug zur Natur. Grelle Farben empfindet er als künstlich und benutzt am liebsten dunkle Töne.

Son style pourrait se nommer la "néo-confortabilité". Morita crée des objets de luxe qui veulent nous émouvoir, offrir davantage que la pure fonctionnalité. Sa préférence pour les matériaux élémentaires comme la pierre, l'acier et le verre et ses formes parfois zoomorphiques sont, toute abstraction retenue, très marquées par des références naturalistes. Il trouve les couleurs vives artificielles, et utilise plus volontiers des tons sombres.

Masaki Morita

*1950
Japan . Japon

Blue Sofa 1989
Blaues Sofa 1989
Canapé bleu 1989

Materials unknown
Materialien unbekannt
Matériaux non connus

Manufacturer unknown

Masaki Morita:

Red Sofa, 1989

Rotes Sofa, 1989

Canapé rouge, 1989

Alfredo Arribas

*1954

Spain . Spanien . Espagne

J. Greystoke chair 1990
Stuhl J. Greystoke 1990
Siège J. Greystoke 1990

Solid beech and anodised cast aluminium frame with fabric-covered, upholstered seat and back

Rahmen Buche massiv und galvanisiertes Gußaluminium; Sitzfläche und Rückenlehne gepolstert, mit Stoff bezogen

Hêtre massif et structure en fonte d'aluminium anodisé, siège et dossier rembourrés et recouverts de tissu

Carlos Jané Camacho, Spain, from 1990

Working primarily as an architect, Arribas launched his first industrial design, the *J. Greystoke* chair, at the Vinçon Gallery, Barcelona, in 1990. In this elegant organic design, Arribas alludes to wild animal forms and the earlier work of Carlo Mollino, particularly through his use of a bifurcated upholstered back.

Arribas, der vorwiegend als Architekt arbeitet, stellte sein erstes Industrie-design, den Stuhl *J.-Greystoke*, 1990 in der Galerie Vinçon, Barcelona, vor. Mit diesem eleganten, organischen Entwurf spielt Arribas auf die Gestalten wilder Tiere und auf die vorangegan-genen Arbeiten von Carlo Mollino an, vor allem durch die zweigeteilte gepol-sterte Rückenlehne.

Architecte d'origine, Arribas exposa ce siège, sa première intervention dans le design, à la Galerie Vinçon de Barce-lone, en 1990. A travers cet élégant dessin organique, il fait allusion aux formes de la vie sauvage et à certains travaux antérieurs de Carlo Mollino, en particulier dans son dossier «fourchu».

Powerplay chair 1990–92
Stuhl Powerplay 1990–92
Siège Powerplay 1990–92

Bent and woven laminated wood

Geflecht aus gebogenen Schicht-
holzstreifen

Bois cintré, lamellé et entrelaçé

**Knoll Group, New York,
from 1992**

Michael Thonet, Alvar Aalto and Charles Eames all made revolutionary developments in the techniques employed for moulding and bending plywood. However, their designs either "had a heavy substructure and then webbing, or an intermediary structure for the seating." Gehry continues: "The difference in my chairs is that the (support) structure and the seat are formed of the same lightweight wood strips... (what) gives it extraordinary strength is the interwoven, basketlike character of the design."[34]

Michael Thonet, Alvar Aalto und Charles Eames entwickelten völlig neue Techniken zum Verformen und Biegen von schichtverleimtem Sperrholz, aber ihre Entwürfe hatten entweder »ein schweres Untergestell und dann noch ein Geflecht von Gurten oder eine Zwischenlösung für die Sitze«, sagt Gehry. »Meine Stühle unterscheiden sich dadurch, daß die (tragende) Konstruktion und die Sitzfläche aus den gleichen, leichten Holzstreifen geformt sind... (was) ihm (dem Stuhl) die ungewöhnliche Stärke verleiht, ist das korbartige Geflecht.«[34]

Pour Gehry, Michael Thonet, Alvar Aalto et Charles Eames apportèrent chacun des développements révolutionnaires aux techniques de moulage et de cintrage du contreplaqué. Cependant, leurs créations reposaient «soit sur une lourde sous-structure, puis sur une fixation, soit sur une structure intermédiaire pour le siège... La différence avec mon siège est que la structure (le support) et le siège sont constitués à partir des mêmes légères bandes de bois... ce qui lui donne son extraordinaire solidité est leur entrelaçage, cet aspect de «panier».»[34]

Frank O. Gehry at work, 1992
Frank O. Gehry bei der Arbeit, 1992
Frank O. Gehry au travail, 1992

Frank O. Gehry:
The Gehry Collection, 1992
Die Gehry Kollektion, 1992
La Collection Gehry, 1992

Frank O. Gehry:
Study for *Powerplay*, 1992
Studie für *Powerplay*, 1992
Etude pour *Powerplay*, 1992

Borek Sípek

*1949

Czech Republic .
Tschechische Republik .
République Tchèque

Sedlak chair 1992

Stuhl Sedlak 1992

Chaise Sedlak 1992

Cast-aluminium and stained
beech frame with integral
foam seat

Rahmen aus Gußaluminium und
gebeizter Buche; integrierte,
gepolsterte Sitzfläche

Cadre en font d'aluminium et
hêtre teinté avec siège en mousse

**Vitra GmbH, Germany,
from 1992**

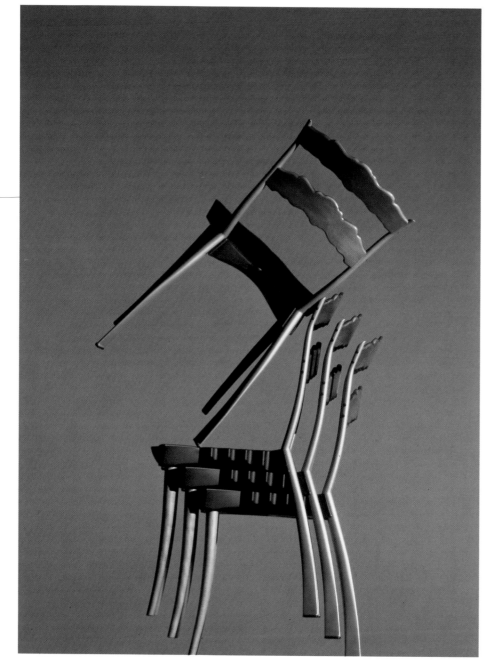

"*Sedlak* combines the decorative with the functional… The chair's parts can be dismantled and exchanged. The materials can be separated for recycling. Despite the fulfilment of functional requirements, *Sedlak* retains its special expression and is unmistakably identifiable as one of Sípek's designs."[35]

»Der Stuhl *Sedlak* kombiniert das Dekorative mit dem Funktionalen… Man kann den Stuhl auseinandernehmen und die einzelnen Teile austauschen. Die Materialien können getrennt wiederverwertet werden. Bei aller Funktionalität hat der Stuhl *Sedlak* einen ganz speziellen Charakter; er ist eindeutig als Sípek-Design identifizierbar.«[35]

«*Sedlak* marie le décoratif et le fonctionnel… Les éléments de la chaise peuvent être démontés et changés. Les matériaux peuvent se recycler. En dehors de ces qualités fonctionnelles achevées, elle conserve son expression particulière et s'identifie sans risque d'erreur comme une création de Sípek.»[35]

Sedlak chairs in café

Sedlak-Stühle in einem Café

Chaises *Sedlak* au café

For recycling purposes the *Louis 20* chair has been constructed in two sections which are joined with screws rather than glue so that the materials remain unsullied by additives. This arrangement also facilitates the easy separation of the main elements. Designed to be used indoors or outdoors, the *Louis 20* can be stacked and is available with or without arms.

Um das Recycling zu ermöglichen, besteht die Konstruktion des Stuhls *Louis 20* aus zwei Teilen, die nicht geleimt, sondern durch Schrauben verbunden sind. Außerdem werden die Materialien dadurch nicht durch Zusatzstoffe verunreinigt und lassen sich leicht voneinander trennen. Der Stuhl läßt sich stapeln und eignet sich für drinnen und draußen; er ist mit und ohne Armlehnen erhältlich.

Pour être recyclable, cette chaise a été construite en deux sections assemblées par écrous et non collées afin que le matériau ne soit pas chimiquement pollué. Cet arrangement facilite également la séparation des principaux éléments. Conçues pour l'extérieur ou l'intérieur, les chaises peuvent s'empiler. *Louis 20* est disponible avec ou sans accoudoirs.

Philippe Starck

*1949

France . Frankreich

Louis 20 chair 1992
Stuhl Louis 20 1992
Chaise Louis 20 1992

Blasted polypropylene body with aluminium "bridge" rear leg section

Hochdruckgeformter Polypropylen-Körper; hinterer »Brücken«-Teil, einschließlich der Hinterbeine, aus Aluminium

Corps en polypropylène soufflé avec pieds arrière en «pont» en aluminium

Vitra GmbH, Germany, from 1992